PiSTOLS! TREASON! MURDER!

listw/ Jtl ed
0 8018 93704

PiSTOLS! TREASON! MURDER!

THE RISE AND FALL OF A MASTER SPY

JONATHAN WALKER

ILLUSTRATIONS CREATED BY DAN HALLET

MELBOURNE
UNIVERSITY
PRESS

PISTOLS! TREASON! MURDER!:

THE RISE AND FALL OF GEROLAMO VANO, VENETIAN GENERAL OF SPIES

BY JONATHAN WALKER

ILLUSTRATIONS BY
DAN HALLETT

MMVI

I uttered these words of his aloud. My voice sounded hollow to me,
quite unreal. How would he have pronounced them?
I knew nothing of his voice, whether it was harsh or soft,
high-pitched or deep. ... I was self-conscious at first, but I persisted. ...
The sounds I began to make were not a stranger's but they were
not mine either. ... It was not his voice, how could it be?
It was not a friendly voice at all. It ended by frightening me.

Barry Unsworth, *Losing Nelson*

I will ... Acquaint you with the perfect spy o'th'time.

William Shakespeare, *Macbeth*

MELBOURNE UNIVERSITY PRESS
An imprint of Melbourne University Publishing Ltd
187 Grattan Street, Carlton, Victoria 3053, Australia
mup-info@unimelb.edu.au
www.mup.com.au

First published 2007
Text © Jonathan Walker 2007
Illustrations © Dan Hallett and Jonathan Walker 2007
Design and typography © Melbourne University Publishing Ltd 2007

Cover design by Peter Long
Text design by Peter Long
Typeset in Scala by Pauline Haas
Printed in Australia by Griffin Press

National Library of Australia Cataloguing-in-Publication data:

Walker, Jonathan Martin, 1969– .
Pistols! Treason! Murder!: The Rise and Fall of a Master Spy

Bibliography.
ISBN 9780522852554.
ISBN 0 522 85255 6.

1. Vano, Gerolamo. 2. Spies—Italy—Venice—Biography.
3. Venice (Italy)—History—1508–1797. I. Title.

945.307

Author's website: www.jonathanwalkervenice.com

CONTENTS

THE ITALIAN STATES

HOLY ROMAN EMPIRE

DUCHY OF SAVOY AND PIEDMONT

STATE OF MILAN

Bergamo

Turin

Milan

Salò

Venice

Padua

DUCHY OF MANTUA

Mantua

PARMA

DUCHY OF PARMA

Genoa

DUCHY OF MODENA

REPUBLIC OF GENOA

Bologna

RIMINI

DUCHY OF URBINO

Florence

GRAND DUCHY OF TUSCANY

CORSICA (GENOA)

PAPAL STATE

Rome

REPUBLIC OF VENICE

KINGDOM OF SARDINIA (SPAIN)

KINGDOM OF NAPLES (SPAIN)

NAPLES

KINGDOM OF SICILY (SPAIN)

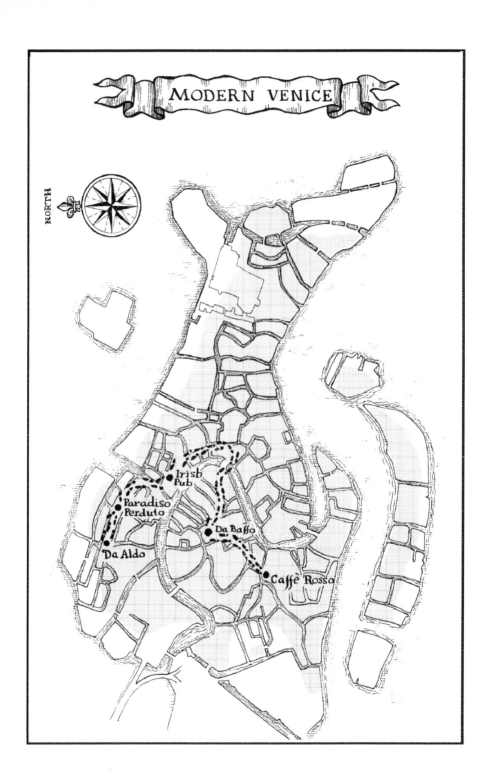

MODERN VENICE

NORTH

Irish
Pub

Paradiso
Perduto

Da Baffo

Da Aldo

Caffè Rosso

FACTS

May 1620 Gerolamo Vano begins to submit regular reports to the Inquisitors of State, the Venetian magistrates in charge of protecting state secrets. These reports are now stored in File 636 of the Inquisitors' archive.

July 1620 The Venetian noble Zuanne Minotto is arrested for revealing state secrets to the Spanish. The evidence comes from Vano.

July 1620 Vano's informant Diego Gomez is imprisoned within the Spanish embassy on suspicion of collusion with the Venetians.

September 1620 The Venetian noble Zuan Battista Bragadin is arrested on charges of passing information to the Spanish and is subsequently executed. Vano's evidence is again crucial to the prosecution.

October 1620 Vano's informant Domenico is sacked from his position as gondolier in the Spanish embassy, after his cover is 'blown' by Diego Gomez. He subsequently teams up with Vano to help run other agents.

December 1620 Diego Gomez is executed by the Spanish in Milan.

December 1621 After appearing regularly in Vano's reports throughout 1620, the Venetian noble Alvise Querini is finally arrested on charges of illegal visits to foreign embassies.

April 1622 The noble Antonio Foscarini is arrested, tried and executed for treason, an event that is widely reported abroad by all the foreign ambassadors resident in Venice.

July 1622 Giulio Cazzari, secretary to Nicolo Rossi, the Imperial resident in Venice, is assassinated.

August 1622 Vano describes the circumstances behind the exposure and 'defection' of Battista, one of his informants in the Spanish embassy. Vano's final report is dated 16 August 1622, when File 636 ends without explanation.

September 1622 An ex-informant of Vano's, Zuanetto, appears before the Council of Ten to claim that he was suborned to offer false testimony in the trial of Alvise Querini. His claims are judged to be false.

August–September 1622 Vano is prosecuted, condemned and executed for unspecified reasons, but rumours suggest that the charge is perjury against Foscarini.

January 1623 Antonio Foscarini is posthumously proclaimed innocent.

I. BETWEEN THE COLUMNS

In Memoriam:

Zuan Battista Bragadin, Venetian traitor, executed September 1620.

Diego Gomez, Spanish spy, executed December 1620.

Antonio Foscarini, Venetian noble falsely accused of treason,
    executed April 1622.

Giulio Cazzari, Italian spy, assassinated July 1622.

Domenico Zanco, Venetian spy, executed September 1622.

Gerolamo Vano, Venetian spy, executed September 1622.

EROLAMO VANO DIED IN MID-AIR, ON A GALLOWS, BETWEEN the columns at the entrance to Piazza San Marco in Venice, the site of public executions under the Venetian republic. Vano is the hero (for want of a better word) of this book, and he has a unique status in the list of names above, since he was, in one way or another, responsible for the deaths of all the other men on it. The place where Vano died is now an empty piece of sky, but if you stand between the columns and reach up—as high as you can—your fingertips might brush the spot where his kicking feet once passed, marking out an irregular spiral. Its limits were set by the arc of the rope from which he dangled, and its central, zero point was reached only when his body stopped moving.

What glory is there in a common good,

That hangs for every peasant to achieve?

That like I best that flies beyond my reach.

The area between the columns was a threshold. It was not only the site where criminals crossed from one world to the next but the spot where important visitors to Venice officially entered the city under the gaze of its two patron saints, who sat on top of the columns. It was also a space in which certain liberties could be enjoyed: for example, public dicing for money was customarily permitted there. I reclaim these defunct privileges as I write on a threshold situated between now and then, where I gamble with different voices and devices, as Vano gambled with his own life and that of his victims. Every chapter is a roll of the dice.

The main narrative is in this typeface. Quotations are in this typeface. **Quotations from documents written by the protagonists of the story are also in this typeface, but are set in bold**. Tape transcripts are in this typeface.[*]

---

[*] Footnotes provide essential background information, whereas the separate endnotes contain detailed references to sources and are intended mainly for professional historians. Snippets from seventeenth-century plays are occasionally used to comment on the action, but it is not necessary to be familiar with the original plays to 'get' their point.

2. WHY VANO MATTERS

ANTONIO FOSCARINI WAS THE VICTIM OF THE MOST infamous miscarriage of justice in the long history of the Venetian republic. In 1622, he was arrested for passing secret information to foreign ambassadors and then convicted and executed only days later, an abrupt conclusion that shocked contemporaries. Nine months afterwards, Foscarini was posthumously exonerated, an even more scandalous development.

No one knew the details of the case except the prosecuting magistrates, and they released no information officially until the announcement of Foscarini's absolution in January 1623, which also arrived without explanation. The trial record remained under lock and key until the republic's fall in 1797, after which it disappeared altogether, but the lack of available information did not prevent many writers from tackling the subject, which exercised a lasting fascination. Throughout the nineteenth century, Foscarini's downfall was re-told in poems, plays and novels and was elaborated with fanciful or invented details. These fictions, and the discussions they inspired among historians, were influenced by a long-standing debate on the nature of the republic, a debate that actually began in the early seventeenth century. On one side were defenders of the so-called 'myth of Venice', who glorified the city's achievements: its longevity and stability, its art and architecture, and its sophisticated political and legal system. On the other side were proponents of the 'anti-myth', who insisted that all this was propaganda to distract attention from the actions of a cynical regime, whose apparent harmony was actually built upon the ruthless repression of dissent. These critics drew particular attention to the magistrates who prosecuted Foscarini: the Council of Ten and Inquisitors of State, who were responsible for public order and the protection of state secrets respectively. Seen in terms of the 'anti-myth', Foscarini's prosecution was exemplary in a negative sense, in that it momentarily exposed the true nature of the Venetian state, where innocent men were vulnerable to the secret accusations of spies. Conversely, defenders of Venice insisted that the execution was regrettable but exceptional, and that the posthumous exoneration of the victim proved the republic's good faith.

Until now, all the attention has been on the wrong man. The victim is not important—Foscarini is a mere dupe; it is the accuser who matters. Although Gerolamo Vano was almost immediately identified as the main witness against Foscarini in 1622, he was otherwise ignored at the time, as he has been since. Nobody is aware of the extent of his activities as **general of spies** in Venice in the early 1620s, when Foscarini was only the most prominent among his many victims. I cannot even remember when I first heard Vano's name, but in the late 1990s I stumbled by chance across a tantalising reference to his surveillance reports. When I first ordered File 636 from the archive of the Inquisitors of State, which is where Vano's reports are now stored, I did so in the naïve belief that they might reveal the truth about Foscarini's death. I was soon disillusioned on that point. Among the hundreds of sheets of paper in Vano's hand, only one contains a substantial reference to Foscarini. It allegedly draws upon information from a source in the Spanish embassy named Battista.

File 636, report from Gerolamo Vano dated 9 April 1622:[*] **Battista, servant of the Spanish secretary, said that last night at four bells a masked man … knocked and asked urgently for the [Spanish] secretary … [and] gave him the news that the Knight F had been imprisoned with his servant. Then he left straightaway. The secretary, greatly enraged and stamping his feet, ran about like a man possessed, and called Nicolo Rossi [the Imperial resident in Venice, and thus a crony of the Spanish secretary] to give him the news straightaway. Both of them armed themselves and said privately, *'We go to warn our friends'*. Battista took a sword and the secretary said, 'Where do you think you're going, *drunken rogue*? You want to come *with me without being asked*? I'll give you a kick'. And he threw him down four stairs. The secretary and Rossi went out … When they returned home, the secretary shut Battista up in a room. After a while he returned … and questioned him at length, saying, 'Battista, tell me *the truth*, I know that some coward has asked you about my affairs … [O]n the King's *life*, tell me who they are, so that I can punish them and I shall forgive you. You will be like my brother and master of my house. I shall give you as much money as you want. I know that these villainous Venetians have been after you and you'll be thrown in the storeroom [if you don't confess]. Tell me to save your life'. … The secretary asked him if he knew that [Venetian?] gentleman *from the other night*. … Battista said, 'Sir, I don't know anyone. I wouldn't know them even if I saw them'. The secretary was enraged, saying, '*I'll make you confess* by force. You won't get away from here', and he shut the room up and left [Battista] there for twenty-four hours without anything to eat or drink. … [When Battista was released] he went to [see] the servants of Nicolo Rossi and asked them, 'Why the hell did my master lock me up? What am I supposed to have done?' The servants replied, 'We don't know anything about you, but your master is behaving insanely, like ours and Don Giulio [Cazzari, secretary to the Imperial resident, Nicolo Rossi]. They've gone cuckoo. They say a gentleman called Foscarini has been imprisoned, … Don Giulio said … 'We are sure to find that this business was started by Gerolamo**

---

[*] All subsequent quotations headed 'File' without further qualification refer to the contents of the archive of the Inquisitors of State, which is preserved in the Archivio di Stato di Venezia.

Vano and Domenico [Vano's right-hand man] and no one else. Our friends know Vano and Domenico well ... and we can hang and drown these villains'. *

Foscarini's first appearance in Vano's reports is thus under the appropriately Kafkaesque designation of **Knight F**, but it is clear who is meant, even before the helpful clarification from the servants—because the report was submitted the day after Foscarini's arrest, which occurred on 8 April 1622. In the context of Foscarini's death, the discovery of this passage is not much of a coup. It confirms that Vano was somehow implicated, but it does not resolve any of the mystery surrounding the case. It is a helpful reference for other historians, and that is all. But something happened while I was reading Vano's reports, and they quickly became addictive reading in their own right.

When did I finally admit that I was writing a book about Vano, in which Foscarini was a minor figure in the background, and not the other way around? When did I realise that I was gambling my career—and perhaps my sanity—on an impossible undertaking? Was it when I spent night after night obsessively retracing Vano's itineraries in Venetian alleys, without ever being able to fix the routes definitively? Was it when I covered every available centimetre of wall space in my office with blown-up samples of microfilmed documents, in a futile attempt to identify each individual contributor to the Council of Ten's archive between 1618 and 1622?

Each story in Vano's reports contains or opens up the possibility of another that undoes or reverses it. Each collapses as a direct consequence of attempts to shore it up. No possible scenario accounts for everything. As I read the reports, I 'crashed' repeatedly: irretrievable error; the system has shut down. I could not leave Vano alone, but he offered no answers to any questions that a respectable historian might want to ask. Instead, he demanded a more daring and radical response, in which obsession itself became a strategy.

---

* The phrases in italics are in Spanish in the original, although it is sometimes hard to tell, with Vano, which language is which.

I had to step inside Vano's virtual world and learn to think like him. What does it mean to 'think like' Vano? Let us begin with an example, using an excerpt from a report in which Vano describes a conversation between the Spanish secretary (his enemy) and Domenico (his right-hand man). The secretary taunts Domenico as follows.

File 636, 11 May 1622: **[Vano] has been paid thousands of ducats, and bonuses on top, and he has a stipend of five hundred ducats, and what about you lot [who work for him]? When's he ever given you a gold coin or two? [No, it's] a** *scudo*[*] **here, four** *lire* **there, just enough for a drink, and no more.**

The first thing to note is that one of the basic premises of this quotation is incorrect. Vano certainly profited from spying, but he received no stipend from the Venetians, and his principal rewards were not rendered in cash. Whether this was a lie or an error on the Spanish secretary's part need not concern us. The more important question is: In what 'tone of voice' does Vano report this comment? He surely would have liked the secretary's claim to be true, but both he and his readers knew that it was not. So is the remark?:

a) Wistful: 'If only I could have such a stipend! But I know that will never happen'

b) Ironic: 'Unfortunately, the secretary is misinformed'

c) Cynical: 'Nobody gets a stipend of five hundred ducats unless they are a noble'

d) Crudely self-interested: 'A five-hundred ducat stipend? Now there's an idea!'

e) Boastful and insubordinate: 'The secretary knows what I am worth, even if you do not'.

It could be any or all of these. As a final twist, Vano disclaims responsibility for the words by attributing them to the Spanish secretary, whose ignorance he mocks in the very act of quoting him.

Vano's reports are an infernal machine that churns out possibilities. I am trapped in that machine, and I cannot turn it off. Inevitably, then,

---

[*]   A coin with an exchange value slightly higher than one Venetian ducat.

this book is not only about Vano but about the process whereby historians assemble stories. Vano challenges us to rethink that process—and to turn it inside out.

Authentic obsession requires no justification. It runs on pure conviction alone. Fortunately, there are more objective reasons why Vano deserves your attention. They have to do with changes in our understanding of 'modernity' over the past hundred and fifty years. In the mid-nineteenth century, historians looked back to the Italian Renaissance as the birthplace of modernity, which they associated with heroic creativity and progress. Jacob Burckhardt, in his groundbreaking study *The Civilization of the Renaissance*, first published in 1860, concentrated on architects, artists and the princely despots who transformed political life by treating the state as if it too were a work of art, which meant that it could be remade and transformed according to its ruler's wishes. Since Burckhardt wrote his book, modernity has lost much of its shine. The alienated, protean figure of the spy, whose existence is defined by bad faith and duplicity, seems more representative of contemporary disillusionment than Burckhardt's heroic geniuses do. Baroque cynicism has replaced sunny Renaissance optimism.

The major issue for seventeenth-century Venetians was not how to assert their individuality so much as how to reconcile competing claims on their loyalties, but this problem itself contributed to the 'birth of the individual'. People became aware of who they were not only by meditating on their own uniqueness but by outwardly pretending to be someone they were not. They began to define identity in terms of what separated them from other people. The origins of this way of thinking lie in the careers of men like Vano, as well as those of courtiers and Burckhardt's artists. It is no accident that, around 1600, some writers began to connect the figure of the spy with self-knowledge as well as with knowledge of others. One such writer was Montaigne, an endlessly curious and reflective essayist, who also had some experience as a diplomat. Each man, he argued, is a good education to himself, provided he has the capacity to spy on himself from close up.

There were no permanent intelligence services in seventeenth-century Europe, so, for most people involved in the exchange and sale of secret information, 'spying' was an occasional activity. Vano is the exception that proves the rule. From 1619 to 1622, he worked exclusively at counter-intelligence. Perhaps he (inadvertently, unconsciously) invented the very notion that spying could be more than a sordid extension of politics or war; that it could, in short, be a trade, with its own special skills. Such a bold thesis is impossible to prove, but Vano was certainly one of the first dedicated, full-time spies in European history, which is why one anonymous denunciation described him as the Venetian **general of spies**.

Vano was a performance artist: less idealised and more democratic than the modernist hero, he lived in a compromised, complicated world rather than existing on some higher, Olympian plane of Truth and Beauty. It was in his mind, as much as that of the princely despot, that the state became a work of art, but his art was ephemeral, improvised and personal. He left no monuments to his genius except a pile of neglected, handwritten notes, but he explored the relationship between the private and the political in highly original ways. He was not above the moral obligations of mere mortals. Rather, he paid for the choices he made with his life—and that of others.

The best contemporary comparison for Vano's reports is perhaps the work of Christopher Marlowe, playwright, murder victim and—not coincidentally—part-time spy. The critic Stephen Greenblatt describes the world of Marlowe's plays as follows.

[His heroes] take courage from the absurdity of their enterprise, a murderous, self-destructive, supremely eloquent, playful courage. This playfulness in Marlowe's works manifests itself as cruel humor, murderous practical jokes, a penchant for the outlandish and absurd, delight in role-playing, entire absorption in the game at hand and conse-quent indifference to what lies outside the boundaries of the game, radical insensitivity to human complexity and suffering, extreme but disciplined aggression, [and] hostility to transcendence.

Vano's literary abilities were undeniably much inferior to Marlowe's, and his purposes far more directly pragmatic, but this quotation perfectly captures the tone of his intelligence reports, which strip descriptions of human interaction down to pure calculation of interest: abstract exercises in game theory played out as black farce, where the loser gets stabbed to death.

For nearly four hundred years, Vano's only acknowledged place in history has been that of false accuser: dishonourable, contemptible, amoral. Myth; anti-myth. White; black. I have another kind of history in mind. This, then, is the biography of a subject about whom I know almost nothing; it is a critical study on an unedited and unpublished bundle of loose-leaf documents written in a barbarous style; it is a celebration of the legacy of a man whose life left no mark on history, except a small stain of infamy. It is both a tribute to an unrecognised genius and a parody of the nineteenth-century idea of genius. It tells stories, and it deconstructs the process of storytelling.

3. DISSECTION / RESURRECTION

THE ARCHIVE IS DISMEMBERED. SECRETARIES SAWED THE story up, disposing of the corpse in pieces to prevent identification. Mutilate the face; pull the teeth; burn the fingerprints. The historian as pathologist: death is our medium, the precondition for our work to begin. An autopsy measures from the moment of death, the moment of origin, in which the document is created. The living body does not exist for us, cannot speak to us, even if the corpse still hosts a different kind of life that has nothing to do with the consciousness that once inhabited it. Rather, this life is parasitical—a swarming mass of signs, continually multiplying, crawling across the page. Their buzzing is loudest around the body's wounds, where the text is most 'corrupt', as the philologists put it. The ligaments and cartilage that once articulated it have rotted away.

The historian as psychic or medium: a romantic alternative to the pathologist. If the dead will not speak to us, then we must dare to speak for them. Words become scar tissue, the means by which a still-living body can reconstitute itself, but at the same time continue to bear witness to the violence inflicted upon it.

Between the order and its execution, between narration and action, between the document as artefact and the document as witness, between the corpse and the bloody, resurrected body, lies a gap that can only be crossed by a leap of faith.

Can these bones live?

Pathologist; medium: there is no contradiction. Both make the connections that beg to be made. Telling the story is an intervention in the story.

4. THE HERO

WHO WAS GEROLAMO VANO? **MEAN FELLOW**, MANIPULATOR, executed by his employers in September 1622, probably for perjury. He was a man of unremarkable appearance, **of average height and build, whose hair is white at the ends**. His principal legacy to posterity is his folder of reports. Reading them is sometimes like reading fiction, in that Vano's words are artful and manipulative as well as dramatic and exciting, but the stories they contain are different from those in either a seventeenth-century play or a modern novel. For the most part, Vano refused to offer explicit interpretations, and in doing so he also refused to organise events into an extended plot. Instead he shuffled the same motifs again and again: a dealer with a limited pack of cards, worn and greasy from overuse. The Spanish ambassador stamps his foot / grinds his teeth / weeps / foams at the mouth. Delete as appropriate. There is no character or plot arc— and no development. The reports are repetitive, and the series begins and ends abruptly, without warning in either case.

Despite these limitations, Vano was a serious writer because he dealt in essences, not in mere appearances—good and evil, loyalty and betrayal—but he summoned these essences with the most ephemeral of surface details: a glance over the shoulder, a cough, a cloak held over the face or a look held too long. The iconography of betrayal, an inverted iconography of desire. Unlike those who wrote for the theatre houses in Jacobean London, Vano's tales also had immediate and violent consequences: betrayal, assassination and execution. He understood that a well-turned phrase could kill just as effectively as a stiletto thrust.

Vano's reports are not an autobiography. They reveal nothing of his interior life or his material circumstances and, as with most of the inhabitants of early modern Europe, we know little of his background. The contrast with Foscarini, his most famous victim, is striking. Venetian nobles were members of an exclusive and hereditary political class with proud and long-established traditions. Vano was nobody, nothing, a shadow—Foscarini's shadow, in fact.

What do we know about this shadow? We can work backwards and outwards from his death, along a chain of names and documents and out to the town where he was born. For example, we know that Vano was fifty-six years old when he died (four years older than Foscarini) and that he was from Salò, a small town on the Venetian mainland. We also know that he had a wife called Faustina, whose existence comes to light only because she is mentioned in the will that Vano wrote in the condemned cell on the day before his death. She is never mentioned before that, in either his intelligence reports or any of the official documents in which Vano's name appears. There were apparently no children from the marriage, or at least none are named in the will.

According to Vano's reports, his enemies referred to him as 'captain', which implies military experience. In the command structure of early seventeenth-century armies, 'captain' usually meant someone in charge of a company, who contracted to lead and pay (and sometimes to recruit) the troops under his command. The size of a given company varied greatly—from roughly a hundred to four hundred men—and the job required a degree of prestige and wealth. Thus captains rarely rose 'through the ranks', although they were not necessarily noble. Alternatively, the title may have been a sarcastic reference to Vano's activities as spymaster. The leaders of the Council of Ten's private police force were also called captains, so the word may even have been a nod to Vano's privileged status as someone with access to resources normally reserved for the police. In any case, we only have Vano's word that the Spaniards called him captain. The Venetians never used the term.

What else? Vano's Last Will also reveals that he was involved in an extended network of debits and credits and at least one legal dispute, although none of the names he mentions in this context appears in his spy reports. This in itself is interesting, since it means that Vano kept his spying separate from the rest of his life, in contrast to many of his rivals. The most useful piece of information contained in the will is, however, an apparently incidental detail, which is important less for what it says than for where it leads us. Towards the end, Vano mentions that his wife's dowry was registered with a notary named Crivelli, whose offices were at Rialto. This is a thread that can be followed out elsewhere.

There are records extant from two notaries with the surname Crivelli around 1620. In the index of documents drawn up by one of them, Giovanni Crivelli, there is an entry under the letter 'F', dated 26 August 1619, which reads: **Faustina, consort of Gerolamo Vano, Dowry**. If you order up the document indicated, you will discover that what Crivelli drew up in August 1619 was not, strictly speaking, a dowry contract. Rather, it was a renewal of Vano's commitment to restore after his death the sum already paid to him in Naples in 1602 by Faustina's family. Under Venetian law he was obliged to do this anyway, so possibly the declaration was intended to reassure Faustina or clear up any legal ambiguities resulting from the fact that the initial contract had been drawn up outside Venice.

The 1619 pledge is revealing. First of all, it shows that Vano once lived in Naples, at that time Spanish territory, and that his wife was presumably Neapolitan. That might explain why he apparently found it so easy to cultivate employees in the Spanish embassy in Venice. Also, the dowry was quite substantial: 2381 Neapolitan ducats, not a sum that would be offered by (or indeed to) a pauper. Finally, the most revealing detail of all can be found in the postscript, which indicates that the contract was not drawn up in the notary Crivelli's office. Instead, it was drawn up in the warehouse owned collectively by the merchants from Salò who traded in Venice, and it was witnessed by members of that community. Why is this important? Because it confirms that Vano was not a shadow to the people who knew him. Rather, he was a valued member of the commune of Salò, publicly acknowledged as such by his fellow expatriates. If others came to know him as the Venetian **general of spies**, the two sides of his character were not entirely unconnected. In one of Vano's spy reports, for example, we learn that the Salodian warehouse served as a message drop, where Vano's accomplice Domenico left letters filched from the embassy.

Crivelli's contract also provides us with another link on the chain leading back into Vano's past, since it contains a reference to a document ratifying a division of inherited property among Vano and his brothers.* This document was registered with yet another notary, this time back in Salò. His records now survive in the city of Brescia, not too far from Venice, where I was able to consult them. They contain many brief references to Vano in the early seventeenth century. He appears both as a participant in legal decisions and as a witness to agreements reached by others. On at least one occasion, he helped broker the settlement of a feud. These appearances in Salò are intermittent, and do not preclude periods away from the area—for example, in Naples—but they do mean that Vano persistently returned to his birthplace, at least before 1618. Even more importantly, when considered together with similar appearances by his two brothers, his father, and other men with the same

---

* Such divisions were common under Venetian law, which did not have a system in which the eldest son automatically inherited the estate. On the contrary, property was presumed to be held in common among all surviving male children, an arrangement known as the *fraterna*.

surname who were probably cousins, they prove that Vano's family was large, prosperous and influential, and that Gerolamo was a prominent member of it.

One of the most important things we know about Vano is so obvious that it would not seem worth mentioning under other circumstances. We know that he was able to write, in a laborious but legible italic script, which he used for all his spy reports. Although he did use some secretarial abbreviations, he also employed a great deal of non-standard or dialect-inflected grammar and vocabulary. Conversely, he never wrote in Latin or made literary references. His reports are strictly functional in tone and style, if we discount the melodramatic conversations he transcribed. He also knew a little Spanish, although he could have picked this up conversationally, probably in Naples. Last but not least, we know that Vano falsely accused Antonio Foscarini of selling information to foreign ambassadors in 1622, an accusation that proved fatal for both men.

For two and a half years, Vano razed reputations and lives. He stripped other men naked while revealing nothing of himself, except indirectly, by the way in which he wrote.

5. IDIOLECT

VANO USES A LANGUAGE THAT IS RECOGNISABLY RELATED to modern Italian but is nonetheless quite distinct from it. Similarly, although many of his words and constructions come from Venetian dialect, he was not really writing in dialect, which is probably just as well, since dialect presents considerable difficulties to a foreigner like me. I still have to mentally pair Vano's words with the 'proper' Italian equivalent: *cifra* with Vano's **ziffra** (cipher), *nemici* with his **inimisi** (enemies), *voglio* with **voio** (I want) and so on. For me, the melody line of Vano's reports is composed of chords, in which the word on the page is silently counterpointed by its modern Italian substitute.

There are other difficulties. For example, like many writers of the period, Vano used many abbreviations and contractions, often omitted apostrophes and sometimes ran words together. For all these reasons, his reports would be virtually incomprehensible to an unprepared reader, even before you factor in the dense network of highly specific references to persons and events that make up their content.

That is why they are exciting.

To adapt a dictum of T. S. Eliot, the beauty of certain sentences is best appreciated before you are fully conversant with the language in which they are written. Approached in this way, the words are strange, unfamiliar objects, whose meaning and sound cannot be taken for granted. They are unstable and treacherous. They have to be handled carefully. In the archive, my reading is slower and more laborious than that of my Italian colleagues. The compensation for this is that I remain aware of Vano's words as *things*, with their own specific physical qualities. They have a particular feel when you say them aloud, a thickness and heaviness that is partly a result of the difficulty they pose and partly a result of the sounds characteristic of Venetian dialect, although in fact Vano's most distinctive coinages are his attempts to render Spanish words and phrases phonetically, such as **zentilhombre** (a hybrid form of **gentleman**). His words taste like red wine—or, to be more precise, bad red wine: acidic, furring the tongue, lips and teeth; intoxicating, yet also prone to induce sore eyes and jabbing headaches. The more of them you speak, the more they numb the mouth and brain, and induce slurring.

They are not subtle, but they do the job.

The paradox is this. I possess Vano's words most fully when I make them available to the reader by translating them into English, but the power of these words resides equally in the phrases and passages that remain untranslatable and are hidden in the notes, or the dots indicating an ellipsis ... My reading slows at these points of resistance, where the words will not yield up sense, either because of a peculiar construction or an unexplained reference. This is not a sobering experience. It does not break the spell, or leave me stranded outside the text. On the contrary, it is at these points that the intoxication is greatest, the senses are most befuddled, and the difficulty of responding coherently is most pronounced. It is then that I stumble and cannot hide how drunk I am— so drunk that making sense no longer seems to matter.

I am no longer self-possessed, but nor am I possessed by Vano. I would not want to be. He is a frightening man.

Report by Gerolamo Vano dated 4 August 1620, reproduced by permission of the Archivio di Stato di Venezia (concession number 70/2005).

6. ODD ONE OUT

ALL OF THE FOLLOWING ARE GENUINE EXCERPTS FROM dialogue quoted in the reports of Gerolamo Vano—except one.

*WITH APOLOGIES TO ROY LICHTENSTEIN.

7. CAFFÈ ROSSO, 7.00 P.M.

Jon: It's your round.

Jim: How d'you work that out?

Jon: Because it was mine the last time we met.

Phil: Which was when, exactly?

Jon: Last June. But that's not the point.

Jim: Spoken like a true Northerner. [To waitress:] *Tre Spritz bitter per favore* [a local drink combining Campari, white wine and soda].

Jon: Once upon a time, being a historian meant spending your career unpicking the minutiae of international diplomacy, but we only have to provide a bit of background here. So why were the Venetians afraid of the Spanish?

Phil: The Venetians weren't just bothered about the Spanish. They were bothered about the Hapsburgs [the royal dynasty] ruling both Spain and Austria.

Jon: And what would a history book be without kings and queens? Go on then—tell us more.

Phil: To the west of Venice you had the [Spanish-governed] Duchy of Milan, and in order to move troops to support their Austrian relatives, the Spanish needed to go through northern Italy, into Germany. So there was a geopolitical reason for Venetian fears.

Jim: The Venetians also had to worry about the pope to the south. A particular concern was that the papacy was under Spanish influence ...

Phil: That's right. And the Spanish also governed southern Italy.

Jim: So the Venetian fear was that a kind of alternative commercial route would develop, because the Venetians—the way they traded was to have all goods go from the eastern Mediterranean to the western Mediterranean up the Adriatic.

Jon: To force people to go along the route they controlled. *

Jim: Whereas the Spanish and the pope were developing an alternative route via Naples to Spain, and that would endanger Venetian trading revenues.

Phil: So in these years, the whole question of control of the Adriatic became central. If we go forward to the period when Vano was active, this whole situation was about to explode. There was war in Germany from 1618, and the truce between Spain and Holland was—

Jon: Due to expire

Phil: —due to expire in 1621. And no one was sure what would happen then.

---

* That is, any merchant ship entering the Adriatic was obliged to unload at Venice, thus ensuring that all goods entered Italy there and so could be taxed by the Venetians.

Jon: Right. There was a Viceroy or governor in southern Italy, the Duke of Ossuna, who was formally under the control of Spain but actually had a lot of independence. Despite the fact that Venice and Spain were supposed to be at peace, the Viceroy's fleet was sailing up and down the Adriatic, into waters claimed by Venice.

Phil: That's right. The Venetians believed the appearance of this fleet was connected to a conspiracy they claimed to have uncovered at the same time. In fact, they believed it was an invasion fleet. Though the Spanish pretended the Viceroy was doing his own thing.

Jon: Right, okay.

Phil: He might actually have been acting on the orders of the Spanish king.

Jon: There are ways in which it was useful not to be fully in control or fully accountable, just as there were different levels of consent and awareness. That was important for Vano's actions, just as it was important at the level of international politics.

Phil: What's interesting is that contemporaries had the same problems as historians have today in understanding what was really going on behind the scenes. Everyone debated these questions openly, even though governments tried to stop them.

Jon: One of the other important things to be aware of is that inside Venice there were, er, different ideas about the best way to respond. An important faction, an increasingly influential faction, favoured neutrality and isolationism. They wanted to avoid attracting the attentions of the Spanish. And then there was another faction, which was, I guess, more and more in a minority, and Foscarini was a member

of this faction, and they were in favour of a more
adventurous, more aggressive foreign policy.

Phil: Europe in the 1610s was a bit like Europe in
the 1930s. Everyone was expecting a major war, and
there were lots of potential flash-points.

Jon: It was just a question of which was going to
spark the powder, to use one of those tedious dead
metaphors that historians love! Venice was one of those
flashpoints, but so was Germany and so was Holland.

Phil: Just as in the 1930s you had Czechoslovakia, the
Rhineland, Trieste and so on. And in fact the 'real'
war finally broke out in Bohemia in 1618.

Jon: There was also a 'cold war' aspect to this, with
a lot of propaganda, misinformation and provocation.

Phil: A paper war rather than a cold war. One of the
key problems in Venetian defence was that they lacked
a proper standing army and didn't have a pool of
surplus labour from which to recruit in times of
crisis, so they relied totally on foreign mercenaries.

Jim: It was said that Venice had two problems: *grano
e gente,* corn and people, because Venice didn't have
the countryside in which to grow corn and didn't have
enough people.

Jon: The background to the Spanish conspiracy of
1618 involved mercenaries. This conspiracy, and its
aftermath, set the scene for the early 1620s. It
created the atmosphere of paranoia in which Vano
flourished and Foscarini's execution took place.
But it's a terribly complicated set of events.
Why is the Spanish conspiracy so controversial?

Phil: Well, this might be the shortest ever summary
of the Spanish conspiracy, the so-called Spanish
conspiracy.

Jon: The disclaimer is now obligatory.

Phil: There are very few undisputed facts, but we can start one morning in May 1618, when Venetians arriving at Piazza San Marco were faced with two corpses hanging from the gallows. A third appeared a few days later. Other executions took place at about the same time in the Venetian fleet.

Jon: Like the morning in 1622 when passersby were confronted with Foscarini's corpse, which also appeared hanging upside down in San Marco. In both cases, the explanations, the storytelling, were retrospective. We begin with a death or deaths, with mute corpses that the Council of Ten forced to speak against their will, and what it forced them to say was, 'Treason, justly punished'. Everything else was a response to that initial statement. We begin at the end and everything unfolds in 'flashback'.

Phil: Yes, and in 1618 it quickly became clear that the executions were the result of a conspiracy.

Jon: So-called conspiracy.

Phil: Yes, but this situation wasn't unique. There'd been other conspiracies, and their memory was an important part of Venetian history.

Jon: And the Council of Ten was actually founded in response to these earlier conspiracies, hundreds of years before.

Phil: In other words, it wasn't impossible for Venetians to imagine a conspiracy that threatened the state's existence. The version of events initially accepted in Venice was that Ossuna, the Spanish Viceroy of Naples, had tried to plant spies and soldiers in Venice, with the aim of seizing the Arsenal, the Ducal Palace and the houses of the most important senators, especially those linked with Foscarini's faction. There are similarities with the Gunpowder Plot of 1605 in London. Potentially, this had serious diplomatic consequences. If it was true, then Spain and Venice ought to be at war. Well they weren't at war, but there were some upsets. The Spanish ambassador Bedmar fled the city, for example.

Jon: There is no real proof that Bedmar supported the plot.

Phil: Yes, but the point is that the Venetian version was credible, at least in the city. However, different versions of events were quickly circulated, in an attempt to justify Bedmar or to justify Spain. And it's impossible to reconcile these accounts. The controversy has continued among historians ever since. One version is that the Venetians over-reacted to a half-baked idea on the part of some discontented mercenaries acting without Spanish approval. Another is that the Ten actually invented the whole thing, to discredit the Spanish, get rid of the ambassador Bedmar and force the Viceroy of Naples to recall his fleet from the Adriatic.

Another problem for Venetians is that Venice was known as the *Serenissima,* the 'Most Serene Republic', free from discord and unrest. The famous conspiracies happened in the fourteenth century, and they were remembered as things of the past, from the 'bad old days'. So, the very existence of a modern conspiracy, even though it was foiled, was a major blow to Venice's reputation.

Jim: Everyone was afraid of conspiracies, weren't they? Kings were being assassinated left, right and centre.

Phil: But many of these 'conspiracies' were encouraged by *agents provocateurs.*

Jim: What—you think they were invented?

Phil: Stage-managed would be a better way of putting it.

Jon: This is precisely the period when Vano's career as a spy took off; that is, during an unstable period in Europe, which caused great anxiety in Venice. So Vano's information on the Spanish embassy in Venice acquired an exaggerated importance. He was the right man in the right place at the right time—or the wrong man in the wrong place at the wrong time, if you look at it from Foscarini's point of view. After Vano's downfall, and as a direct result of Foscarini's exoneration in 1623, the mood changed, and rumours about Spanish plots were treated with greater scepticism.

Jim: Who's up for another drink?

[Non-applicable conversation follows.]

8. THE FILE

ACH OF VANO'S REPORTS IS WRITTEN ON A SINGLE OR double sheet of cheap paper and has a hole in the middle, where a secretary originally stuck it on a paper spike. Some have brief annotations identifying them as **from Vano**, or indicating important topics broached within. On average, Vano composed three or four such reports a week. There were active periods when he produced two or three updates a day but there are also weeks or months with no material at all. The original audience consisted firstly of the secretary of the Inquisitors of State, and then of the three Inquisitors themselves, who changed office annually. The Inquisitors of State are not to be confused with the church Inquisition. Rather, they were responsible for protecting state secrets, and as such they sponsored spying, although their executive powers were limited. In effect, the Inquisitors were a sub-committee of the Council of Ten, a magistracy with a much wider mandate for ensuring public order and state security.* The Inquisitors were elected from within the Ten, and their decisions had to be ratified by the larger council, so although the two magistracies had separate archives (both of which are quoted in this book), their membership and activities overlapped. When Vano's information required an official response—for example, an arrest—excerpts from his reports were read out to the Council of Ten, who made the appropriate decisions and then transferred or copied the relevant supporting information into their own archive for future reference.

Vano's reports are not literally in cipher, because he handed them directly to the Inquisitors' secretary, and so there was no need to actively disguise their content. In a sense, it would be easier if they were encrypted, because then their interpretation would be a purely technical problem. The Venetians used a syllabic system, and it is not difficult to crack. Vano's reports present more insidious problems, even though they look much more straightforward at first glance. The first one opens as follows.

File 636, 2 May 1620:

Don Francesco the Spaniard and the *Clarissimo* ** Minotto have changed the place where they meet. They don't go to the church of Sant'Andrea any more, but speak elsewhere. The *Clarissimo* Minotto said to him, 'That Jew of an Ambassador doesn't want to give me the money'. The Spaniard replied, 'He will give you what he promised. Watch out. We should not meet so openly'.

We are immediately dropped into the centre of things, but that is the problem. Who are the mysterious Don Francesco and the *Clarissimo* Minotto? We have to work that out for ourselves. And who is the source

---

* Rather confusingly, the Council of Ten actually had seventeen men sitting on it: ten 'ordinary' elected members, plus the doge (the elected Venetian head of state) and six ducal councillors. The latter seven were *ex officio* members who were simultaneously members of the Venetian cabinet, which set the agenda of business put before the much larger Senate. Two of the three Inquisitors of State were elected from among the 'ordinary' members of the Ten, while the third was always a ducal councillor.

** A title reserved exclusively for Venetian nobles, which roughly translates as 'Most Illustrious'.

for this account of a private conversation between them? Vano takes our complicity for granted, and continues to do so. He piles name upon name and incident upon incident. The merciless pace never lets up until his own arrest in August 1622. Without any context or cross-referencing, it quickly begins to resemble the gibberish of enciphered text.

Vano did not always know the significance of what he was saying; he was not able to compare it with information available from other sources; he was not aware that some of his 'news' was pitifully thin, irrelevant or obsolete from the Inquisitors' point of view. Nor was he always able to tell when he had hit upon something important. To a certain extent, he was guessing about what the Inquisitors wanted to know. They were not always willing to confirm if his guesses were right. Not only was Vano ignorant of what was important, but he had no idea what was likely to become important, even if it currently seemed irrelevant. Therefore in every report he emptied out a rubbish bin of scraps and left his readers to sift through it.

If we cannot swim in the stream of information as the Inquisitors did, then we can at least try to avoid being washed away by anchoring ourselves with some specific questions. For a start, how did the collection of reports now preserved in File 636 come to exist? They describe a relationship: between Vano and the Inquisitors, but by the time the file begins in May 1620, that relationship was already established. How then did it begin?* There are hints elsewhere in the Inquisitors' archive.

The earliest surviving document relating to Vano is a paraphrase of an interview dated August 1617. It is typical of the material offered to the Inquisitors during this period by other potential informants. It describes a casual conversation about foreign policy between Vano and a man who claimed to be from the Spanish embassy. However, since the conversa-

---

* File 636 in its current form is the creation of a nineteenth-century archivist. Besides Vano's reports, it contains those of numerous other informants from various epochs whose surnames begin with 'V', each set slipped within a separate cover sheet. Nonetheless, the fact that the reports survive as a group together suggests that they were originally stored that way.

tion was extremely vague, the report was practically worthless, except possibly as a guide to rumours circulating in Venice.

After this isolated and rather unimpressive debut, there is no trace of Vano for eighteen months. What was he doing during this period? In a petition written in March 1619, he provided a retrospective summary of his activities. Among other things, he had twice journeyed to Rimini to spy on pirates operating there against Venetian shipping. A subsequent assassination attempt on another group of pirates was aborted when the targets withdrew to Naples. In a later petition written in May 1622, Vano described himself as having been engaged on **matters of the highest importance** on behalf of the Ten for five years, implying fairly consistent employment from 1617 onwards. All this suggests a man anxious to ingratiate himself.

Am I not here? whom you have made? your creature?

It remains unclear what Vano did before 1617 and whether he continued to practise any trade other than spying after his arrival in Venice. He was clearly ambitious, but strong-arm expeditions into Spanish territory were not the best way to guarantee a future income, especially for a man in his early fifties. If Vano was indeed an ex-soldier, he may have been looking for another way to exploit his skills at recruiting and leading men. For example, the supply of information from regular, established sources was a specialised (and relatively sedentary) activity, in which the quality and identity of those providing the service were critical. Recruiting a privileged source was the best way to become indispensable.

The next trace of Vano's slippery progress into the Inquisitors' confidence is hidden in their files of correspondence. In 1617, a Venetian noble called Hieronimo Grimani escaped to Naples after being convicted of working for the Spanish. Over the next few years, the Inquisitors kept a close eye on Grimani, whom they first made tentative plans to assassinate and then recruited as an informant. Hence, from 1618 onwards, much of the Inquisitors' correspondence with the Venetian resident in Naples concerned Grimani's activities and declining fortunes. Inserted among the official despatches on this topic are numerous intercepted copies of letters exchanged between Grimani and his wife and daughter back in Venice. They were probably misfiled at some point in the nineteenth century, since the accompanying despatches do not refer to them and the dates do not always correspond. The important point for our purposes is that many of these letters are annotated as **presented by Hieronimo Vano from Salò**, or more simply **from H. V.** (using the Latinate form of Vano's name, as secretaries tended to do). There is of course no explanation in the file as to how Vano got access to the correspondence.

After the Grimani letters, the next set of references to Vano comes in late 1619 and concerns his recruitment of an informant in the Spanish embassy in Venice, Diego Gomez, whose story we shall return to. There is again no account of how the two men met, but it presumably did not happen by chance, and again Vano's initial access to Gomez and the embassy may have been related to his Neapolitan connections.

At the end of this trail, we return to the place where my archival research started: File 636, which contains hundreds of Vano's surveillance reports, beginning in May 1620 and continuing for the next two and a half years, until 16 August 1622. We are now in a position to suggest why the file begins where it does.

Hypothesis: it was only in 1620, and as a direct result of the recruitment of the Spaniard Diego Gomez, that Vano made the jump in the Inquisitors' estimation from occasional employee to trusted confidante. In the period between his first tentative report in 1617 and the reports contained in File 636, it is obvious that Vano's expertise and his ambition grew exponentially. The creation of a separate 'file' was thus the consequence of an increase in both the volume of material Vano produced and the importance attached to it. Before May 1620, the few references to Vano's progress are scattered throughout various locations, in various different kinds of document, almost none of which was written by Vano himself. After May 1620, that all changed. Henceforth, Vano took charge of his own story—and that of others.

9. THE INQUISITORS OF STATE

I f Vano's recruitment of Gomez explains the opening of File 636, there is still no guarantee that it is complete, since the first report begins abruptly *in medias res* and the last one also ends that way. Worse, the archive of the Inquisitors of State was disfigured by nineteenth-century attempts to rationalise and reorder its contents. As a result, it is not clear how meaningful either its order or disorder are. There are more problems: gaps inside the file as well as a ragged beginning and end. Weeks and months have been razored out of the years 1620, 1621 and 1622. What do these gaps represent? Vano's deliberate omissions? A secretary removing material for incorporation in trial records that were subsequently lost? A nineteenth-century archivist trimming material considered unimportant? Or were they simply periods during which Vano had nothing to say?

We might understand the file better if we explore in more detail Vano's relationship with his employers, the three Inquisitors of State, who were elected from the members of the Council of Ten. As a permanent body exclusively dedicated to protecting state secrets—what we now call counter-intelligence work—the Inquisitors were virtually a unique institution in seventeenth-century Europe. Elsewhere, such intelligence was gathered by networks run by individual diplomats or statesmen as part of their attempts at personal advancement. Even so, the Inquisitors were not a modern intelligence service. Not only did their membership rotate annually, but they had no permanent staff, with the single exception of their secretary, who was always nominated from among the four employed by the Council of Ten, a post he continued to hold concurrently.

The Inquisitors' secretary was the person Vano dealt with most frequently on a day-to-day basis. In 1619 and early 1620, this man was Zuan Battista Padavin, a very experienced bureaucrat, who had also carried out many sensitive diplomatic missions. He was not, then, a naïve reader, and it would have been hard for Vano to fool him. In October 1620, however, Padavin was replaced by Roberto Lio, who 'ran' Vano for the next two years, until Vano's career met its ignominious end in 1622. Lio was no fool either—he had been a member of the Venetian chancery for more than thirty years—but he had no previous experience of assessing information obtained by spying, and this fact was probably crucial. Lio's period of office as secretary to the Inquisitors was thus a 'gap' or window of opportunity that Vano was able to exploit.[*] His early reports—to Padavin—were probably (more or less) reliable and the men denounced in them were all guilty as charged. It was only in 1621 that the names of innocent men started to appear.

Although Vano co-ordinated surveillance operations with the Ten's small police force, he essentially remained freelance. He was never a state employee. That was how the Venetians ran things. Tender and subcontract. Co-opt and disassociate. Sever nerve tissue and sensation. Righteous indifference. Vano's foot was in the door, but he always had to

---

[*] None of the three inquisitors who requested the arrest of Foscarini on 8 April 1622 had served in the office before, or at least in the previous ten years. By contrast, the men who presided over Foscarini's absolution in January 1623 had all dealt directly with Vano in the previous three years.

compete for the right to supply information. His competitors appear occasionally in his reports, generally in a negative light. His area of expertise was the Spanish embassy and contacts between its staff and other foreign representatives in Venice. After the coup in recruiting Gomez, he went wherever the availability of information took him—in particular, to the Imperial residence and that of the Duke of Mantua, allies of Spain. These were the obvious targets for an ambitious spy in the early 1620s.

Since he was not an official employee, Vano's payments were irregular and gratuitous rather than guaranteed and fixed. Income depended on Vano producing results and on his ability to transfigure the greed of informants into moments of patriotic grace. Money was the informants' only absolution, and this was the measure of their degradation. They were required to repeat a penitential cycle of betrayal to get at it. A significant portion of their 'information' consisted of complaints that they were not being paid enough. As the Inquisitors noted in 1618, it was best to **reward irregularly and never with large individual sums ... because we find [that] ... an uncertain or unreliable income produces better results**. The Inquisitors knew that fasting was good for the soul.

Grace also meant turning a blind eye to minor financial irregularities. Vano did submit accounts, but who knows how trustworthy or complete they were? His freedom mirrored similar privileges that the Inquisitors had in relation to the Venetian fisc. They too were indulged by larger councils to which they were technically accountable. For Vano, as for many other recipients of official gratitude, certificates of indulgence came in the form of blank pardons to be sold on to others. Vano received at least five during his career.

The use of such pardons in early seventeenth-century Venice was a response both to the difficulties of law enforcement and a lack of hard cash. In the Venetian legal system, there was little effective policing, and so many criminals absconded before being arrested. They were then outlawed *in absentia*, which explains the buoyant market for blank pardons among the bandits infesting the Venetian state. Capture an outlaw and deliver him into the hands of justice, or murder him if you prefer. Get a pardon in return and sell it to another outlaw.* Round and round it went. The state offered shares in forgiveness. Adventurous speculators with good contacts could make a killing.

While they waited to negotiate the purchase of a pardon, some bandits sought protection in the legal enclaves of the various foreign embassies in Venice. So, in 1611, twenty-four men convicted of capital crimes were alleged to be lodged in the Spanish embassy, out of police reach. Bandits therefore appear frequently as spear-carriers in Vano's reports: dogs of the house of Spain, barking at nosy spies, keeping the neighbours awake at night.

Vano had more in common with these men than with the Inquisitors and their secretary. He was not a bureaucrat. He did not need to write everything down, since he met regularly with the Inquisitors' secretary. Some of the information 'missing' from his reports must therefore have been conveyed verbally for reasons of security and immediacy. As Diego Gomez put it, **Vano will tell you everything in more detail by mouth**. The Inquisitors also summoned Vano regularly to appear before them in person. Meeting face to face was an opportunity for them to observe the quality of the person and measure this against the apparent quality of the information. Hence Vano continued his visits to the Ducal Palace, despite the fact that his enemies were able to monitor them. When they could, the Inquisitors also interviewed Vano's informants directly, at least in the early stages of his career. Ultimately, Vano always had to justify himself. In Foscarini's case, he did so on the gallows.

---

* Those claiming such rewards sometimes had to prove that the killing had taken place (with a severed head, for example). Police agents were also given pardons as bonuses for apprehending outlaws or other dangerous criminals. Indeed, this was their major source of income, since salaries were low and paid irregularly.

10. DIPLOMACY

B Y THE EARLY 1620S, A EUROPE-WIDE SYSTEM OF PERMANENT embassies was already well established, although these 'ordinary' embassies were still frequently supplemented by 'extraordinary' missions, sent for particular ceremonial and diplomatic ends. Technically, however, only the European monarchies and Venice sent ambassadors to one another. The representatives of smaller states were given the lesser title of 'residents' or 'agents', and therefore occupied 'residencies' rather than embassies. Similarly, states like Venice, who sent full ambassadors to England, Spain and France, maintained only residents or consuls in smaller states like Switzerland or in dependent territories such as the Spanish viceroyalties of Milan and Naples. Finally, there were also temporary, *de facto* residents, secretaries lacking the wealth and social status expected of an ambassador, who took over when an ambassador was recalled, remaining as a stopgap until a successor arrived.

The division between ambassadors and residents or agents can be clearly observed in Venice in the early 1620s. The French and the English maintained embassies, as did the Spanish until the recall at the end of 1620 of the ambassador Bravo, whose secretary Andrea Irles then took over as temporary resident. The fact that the Emperor had only a resident was also due to the temporary lack of a qualified ambassador. Conversely, the representatives of smaller Italian states like Mantua were defined as residents because they were not entitled to the higher status, rather than because they chose not to make use of it.

In the early seventeenth century, diplomatic practice was still complicated by problems resulting from the Reformation. The division of Europe into Catholic and Protestant states had destroyed the fiction of a united Christendom that underlay the practice of medieval diplomacy, and states of different religions had yet to formally admit that they had a reciprocal right to existence. As a result, there had been no embassies from Protestant countries to Italy during the latter part of the sixteenth century. In the years after 1600, however, the system of resident embassies was gradually restored, although the papacy continued to have no diplomatic relations with Protestant powers.[*]

Resident ambassadors represented the authority and interests of their masters—in the practical sense of communicating and defending their actions and decisions as well as in the symbolic sense of substituting for them on ceremonial occasions. Hence, precedence and ceremonial rights were among the major preoccupations of diplomats during this period, just as honour remained one of the most important principles of international relations. As one commentator put it, **Princes and soveraigne estates doe hold many-times more deare, the conservation of their degree and dignitie than of their lands and possessions.** Vano's total indifference to such matters clearly distinguishes his reports from official ambassadorial despatches and is a sign of his unusual specialisation in counter-intelligence work.

Resident ambassadors were also expected to gather information—in other words, to engage in extra-diplomatic activities, which were not part of the official public duties declared to their hosts but were tacitly

---

[*] The pope's diplomatic representatives were called 'nuncios', and in some respects they constitute a special case.

accepted within certain bounds. In pursuit of such information, ambassadors frequently ran networks of informants. This part of the ambassador's job was described with considerable distaste by many writers of treatises; hence the famous, contradictory description of ambassadors as honourable Spies. The limits of acceptable behaviour in this area were unclear, but the Spanish ambassador Bravo was clearly felt to have contravened them in Venice by suborning the nobles Zuanne Minotto and Zuan Battista Bragadin, whose treachery was exposed by Vano. So the Mantuan resident noted in a despatch of 18 July 1620 that **The nobles complain … that he behaved very badly in corrupting an innocent youngster like Minotto, a wealthy man with an income of about six thousand ducats a year, … [They argue that] a minister can legitimately use spies, but not exploit treachery such as this.** Nonetheless, Bravo remained in office after Minotto's exposure, at least for a few more months, and no official complaint was made to his master, Philip III.

I said above that ambassadors 'represented' their king or master, but that did not mean that they were civil servants or bureaucrats. Rather, most had a close personal relationship with the sovereign—and were appointed because of it. If they sought to cultivate potential informants as their personal clients, they were also clients of their king, for whose favour they competed. Contemporary treatises all recommended that ambassadors be wealthy men of good birth, so that their service would give honour to their ruler. Some were men of considerable influence in their own right, who (as Montaigne puts it) do not simply carry out, but also by their counsel form and direct their master's will. They sometimes acted on their own authority or exceeded their mandates. This was frequently the case for Spanish ministers in the early seventeenth century, and it was also true of Antonio Foscarini, who had been Venetian ambassador to France and England in the 1610s. In any case, far from home, ambassadors were frequently required to interpret very general or outdated orders and apply them to new or changing contexts.

Today, embassies are treated as legal islands, not subject to the laws of their host country. This legal fiction of 'extraterritoriality' had not yet been formulated in the 1620s, although the treatment of ambassadors with different religious beliefs perhaps hinted at it. By the 1620s, the usual solution to this problem adopted for both Catholic ambassadors in England and Protestants in Venice was to allow them to worship according to their own rites in a private chapel in the embassy. Certainly the idea of diplomatic immunity was universally acknowledged, but what it meant in practice was a matter for debate. Ambassadorial privileges therefore varied according to custom, from country to country. Matters such as the ambassador's liability for debts contracted during his stay and the right of police to arrest embassy employees guilty of common crimes were particularly sensitive topics, resolved on a case-by-case basis. Treatises of the period sometimes gave potentially contradictory advice on this point.

Early seventeenth-century ambassadors were not modern diplomats. Rather, their role and activities were the natural expression of the political regimes they served: for the most part, absolutist monarchies, where the king's relations with powerful subjects were determined on the principle of patron–client relations.

II. HONOUR AMONG SPIES

To understand Vano's progress, we need to trace the lines along which information travelled—the cat's cradle of entanglements out of which his words were woven. We need to thread our way through the moral and physical maze of Vano's Venice. Names are the most reliable markers. Follow them like a flag held by a tour guide. Start with Diego Gomez, whose relationship with Vano predated (and probably precipitated) the special arrangement with the Inquisitors that File 636 represents. Link him to Zuan Battista Bragadin, the first Venetian traitor to die because of Vano. Their destinies were closely intertwined. One was Vano's first informant; the other, his first victim.

The story is complex, but that is why it is useful. It begins with Vano as one among many potential informants and ends with him consolidating his position as Venetian **general of spies**. This change in Vano's status affected the nature of the evidence that has survived. The story ends in File 636, with Vano in control and submitting regular reports, but it begins elsewhere, in File 1214, which is a miscellaneous ragbag, where traces of Vano's early career are scattered among many other, unrelated documents. Even though the Inquisitors of State were a sub-committee of the Council of Ten, their archive was and is quite different from that of the larger council. The Inquisitors' secretary had exclusive control over it and complete discretion as to what should be recorded. His practice was therefore inconsistent and unpredictable. In effect, the Inquisitors' archive, such as it was, consisted of all the material that the secretary no longer needed. When something was officially 'archived', that meant it was locked away in a chest. Documents required for day-to-day consultation were kept separately and close to hand, while anything needed for future reference was transferred into the Ten's archive and filed there, since important matters ultimately had to be referred to the larger Council anyway. All this explains why File 1214 is so messy and incoherent: because it is not a real 'file' at all.

It would be incorrect, then, to say that I have 'reconstructed' this story, because it has never existed in this form before. It is made up of anonymous denunciations, notes from Vano and Diego Gomez, records of official proceedings and resolutions, interrogation transcripts and secretarial memoranda—all jumbled together. Most of these documents have no accompanying contextual information. History does not just 'happen'; it is made, and out of the most unpromising of materials. My account is a collage stitched together by the thread of a series of names: Diego Gomez, Zuan Battista Bragadin and Gerolamo Vano. My job is not to hide the joins but to show how the various pieces fit together. There is no apex or vanishing point and no vantage from which the contents of the entire archive can be surveyed or integrated. You must descend to ground level, into the warren of alleys and dead ends, to the exact point where the dagger draws blood and the pen blots the page.

File 1214, 21 December 1619, a speculative report from Vano: We begin five months away from the first report in File 636, with Vano angling for official recognition. The bait is this: Gomez can identify a mysterious visitor to the Spanish embassy. The technique is this: Vano presents a problem only when he can simultaneously offer a solution. The key to solving the problem turns out to be defining it precisely. To put it more plainly, there is a traitor, who is selling Venetian secrets (or rather there are traitors, plural, but one is more important than the others). Gomez can expose him, and Gomez is Vano's man.

File 1214, Christmas Day 1619, notes written by Zuan Battista Padavin, the Inquisitors' secretary: Padavin takes minutes for a secret meeting between the doge and the Inquisitors on one side, and Vano and Gomez on the other. It is a ceremony of initiation, in which Vano sponsors Gomez and asserts his moral rights in the matter. Padavin notes that Gomez is **a man of slightly below average height, about thirty years of age, with a light beard, dressed in cloth made of black silk ... [who] speaks Italian excellently**. He offers to serve, **sincerely, endangering his life and honour** in exchange for the recognition the republic is accustomed to grant for such service—which means cash and blank pardons.

Honour among spies is a difficult notion to define, since honour consists in the public recognition of a publicly valued role. Arguably a double agent like Gomez handed over his honour for at least the duration of his employment, if not permanently, like a woman handing over her chastity to a seducer. He received only periodic cash payments as security for the loan, and he had nothing to protect himself against public disgrace at the hands of those he had betrayed should they discover his treachery. Spying had its own forms of street theatre, as we shall see, but the double agent was paid in ways that were pitifully shorn and denuded of ritual significance, since neither he nor his employers could afford to acknowledge that payment had taken place. Spies were therefore the only crude economic rationalists in early seventeenth-century Venice. In their world, there were no ceremonies, no symbolic gift exchanges and no ritualised gestures.

Gomez was sent out shivering and naked. He could never see his true worth reflected in the faces of others. His worth was in fact directly proportional to the degree of his potential dishonour in the eyes of those he betrayed. This may explain why Gomez proved keen to recruit accomplices in the embassy. Perhaps he needed others to share his secret: to share his vision of himself as a man putting his honour on the line. Gomez remained obsessed with this theme throughout his short career, returning to the word honour like someone touching a sore tooth.

After the Christmas Day audience, Padavin, the secretary of the Inquisitors, was ordered to hand over one hundred ducats to Gomez. He noted that payment was made **through Vano, who gave me a receipt**. Vano was the symbolic broker of the deal, whose signature was on the receipt instead of Gomez's. Part of Vano's strength lay in his ability to control access to his informants. This too was how the Venetians liked to run things—using middlemen. Indeed, the trade of broker was in general an important one in Venice, practised in everything from gambling debts to marriages, as well as in fixing the terms for acts of betrayal. Vano, the spymaster, therefore acted as his informants' 'agent' from the start. Later, and more problematically, he also served as their 'ghostwriter'.

The first payment was the critical one. It left Gomez vulnerable to blackmail if he tried to back out of the deal. His honour was mortgaged for one hundred ducats. The only remaining question was at what point it would become forfeit. The best he could hope for was that his situation would not become any worse.

In the meantime, Gomez had the enthusiasm of a convert. Important intelligence on Spanish relations with other powers was immediately forthcoming on 26 December. Vano again performed the physical handover of the papers to Padavin. If Vano was Gomez's broker and cut out, then Padavin performed the same task for his masters. All the day-to-day work was carried out by intermediaries.

By 29 December, Gomez was having second thoughts. No doubt he had decided that reports written in his own hand were too compromising. Gomez's indecision on this matter continued. For example, a later report in File 1214 has the unintentionally ironic etiquette, **copy of a paper of Diego Gomez submitted by him on 2 March 1620 and returned to him at his request by order of the most excellent lords Inquisitors on 27 June by means of Gerolamo Vano**. Gomez presumably did not intend for the

Inquisitors to retain this copy. The obvious solution to this problem was the one later adopted in File 636, where Vano paraphrased information delivered to him orally by Gomez.

Back in December 1619, Gomez claimed to have used his one hundred ducats to recruit the ambassador's undersecretary.[*] Presumably this was a hint that he wanted more money, as was a boast of his **great merit**. There is no evidence that more money was forthcoming.

File 1214, 4 February 1620, a report to the Inquisitors from Gomez: It describes the routine for receiving a mysterious visitor to the embassy, who dresses as a priest. The lights are extinguished and the servants sent out. Pseudo-priest speaks alone with the ambassador and his secretary for half an hour. Gomez and another man try to follow him when he leaves, but he is too slippery. Gomez can provide two witnesses to support these accusations. He also suggests a list of questions for any eventual interrogation of pseudo-priest. He wants immediate payment or a written promise of payment.

Padavin, the Inquisitors' secretary, added an appendix to this report, noting that Vano had delivered it. Padavin explained to Vano that action could not be taken without conclusive proof that something illegal was taking place. Maybe pseudo-priest was a Spaniard, in which case arresting him could prove very embarrassing. Gomez must identify him as someone who was forbidden to visit the embassy.

I'll see before I doubt; when I doubt, prove.

Vano then left Padavin for a rendezvous at San Marco with Gomez, who was waiting to see if the witnesses were needed. Later on the same day, Vano returned to give Padavin an update. As a result, Padavin added a second appendix to Gomez's original report.

There are no neat, plodding chronicles here. Instead, there are notes, drafts, annotations and revisions. The story does not go straight from A to B. It doubles back and forth, crosses and re-crosses its own footsteps, and then lurches off abruptly down an alley as you try desperately

---

[*] He may have meant 'Zuanetto' (see below and Chapter 23, '2 + 2 = 5').

to keep up. It is easy to get confused or lost. Reorient yourself. YOU ARE HERE: at Padavin's second appendix to Gomez's original report.

File 1214, 4 February 1620: Vano met up again with Gomez after speaking to Padavin, and explained the latter's reservations. Gomez replied that he could not provide a name, although he swore he could pick the man out from a hundred others by sight. There was nothing more to do at that point, so Vano and Gomez left San Marco. They split up, but Gomez immediately doubled back to intercept Vano. He had seen pseudo-priest entering the church. Vano returned to San Marco. He waited for pseudo-priest to finish his (pseudo?) prayers, and followed him up towards Rialto. Vano approached a servant. Am I right in thinking that your master is Monsignor Arighi from Florence? (The question was of course a pretext, and the name an invented one.) The servant replied that no, his master was a Venetian gentleman from the clan of Bragadin. Ah, my mistake.

Pseudo-priest stopped to greet a foreign gentleman just before Rialto. After the two parted company, Vano followed the foreigner.

Was that priest Monsignor Arighi from Florence?

[The foreigner] replied that, no, he was a Venetian noble. He told me that he was either a son or a nephew of the Bragadin who was skinned in Cyprus;[*] **I can't remember which.**

Vano now had exactly what he needed to justify the target's arrest, since it was illegal for Venetian nobles to visit foreign embassies without explicit permission from the Council of Ten.

4 February 1620: Padavin wrote his account and passed everything on to the Inquisitors.

Follow the path of the signal: Bragadin to Gomez. Gomez to Vano. Vano to Padavin. Padavin to the Inquisitors. The Inquisitors back to Vano. On other occasions the loop was extended even further. For

---

[*] Marc Antonio Bragadin, commander of the Venetian garrison on Cyprus during the war of 1570–71, was captured and skinned alive by the Turks. In fact, the witness here was mistaken. Zuan Battista Bragadin was not closely related to Marc Antonio.

instance, the Spanish ambassador was inclined to confide in his wife. She was inclined to confide in her servant girl; the girl was inclined to confide in Gomez, with whom she was in love. Gomez to Vano, etc., etc. When the Inquisitors were ready to act, though, they preferred to cut out the cut-outs. Bypass Vano and Padavin, and bring in Gomez's witnesses. Immediately, the Inquisitors began to tighten the loop in a noose around Bragadin's neck.

File 1214, 5 February 1620, an interrogation transcript written by Padavin: It records a deposition from a young man of about twenty-six with a light beard. The man was described **by Gerolamo Vano (who accompanied him) as the gondolier of the Ambassador of Spain, or at least that was what Diego Gomez had told [Vano].** Men could not speak on their own authority, at least at first. Every fact began as an attribution.

Q. What is your name?

A. Menego from Venice, son of the late Zuanne of Friuli, but I was born in Venice. I don't know which part of Friuli my father was from.

Q. Justice has been told that you are willing to shed some light on the individuals who come secretly at night to meet with the Ambassador, [circumstances which] suggest that they intend to reveal the republic's affairs. Say what you know about this matter and list every detail with total honesty.

A. I can say truthfully that a man who dresses as a priest comes regularly almost every Friday about an hour after sunset. He hides his face with a handkerchief and he goes straight to the door of the Ambassador's room and knocks, and it is immediately opened. Everyone inside is sent away and the two go up to the platform on the roof.[*] **This man speaks to the Ambassador alone ... locked in the room for half or three quarters of an hour. Then he leaves by the darkened stairway, so that we can't see his face for the shadow and because he always holds his cloak over it.**

Armed with this information, the Inquisitors referred matters to the Ten for a decision, as they were constitutionally obliged to do.

---

[*] Such platforms were a common feature in Venetian houses.

File 1214, 6 February 1620, a draft resolution by the Council of Ten: **Authority is hereby given to our Inquisitors of State to use whatever officials or other means they see fit to arrest the man who secretly enters the house of the Ambassador of Spain … in the manner described in the papers now read. This action must be executed outside the Ambassador's house in the public street under pretext of looking for weapons or stolen goods.**

For 'officials', read the Ten's captain of police. For 'other means', read Gomez and Vano. The target's precise identity was still unclear because his first name was unknown.

The patchy material in File 1214, which we have been relying on so far, tells us little more, but at some point the operation must have been temporarily suspended pending further investigation, since Zuan Battista Bragadin, son of Alvise (to give him his full name) was not actually arrested until September 1620. In the meantime, we cut to File 636. From now on, we are forced to rely on what Vano chooses to tell us. Gomez never spoke directly to the Inquisitors again.

File 636, 8 June 1620: **Diego [Gomez] told me that he has important information about the highest in the city at his fingertips, but he doesn't want to reveal anything because he's disgruntled and [thinks that he] deserves a thousand gold coins. If he runs into [the secretary] Padavin, even if it's in the middle of the [P]iazza [San Marco], he's going to give him a piece of his mind, and he wants his papers back.**

[He said to me], 'I don't believe any more. I want your money and I will do nothing otherwise. If I betray my king and my master, if I risk my life and honour, I want gold coins from those big old men [i.e. the Inquisitors], who have no greater enemy than us Spaniards'.

Again we see the impeccably Aristotelian distinction between honour and profit, with the two balanced against each other in the scales, but the tone has changed. It is no longer that of Gomez's elegant but wheedling requests for money. Now we hear Vano's voice, and it is vivid and direct. He emphasises that Gomez is both a valuable asset and a potential threat. He is greedy and unstable, but Vano can control him, and the secretary Padavin need not fear any embarrassing confrontation. The subtext is: You cannot trust Gomez any more, but you can trust me.

The balance of power has shifted decisively.

As in every failing relationship, the more Gomez complained, the less impressive he appeared. **I don't believe any more.** Does this admission indicate that Gomez's understanding of his relationship with the Inquisitors had changed? Gomez now knew what he was worth to the Venetians: exactly what he could get out of them, and no more. Or does his statement represent self-knowledge? What exactly did he no longer believe in?

In any case, Gomez was fighting on the wrong front. Vano was unlikely to be impressed by appeals to honour, since his reports ironi-cally undermine the Spanish obsession with it at every opportunity. It was precisely because the ambassador Bravo, in his soldierly naïvety, relied on honour to guarantee the good faith of his employees that he was no match for Vano. For example, one night the gondolier Domenico (a.k.a. Menego, recruited by Gomez and now established as Vano's most important informant) arrived back at the embassy to find it empty—except for the ambassador Bravo, who was waiting to speak to him.

File 636, 9 October 1620: **'You are a brave man, Domenico, to refuse to confess. If only the king of Spain had a vassal as … [loyal to him] … as you are to your republic … But if you decide to reveal everything you know, the lord governor of Milan will give you a piece of bread [and] your own place, you and your relatives'. Then he got up and went to the desk and took a bag of gold coins in his hand and said, 'I want you to have these, you and your [women]. For the love of God, confess'. … And he asked if Diego [Gomez] met sometimes with that captain Gerolamo Vano from Salò, who lives in Blacksmith Alley.**

Domenico said, 'I don't know anything; I've never met this captain'.

Vano describes the Spanish as prone to suspicion but easily satisfied if the informant could keep bluffing; that is, if he refused to take Spanish notions of honour seriously. Vano never mocks Bravo openly, in keeping with a general reluctance to offer explicit interpretations. Nonetheless, the transcription of conversations in which informants continually insist *that they have never met Gerolamo Vano* has an obvious ironic subtext.

File 636, 2 July 1620: Gomez drops dark hints to Domenico that he will denounce Vano to the ambassador Bravo and have him murdered. Gomez blames Vano for his failure to obtain the **thousands of gold coins** he had hoped for from the Inquisitors. Gomez surely knows that Domenico will pass this on to Vano. Sending oblique messages through intermediaries has now become standard technique in Vano's world.

Part of Gomez's problem was that Domenico was rapidly taking his place in Vano's affections, a place he would continue to occupy until the two men were executed in September 1622 (the ultimate intimacy, perhaps—to die together). Gomez's disillusionment made him unpredictable, which in turn made him dangerous to Vano. Fortunately for Vano, if not for Gomez, the situation was about to resolve itself. The catalytic event occurred in early July 1620, when the Inquisitors arrested another noble, again acting on information provided by Vano.

Council of Ten criminal register, 10 July 1620: **Our Inquisitors of State are to bring sir Zuanne Minotto, [recently] arrested, to the place of torture. He is to be informed in the name of this Council, that [there is enough evidence to convict him] of close familiarity and secret dealings with Don Francesco the Spaniard. [He has] confessed this himself at various points, and it is confirmed from the investigation. ...**

Item: that he has finally confessed to knowing Zuanetto the servant of the Ambassador's secretary and that the said Zuanetto [used to?] work for him. Also, Minotto has been seen by persons that know him very well on more than one occasion entering and leaving the house of the said Ambassador ... [He was] granted one hundred *scudi* ... [for] providing information on public matters ... We want to know who gave him the information he passed on to the Ambassador ... since Minotto has never been a member of the Senate. ... [We also want to know] who worked with him and was aware of what he was doing.

Minotto was Zuan Battista Bragadin's accomplice, and the last part of the resolution quoted above hints that the Ten needed his testimony to help convict Bragadin, who was the ultimate source of the information

being leaked from the Senate. From the Ten's point of view, it was important for Minotto to admit to knowing Zuanetto (another of Vano's
informants), because Zuanetto was the principal witness against him.
Zuanetto did not have a high opinion of his former employer, whom he
referred to as **that big dickhead fuck Minotto. My master wants to have him
killed.**[*]

The Spanish ambassador Bravo received news of Minotto's arrest
almost immediately. His response was to imprison Gomez in the
embassy. Vano's other informant, Zuanetto, was also questioned but
allayed Bravo's suspicions and therefore remained at large.

Five guards on the embassy doors. Who do you want here? Get lost.

Minotto's arrest was a disaster for Bravo. Not only did it deny him an
important source of information but it exposed him as both devious and
incompetent, a disastrous combination. Meanwhile, in the Spanish
embassy, Gomez was desperate to get out, while Vano was powerless to
intervene.

19 July 1620: Gomez is in chains under guard. Spanish plans are afoot
to smuggle him to Milan.

27 July 1620: The Council of Ten sentence Zuanne Minotto to life
imprisonment in a cell without direct sunlight.

27 July 1620: Gomez is interrogated in the Spanish embassy **until five
hours after sunset** by a man **dressed as a priest** sent specially from Milan
for this purpose.

Shortly afterwards, Gomez was taken to Milan, and he thus disappears
from File 636. Not surprisingly, he was persuaded to denounce Vano and
Domenico; hence the latter was sacked and expelled from the Spanish
embassy in October 1620. A month before Domenico's dismissal, on
7 September 1620, Zuan Battista Bragadin was also finally arrested,
interrogated under threat of torture, sentenced to death a day later and
executed on the morning of 10 September before daybreak. The Ten

---

[*] The **master** here may have been Vano, or Zuanetto's official employer, the Spanish ambassador's
secretary, Andrea Irles.

wound up the prosecution like a pistol, so that when they pulled the trigger in September, the charge detonated instantaneously. No misfires.

Vano omits the story's ending because, once arrested, Bragadin was outside Vano's sphere of influence and therefore ceased to be of interest. We have to turn elsewhere—to despatches sent home by foreign ambassadors in Venice, for example—to discover that Bragadin confessed everything immediately when they showed him the cord.* After being sentenced to death, he married his concubine, so that she would be able to inherit anything the republic did not confiscate, and perhaps claim a pension from the Spanish. He reportedly told his confessor: **I console myself that even though I die hatefully and infamous in my country my name will live glorious in Spain**. After his execution, Bragadin's corpse hung by the foot on the gallows all day, as would Foscarini's eighteen months later. At the end of 1620, Gomez was similarly executed **three hours after sunset by torchlight in the castle at Milan**.** Vano met both events with equal indifference.

Throughout Vano's reports, characters like Gomez and Bragadin come and go without explanation, or at least Vano's decision on whether or not to include an explanation seems arbitrary. Moreover, people are prone to disappear from the reports just before something bad is about to happen to them. The pattern is consistent. Characters appear, move about, rendezvous, whistle and whisper, with varying degrees of furtiveness and paranoia; then they disappear without warning, and when they reappear, they are in prison or on a gallows. Vano cuts away from the decisive moment, the moment of 'impact' so to speak, and the reader

---

* The standard form of judicial torture used by the Ten, in which the prisoner's hands were tied behind the back. He or she was then lifted up, resulting in possible dislocation of the shoulders.

** His execution ruffled some feathers. The ex-ambassador Bravo was offended that it was not carried out secretly to save further embarrassment. Conversely, the Milanese Senate was offended that it had not been consulted regarding the initial sentence, which specified that Gomez was to be pulled apart between four horses. The Spanish governor felt it necessary to conciliate the Senate with the 'lesser' punishment of hanging, an amendment for which Gomez was no doubt duly grateful.

becomes aware that this cut has taken place only retrospectively, when the gaping hole in the story becomes apparent.

There is a commonsense reason for this: Vano did not need to tell the Inquisitors about their own actions. Instead, he provided 'reaction shots' to let them know what effects their intervention had produced. The only substantial report on Foscarini, quoted in the second chapter, is a classic example. In it, Vano does not describe Foscarini's arrest directly, and he similarly ignores the execution later. What he provides instead is a vivid account of reactions to the arrest inside the Spanish embassy.

The story of Gomez and Bragadin begins with Vano fighting to be heard among competing voices, and trying to prove his credibility. It ends with him established as the most important source of information on the Spanish embassy. It begins in File 1214, a disordered miscellany of documents, and ends in File 636, a homogenous and continuous series of dated reports, stored in chronological order. Gomez's recruitment and the consequent execution of Bragadin a few months later are the two landmark events that bookend Vano's rise to power. A Spaniard who sold information to the Venetians, and a Venetian who sold information to the Spaniards: both men died to advance Vano's career.

A receipt for one hundred ducats. Scribbled notes. Pseudo-priest with a cloak over his face. Gomez, Vano and Bragadin criss-crossing and double-crossing around San Marco in complicated dance steps. The smell of fear (a phantom odour, like the sensation in an amputated limb). A cord hanging from the ceiling in an interrogation chamber. Wedding vows. The bride wore black. Gomez in chains, gaping on a castle wall in Milan. Pens scratching. Paper on spikes.

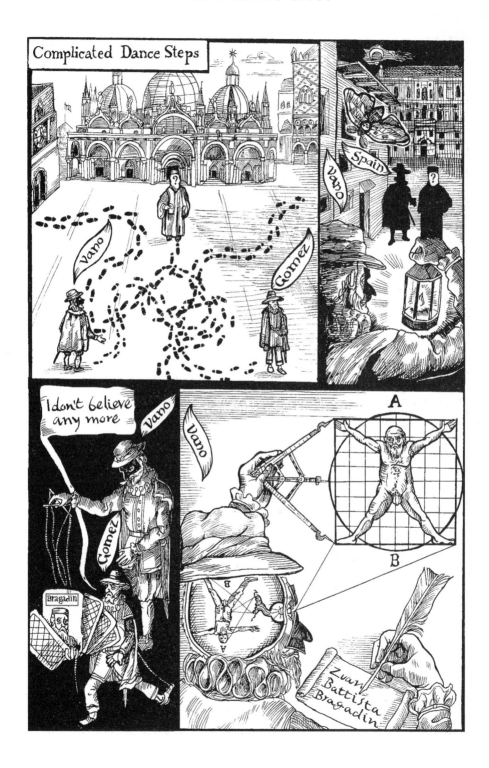

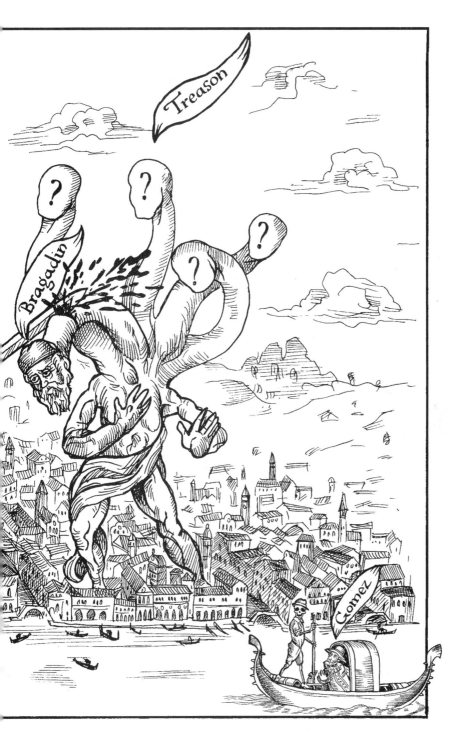

12. DA BAFFO, 8.45 P.M.

Phil: One medium pseudo-Belgian beer for you and me.
One large pseudo-Belgian beer for Jon.
[Sounds of clinking glasses]
Jon: The head's too large, but it doesn't matter.
Jim: So drink wine! It's cheaper anyway.
Jon: How many ducats do you reckon Vano would've had
to fork out for a round of drinks? If we don't know
what a ducat was worth, then we can't understand what
it meant for Diego Gomez to get a hundred for selling
out the Spanish.
Jim: That's a really complicated question, but let's
have a go. A ducat wasn't a huge amount of money. A
journeyman, who was just your average worker enrolled
in a guild, nobody special, he could probably earn
a ducat for three days' work—say, two ducats a week.
Jon: So if we discount all the holidays and saints'
days in a working year, a hundred ducats might be
the salary of an average semi-skilled worker.

Jim: Although it was common to receive part of your salary in goods, like chickens and eggs or wine, on top of the monetary payments.

Jon: To compare this with the 'footsoldiers' in the world of espionage, the Ten's captain of police paid a third of a ducat a day to people employed as casual labour for surveillance operations. This seems to have been a fixed rate, which is interesting.

Phil: For following people, you mean?

Jon: Or for hanging around outside the embassy and keeping notes on who went in and out. There was obviously a regular pool of thugs that the Ten's police captain Francesco Ongarin drew upon when he needed extra manpower. Vano had access to this labour pool for his own surveillance operations, which makes him quite unique—I mean because he wasn't officially part of the Ten's police force.

Jim: So these thugs earned roughly the same amount as a semi-skilled labourer?

Jon: Well, except that surveillance work was casual, so the income was less reliable. There is a related question of how long a spy's working day was. I mention this because Ongarin sometimes lists separate payments for the 'night shift', which are (surprisingly) lower than the normal sums.

Jim: Maybe the night shift was shorter.

Phil: Did assassins get more?

Jon: Oh yes. They were usually bandits. The killers of Giulio Cazzari, the Imperial resident's secretary and Vano's enemy, got about two thousand ducats to be split among them. And the escaped Venetian traitor Anzolo Badoer, he had a ten thousand ducat price on his head. But most of Vano's informants got the same

miserable rate as Ongarin's flunkeys. Even Domenico
only seems to have got about ten ducats a month.
When he was in the embassy, working as a gondolier,
these payments from Vano doubled his salary. After
he was sacked, his wages as Vano's accomplice didn't
go up, which I find surprising. I mean, if he no
longer had his 'official' job as a gondolier, then
he was taking a cut to continue working for Vano.
Maybe Vano shared the proceeds from selling blank
pardons with him.

Phil: How do you know all this?

Jon: Because I've seen the monthly account sheets
drawn up by the Inquisitors' secretary, and the
expense claims submitted by Vano. His expenses were
roughly forty-five ducats a month, most of which he
paid out in dribs and drabs to various informants,
usually at two to five ducats a go. The informants
are listed by name, which is a useful way of keeping
track of them actually, because they aren't often
named in the reports.

Jim: But that wasn't his entire income?

Jon: No, just his expenses. The blank pardons he
got for particular coups were the most lucrative
rewards.

Jim: What about incomes at the other end of the
social scale? If you were a poor noble, your family
might get about three hundred ducats a year. I say
family, because most of it would be from hereditary
rents and investments and offices, and they were
shared. This was perhaps more than a master builder
(it depends on how thinly it had to be spread), but
on the other hand there were different expectations.

Jon: You had certain standards to maintain.

Phil: Venice had a lot of poor nobles, which is one reason why it was so easy for the Spanish to buy information.

Jim: On the other hand, very rich noble families commonly offered dowries of more than twenty thousand ducats. Another point of contrast: If you were a poor noble trying to earn a living from an elected government office—and some of these offices were created to subsidise poor nobles—you might get a salary of four hundred ducats, but that wouldn't be a regular income.

Phil: Though you might earn something on the side from bribes.

Jon: For the highest offices of state, there was no salary at all. You got no pay for being a member of the Council of Ten.

Jim: What about prices, though? The ducat was worth 124 *soldi*, which is what most prices were given in. So, for 124 *soldi*, you could buy 100 oysters, or slightly fewer eggs. An egg was just over one *soldo*.

Jon: I presume oysters cost less than eggs because Venice was a community of fishermen who caught oysters regularly, whereas they didn't catch chickens.

Jim: Eggs are difficult to transport as well. They're delicate. Ham came in at about fifty-five *soldi* a kilo, so you could buy about two kilos with your ducat; half a whole ham. I'm trying to think in physical, concrete terms. You could also buy about two kilos of butter. You could get a melon for six to ten *soldi*, so that's ten to twelve melons for a ducat. Is this helping you imagine what it was worth?

Jon: Melons were quite expensive then.

Jim: That's one of the problems of trying to work out how much money was worth. The comparative value of commodities changed.

Jon: Which is why beer is four quid a pint and wine is seventy-five pence a glass in modern Venice—a sore point of mine.

Jim: Just as caviar was cheaper than cheese in seventeenth-century Venice.

Phil: I wonder what they were referring to when using the word *oyster*, though.

Jim: It's pretty clear that 'oysters' meant the same thing as it does now, and they were cheaper because they were much more plentiful. Even Samuel Pepys, later on in London, typically ate a barrel of oysters on a night out with the boys.

Jon: You know that the ducat didn't actually exist physically. It was a fictional money of account, with a fixed value in real money, of 124 *soldi*, as you said.

Jim: That's right. The *soldo* was a real coin, but its silver content fluctuated, so the amount of precious metal included in a 'ducat' at any given moment changed, even though the value on paper remained constant. Another point is that, in contrast to today, all sorts of coinage circulated in Venice, from the areas with which Venice traded.

Jon: *Ongari,* Hungarian gold coins, are mentioned a lot.

Jim: Also, there were shortages of coin, because the amount you could mint depended on the supply of precious metals. Government salaries were often in arrears as a consequence.

Jon: It must have been galling for the Inquisitors' secretary to hand over a hundred ducats cash if there was no money in the coffers for his own wages.

Jim: The widespread use of credit helped to compensate for this. People were willing to set off one thing against another. So, although coinage was used as a measure of value, coins didn't appear that much in transactions, apart from very low denominations. People always offset credits one against the other until a final reckoning, which they might settle in cash or might settle in goods.

Jon: It's also one of the reasons why blank pardons became almost an alternative currency—and a major way to reward employees. But cash was more important for many spies because it left fewer traces and didn't create a paper trail; or because they were in impermanent relationships, where they had limited access to credit networks. Spies had this in common with gamblers: both were brutally reductive. They wanted immediate payment, preferably in cash, because the debt couldn't be enforced legally or even acknowledged publicly.

Jim: In any kind of black economy, people prefer to be paid 'cash in hand', but I thought gamblers worked on credit.

Jon: They did, but it was difficult for them to base things on trust. Vano's informants were always saying 'I want money now'.

Jim: So they were highly insistent creditors, if they became creditors.

Jon: And this insistence was actually a sign of their vulnerability. Anyway, the one hundred ducats paid to Diego Gomez was a lot to a servant or a semi-qualified worker, maybe a year's or six months' wages. For a noble with expensive habits, it was the cost of a night's entertainment. Gambling debts of a hundred

ducats were commonplace, a thousand not unheard of.
For Gomez, it was probably a month's salary, or two
or three at most. And we don't know precisely what
form Gomez received his one hundred ducats in, though
let's hope it wasn't in chickens and eggs.

Jim: Or barrels of oysters.

Jon: But it could have been in various kinds of coin.

Phil: Gomez came quite cheap, you know. We've been
comparing his income to that of tradesmen and police
thugs, but the Spanish paid a lot for their noble
spies, partly because the nobles were risking their
lives, and partly because they had higher expectations.
For instance, the noble traitor Anzolo Badoer—you
mentioned him a moment ago. He received two thousand
ducats a year, if his stipend was paid regularly,
which is admittedly a big 'if'.

Jon: I'm sure Gomez got more than one hundred ducats
out of the Inquisitors, but I don't know exactly how
much. If you want to compare all this with Vano's
income, it's difficult. We don't know how much he got
for the blank pardons, but they could be sold for
up to a thousand ducats or more. So Vano could have
been making more than a thousand ducats a year, not
counting any other, legal sources of income, which is
not bad going.

Phil: I'll pay the bill.

[Non-applicable conversation follows.]

13. RIVALS

MPLOYERS, INFORMANTS AND VICTIMS. THE NEXT LOGICAL step is to consider Vano's rivals. In late 1619 and early 1620—that is, in the period when Vano was attempting to outbid rival suppliers of information on the Spanish—his principal competitor was a man named Alessandro Grancini, although the two men never betray any awareness of each other's work for the Inquisitors, perhaps because they worked quite differently. Grancini's history is outlined in an autobiographical sketch he wrote in 1620, which can be paraphrased as follows (with appropriate additions from other sources).

1608: Callow Alessandro arrives in Venice from the provincial town of Bergamo, near the border with the Spanish-controlled Duchy of Milan. To his credit, Alessandro has aims other than fame and fortune. He hopes to help his father, Nicolo Grancini, who is in prison in Venice as a suspected grain smuggler. The plan is to get on the good side of the Marquis of Bedmar, Bravo's predecessor as Spanish ambassador, and ask him to petition the Venetians on his father's behalf (since the latter is a Milanese citizen and therefore also a Spanish subject). Diplomatic interventions of this sort were fairly frequent. Then, as now, it was one of the jobs of an ambassador to help distressed nationals. Unlike now, such favours were used to create patronage networks.

1609: Alessandro takes a room near the Spanish embassy and makes a meagre living copying documents. He just happens to live in the same boarding house as Antonio Meschita, whom the Inquisitors later described as the Spanish ambassador's **most important agent, but also his most secret. He is always involved in the most important affairs. He is highly ingenious, clever, cunning, and deceptive, full of schemes, and capable of convincing [anyone] of anything ... In practice, the Ambassador loves and values no one more than him, but he gives no public indication of this.** Meschita promises Grancini an introduction to the ambassador Bedmar, and so Alessandro, eager to please a potential patron, does some work for Meschita, including copying letters to Spanish contacts on the Venetian mainland. Meschita employs a lot of copyists, since he is a *novellista*—a seventeenth-century cross between a journalist and a spy— who gathers and sells news in manuscript copies to a private network of subscribers and correspondents.

The two men become friends. Months pass, but Grancini's father is no closer to liberation. Meschita has a woman, Cecilia, with whom he has been involved for six years. They have children, but he cannot marry her because he is an apostate priest, hiding out from God in a spy's disguise. The situation is clear: Cecilia needs a respectable cover story, while Meschita needs an easily manipulated dupe. Alessandro, at eighteen, has little experience with women, and Cecilia is not unattractive. A bit of 'carnal commerce' never did anyone any harm. All of a sudden, Alessandro finds himself engaged.

1610: Nicolo Grancini knows what is going on, but what can he do from prison? He attempts to intercede with the Patriarch, the head of the Venetian church, but Meschita knows the Patriarch's secretary, who is well placed to hurry things along. The happy couple wed in the church of Santa Sofia. Meschita has the place of honour at the feast and continues to make use of Alessandro's labour and his wife's favours. Nicolo Grancini, understandably concerned, recommends that the two men separate. Alessandro moves his new family (including one of Meschita's daughters) to San Samuele, but Cecilia's passion is only enflamed by her lover's absence. Meschita visits often when Alessandro is out of the house.

Grancini makes concerted efforts to sever contact with Meschita, but the ex-priest responds by threatening him. Don't you know that you're in a dangerous position? You're a Venetian subject associated with the Spanish embassy. You should be scared. Any day now you could be arrested as a spy. At this time—we have now reached 1612—a flurry of arrests does in fact occur, adding force to Meschita's warning. Alessandro retreats to the Spanish embassy, where he enjoys the ambassador Bedmar's full protection. There are plans afoot to ship him to Milan, out of harm's way. Grancini knows too much, so it would be best not to tempt his undoubtedly strained loyalty by keeping him around. Cecilia leaves first, together with a daughter newly born to the happy couple.

According to Alessandro's account, this is the moment of truth, when he decides to change sides. He goes to the house of the Inquisitor of State Nicolo Contarini to offer information. Contarini's is a name worth noting. He is a prominent member of the anti-Spanish faction in Venice and a friend of Antonio Foscarini, whose posthumous absolution he will help secure in 1623. In 1612, he accepts Alessandro's offer, and as a result Grancini decides to stay in Venice. Soon Cecilia returns from Milan, suspicious at her husband's prevarication. She and Meschita rifle through his papers and steal his letters. They want to remind him that he is not his own man, and that his life has been planned out for him, but Alessandro demurs—in Venetian ears.

1617: Alessandro is obliged to leave the embassy again because his wife is sleeping with men there behind his back. He is also in a sweat at the prospect of a private conversation in the Milan castle dungeons. So, **for eight or nine years Alessandro has run great risks because of this woman, as well as being offended in his honour by her not just with Meschita but with**

many others, whoever she felt like. Worse, she does not behave like a wife even when he hits her.

This last point was meant to prove Alessandro's good faith. He was explaining (according to the norms of the period) that he had tried all reasonable means to repair his marriage, including physical discipline. In other words, he had not shirked his responsibilities as a husband, which included the exercise of authority.

He leaves Cecilia twice, but he listens to the friends who urge reconciliation, even when Cecilia the shrew complains that he has another woman. She uses **malign men** to find him. She bawls him out with **infamous words** for the whole city to hear.

1618: The ambassador Bedmar flees Venice under suspicion of plotting to bring the government down. Meschita goes with him. Cecilia is not happy at this turn of events. She **cannot tolerate Meschita being out of her sight**. They correspond secretly, using a priest as postbox. The priest is paid with the usual carnal currency to stay quiet.

1620: Enough is enough. A man's patience has limits, and Alessandro is now ready to take the final, drastic step. He wants a formal separation, to be secured by Cecilia's imprisonment. He wants his life and his reputation back. He wants custody of his daughters, and he has witnesses who will confirm his version of events.

This ending reveals why we have been privileged to hear these sordid details. Grancini's account is not an intelligence report but, rather, a petition addressed to the Patriarch of the Venetian church, which had jurisdiction over such matters. This petition was submitted through the Inquisitors of State, whom Grancini no doubt hoped would support his application. Things did not work out quite as planned, since Grancini was arrested in July 1620, shortly after submitting his petition. It never reached the Patriarch, and is thus still in the Inquisitors' archive. The moral of the story is: be careful what you wish for. Grancini got his separation, only not quite how he imagined it.

Obviously Grancini was playing with ideas about male honour to strengthen his case. In itself, that does not make him a liar. Indeed, it helps us work out what 'truth' might mean in this unusual context. Nonetheless, we are reading a self-serving account, which is inconsistent with other, briefer autobiographical comments that Grancini made elsewhere. For example, he brushes over his motive for approaching the Venetians, but we do not have to look hard to find one: revenge. And in fact the Inquisitors remained suspicious that he was shielding Meschita, despite the alleged bad blood between the two men.

Nor was his relationship with the Inquisitor of State Nicolo Contarini quite the cosy one he implied. Although Grancini was obviously keen to be associated with such an important politician, Contarini was notably less enthusiastic and even took steps to avoid him. On 12 May 1612, Grancini wrote to Contarini that he had **always considered and will continue to consider [him] a Patron**, even though Contarini had refused to receive him at home. Since Contarini had recently ceased to be an Inquisitor, he probably considered it improper to talk privately with a known associate of the Spanish ambassador. In fact, the noble Vido Diedo was Grancini's usual contact throughout the 1610s. The sequence of events in 1612 is also a little dubious. Grancini neglected to mention that his offer to spy for the Venetians was partly intended to pre-empt his imminent arrest by them. He was so terrified that he tried to insist on an official safe conduct for his first meeting with the Inquisitors.

Grancini's father also seems to have been forgotten in all the excitement. In fact, he died unremarked at some indeterminate point in this story. And was he really only a poor, unfortunate smuggler? Elsewhere, Grancini claimed that his father was involved in Spanish plots and that it was he, and not Meschita, who introduced the young Alessandro into the ambassador Bedmar's household. These details do not appear in the petition, for the obvious reason that they are inconsistent with the image of Alessandro as a loyal Venetian subject led astray by wicked men.

We can try to trap Grancini in a web of other references, although any such attempt brings out problems familiar from Vano's reports. For instance, Gomez described him as a frequent visitor to the Spanish embassy at the end of 1619. Another informant accused him of writing to various members of the Hapsburg family, the Duke of Mantua and a cardinal. This is actually an incomplete list: we can add to it the dukes of Parma and Savoy, the English ambassador and numerous cardinals in Rome. Grancini picked up denunciations (and correspondents) like his wife picked up lovers. Like his mentor Meschita, he too aspired to be a newswriter, or *novellista*, someone who swapped pieces of news and passed them along an extended network of informants. **News is a commodity that, like all other commercial goods, is acquired either by purchase or exchange**, as a slightly later commentator put it.

Grancini played various employers off against each other, increasing his credibility by flaunting his contacts, which he simultaneously abused to obtain information for others. Some of his customers were very pleased with the product he supplied. For instance, the Duke of Savoy considered his reports invaluable. Others were less impressed. Bedmar, for example, described him as a **destitute young man, who earns his living inventing news, reports and other things adapted to the interests of various Princes ... but who in effect knows nothing that is not openly discussed in the piazza**. Both the papal nuncio and the Mantuan resident similarly belittled Grancini to their masters, with the latter insisting that he was not worth his nominal salary of ten ducats a month (payments of which were obviously in arrears).

The resident's dismissal was hardly disinterested, however, since the Duke of Mantua used Grancini to provide independent corroboration for official despatches. A fellow spy confirmed to the Inquisitors of State that his **news is not the ordinary stuff that newswriters send, which many people call the Gazette, because the [Mantuan] Resident usually sends this [himself]**. Grancini also acted as a conduit for informal approaches to the Duke by Venetian nobles, who were forbidden to approach the official resident directly.

Perhaps Bedmar did not realise that he was only getting leftovers, while the real meat was being passed under the table to others. Grancini was too busy spying on Bedmar to spy for him. While Bedmar was dallying with women in the bedroom, Alessandro was stealing his keys, going through his desk and taking copies of his letters.

Or, rather, this was what Grancini promised to do, but he often had problems in keeping his promises. This is not surprising, since he was trying to juggle a number of mutually exclusive commitments. In May 1615 the Inquisitors complained that **it is clearly apparent that his only purpose is to get money with hints, promises and suggestions**. Perhaps Bedmar had a point after all. In any case, Grancini frequently crossed the line between *novellista* and spy, as Meschita had before him. It was not a difficult line to cross, since it was never clear exactly where it lay.

Gomez may have been a bashful maiden seduced and abandoned by Vano, but Grancini (like his wife) was rather more promiscuous in his affections. Why did the Inquisitors tolerate this promiscuity? The answer was that Grancini was a useful conduit, who was granted **some tolerance in the hope ... of bringing about some greater public good**, as the Inquisitors put it in 1618. His established role as *novellista* and Spanish crony gave him access. Indeed, one of the reasons he left the Spanish embassy was so that he could receive visitors and couriers in a more neutral and discreet location. His usefulness to the Spanish guaranteed his usefulness to the Inquisitors, as long as the information he supplied to Venice outweighed the information on Venice that he sold to other customers. The denunciations against him therefore have to be understood in the light of positive recommendations elsewhere in the Inquisitors' archive, particularly from his noble patron Vido Diedo. The Inquisitors knew he was holding out on them, but this became a serious problem only when his information was obviously inconsistent with that from other sources.

More specifically, the Inquisitors left Grancini at large because they hoped to use him to get to Meschita. This is revealed by a series of communications with the Venetian ambassadors in Rome and Turin in 1618. Both ambassadors had independently intercepted newsletters sent by Grancini to correspondents in their respective cities. They were worried about the consequences of his reporting, which was clearly slanted to confirm the prejudices of his customers. As the ambassador in Turin put it, **[h]e claims to write ... everything that happens in the Most Excellent**

Senate, the contents of despatches from Ambassadors abroad, the resolutions passed, and the debates surrounding the proposals put forward. He splits the Senate up into factions, according to his own interpretations. This latter point was particularly worrying because it made Venice appear divided and weak to hostile foreign powers. Perhaps, the ambassador suggested, autograph copies of the newsletters could be obtained by opening a fake subscription under a cover name, with the co-operation of a suitable priest? Then it would be possible to prove Grancini's authorship and move against him.

The Inquisitors advised restraint and explained that **[t]he only thing that holds us back is the hope of uprooting this evil plant entirely, which has many branches all flourishing in producing the same cunning fictions**. Grancini's newsletters were only a small sample of the plant's poisonous fruit. Meschita was the real source of the problem, and Grancini remained under his thrall, despite the complicated history shared by the two men. Confiscating Grancini's newsletters was therefore a bad idea, not only because they were addressed to important people who would resent the interference, but because the action would warn Grancini and his masters of the extent of the Inquisitors' knowledge. This was in 1618, at the height of the political crisis caused by the so-called Spanish conspiracy. By 1620, Meschita was less of a threat, and consequently Grancini was less of an asset.

The final nail in Grancini's coffin was perhaps the arrest of the noble Zuanne Minotto in early July 1620. The problem was that Grancini's reports to the Inquisitors did not even hint at Minotto's existence until after his arrest and, when he did finally get around to the subject, he trivialised it. Why? According to the Mantuan resident, Grancini was implicated in the affair, and was presumably trying to cover his tracks by downplaying its importance. With this in mind, the Inquisitors might have decided that he had finally become a liability. What he was hiding now outweighed what he was revealing. *Ergo*: Alessandro was arrested in July 1620—a simple mathematical equation of profit and loss.

How does Grancini compare with Vano? The two men adopted different strategies in 1620, the only period in which it is possible to make a direct comparison between them. The reports in File 636 are immediate: that is their strength and weakness. Vano wrote straight after the events he described; he rarely referred to anything that had happened before the previous report; and he churned them out in a relentless stream. There is no sense of distance, and no horizon or broader context for specific pieces of information. Vano left it to the Inquisitors to provide this context and to interpret the significance of events.

Before 1620, many of Grancini's reports had a similar air of topicality, although they were also padded with repetitions, courtesies and excuses, but in one sense they were better than Vano's, because Grancini was more likely to supply written corroboration in the form of copied letters and other documents. Unlike Vano's, his reports from the 1610s are also bound in folders, complete with annotated indices by the Inquisitors' secretary and various notes telling us what the Inquisitors thought about the information. At first glance, this suggests a degree of official recognition that Vano (whose reports remain in loose leaf) never achieved. However, there is a quite specific explanation for this change in secretarial practice, which requires a brief digression.

In August 1619, the regulations for appointing the Council of Ten's secretaries were changed as part of a short-lived reform.[*] At the same time, Bartolomio Comino stepped down as the Inquisitors' secretary, a post he had held for more than ten years. He was replaced by Zuan Battista Padavin. This changeover explains why the reports of Grancini and Vano were edited differently. It was Comino who bound Grancini's reports, annotated them extensively and placed them within files whose organising principle was that of particular surveillance operations, and not individual informants. In these folders, Grancini's notes sit next to

---

[*] Secretaries working for the Venetian state had a clear promotion structure, but for most of them, Senate secretary was the highest post to which they could realistically aspire. Only a very few reached the next level, secretary to the Ten, because only four men held this office at any one time.

those from Francesco Ongarin, the Ten's captain of police. By contrast, Zuan Battista Padavin, who dealt with Vano in 1619 and 1620, appears to have been less systematic in his record-keeping, but also to have respected the integrity of specific sources more. No doubt this also explains why the material submitted by Grancini in late 1619 and 1620, during Padavin's incumbency, remains disordered and unbound.

As we have already seen, Padavin 'ran' Vano during the first phase of his career as a spy. This would be a natural reason for him to favour Vano, but there was also a qualitative deterioration in Grancini's material in late 1619. The reports from the period immediately before his imprisonment consist primarily of character studies and descriptions of networks (that is, who was in contact with whom), but they were made up of undated anecdotes and vague generalisations, all of which were recycled more than once. Grancini padded and almost never specified sources. Since these **memoranda** do not really have a narrative structure and contain few dates, it would be impossible to say which information was up to date on the basis of internal evidence alone, but the impression they give is that Grancini was playing for time. He warned the Inquisitors repeatedly about Bedmar's men, but Bedmar was long gone by 1620 (and this retrospective tint may explain the otherwise puzzling lack of overlap in subject matter between Vano and Grancini in this period).

So the changeover between Grancini and Vano corresponded not only with a related changeover of secretaries but also with a difficult patch for Grancini. In 1620 at least, Vano comes across as more focused and professional, controlling and developing sources more efficiently and self-consciously. He never used more than the bare minimum of courtesies, he never moralised and he never complained about lack of payment. Rather, his requests for money were confined to separate petitions written specifically for this purpose. Grancini made excuses; Vano never did. He was more impressive because he was more limited and more intense. He concentrated all his energies on a few targets and supplied product only to the Inquisitors. In other words, Vano was quite clearly a spy—or rather a spymaster—and not a *novellista*. Precise dates and references left him vulnerable to direct contradiction and falsification, which made him more valuable. Grancini was more cautious and vague. He never exposed himself more than he had to.

This last point was related to the two men's different working methods. Grancini collected some of his information from people who were not aware that they were providing it to him (or at least did not know what precisely he was using it for). He was personally implicated by his spying. Vano kept his distance from his targets and self-consciously assumed the role of **general of spies**. He encouraged others to betray their friends and employers, but he never betrayed anyone himself. Vano was proud to be associated with the Inquisitors because his reputation testified to his success and made it more likely that those with information for sale would approach him. Grancini's effectiveness as a spy depended on him not acquiring such a reputation, although his activities as a *novellista* and information broker were certainly well known.

Despite the Inquisitors' increasingly sceptical attitude towards Grancini, in the 1610s he had helped to break Bedmar's spy network. By 1620, his words left only faint echoes elsewhere in the archive, and a few, isolated references to names that Grancini mentions. One man warned against associating with Spaniards in August 1620 claimed to have ceased all contact two years before, which might suggest how stale some of the later information was. All in all, this was a pitiful haul compared with his earlier successes. In 1620, therefore, Vano's commitment to precision consistently outbid Grancini's evasiveness.

From July 1620, Grancini was detained without charge for the entire period in which Vano was active. It was very helpful for Vano, to say the least, that his major competitor was put out of the game at this early stage. Two months after Vano's execution, in November 1622, a formal prosecution against Grancini finally went ahead, but it was immediately dismissed for lack of evidence. The timing of both events is circumstantial but suggestive nonetheless. After being **buried alive for twenty-nine months**, Grancini got out of prison in December 1622. He proved unable to benefit from Vano's absence, perhaps because he was out of touch.

Two years was a long time in the world of spies, where information became worthless almost as fast as it was written down. Never mind. No doubt his dutiful wife Cecilia was waiting patiently.

Vano and Grancini were both professionals in the sense that gathering information was their permanent and full-time job, even if Grancini was not really a 'spy' in the same way that Vano was. Other men might be described as semi-professional, in the sense that their involvement seems to have been periodic or opportunistic. A further group were one-off contributors or occasionals. They were in the kind of trouble that Grancini was facing at the beginning of his career, or they were bandits with a price on their head who could not afford to buy a pardon, or they stumbled across something specific and recognised its value, or they knew someone important and decided to exploit their proximity. The vast majority of these men offered their services unsolicited. I know of no cases where the Venetians attempted to entrap or blackmail a potential informant, but these volunteers were not idealists either. On the contrary, just as the Venetian land army was staffed by mercenaries, so most of the spies working in Venice were also 'mercenaries'. They were not motivated by principle and they often changed sides according to opportunity or threat of arrest.

The Inquisitors did not care. They were not priests but bureaucrats, and so they were not particularly interested in motives, except insofar as these were relevant for assessing the degree of guilt in criminal investigations. Thus most of their informants never become characters in any meaningful sense of the word, even if their names designate real people. They are perennially restless, but they seem to learn nothing, and ultimately they achieve nothing. Any account of their activities would be both endlessly complex and endlessly repetitive, but it is precisely the murderous self-containment of this world, and the minimalist nature of its self-analysis, that makes it interesting. It was incestuous and self-regarding, but its violence often spilled outside its boundaries. Pull any thread and others come up with it. If we untangle the names of some of the minor or occasional spies active in Venice at the same time as Vano, and lay out the connections, then the picture that emerges looks a little like the diagram overleaf, in which a pointing finger indicates that one individual denounced another to the Inquisitors of State. (I have not included obvious intelligence targets, such as the Spanish ambassador and the Imperial resident.)

How were these men connected?

Giulio Cazzari: He worked for both the Spanish and the Imperial resident, and so was a natural and obvious target for denunciations. He was assassinated in July 1622.

Alessandro Grancini: After Grancini was arrested, Vano made various negative references to him. Antonio Calegari, a minor spy from Grancini's home town of Bergamo, also denounced him, which was only fair, since Grancini had already denounced Calegari.

Zuan Paolo Ferrari: He seems to have worked as a *novellista*, if the huge number of surviving letters addressed to him is anything to go by. He provided information to the Inquisitors on priests, friars and an assortment of other individuals, including a couple of Venetian nobles. He was active from at least 1618 but, like Vano, his surviving reports begin only some time afterwards, indeed at approximately the same time as Vano's. References to him dry up in August 1621, until he reappears in 1625, when he was executed by the Ten on unspecified charges.

Antonio Calegari: He appears regularly in Vano's early reports as an associate of the Spanish ambassador, of Cazzari and especially of the provincial noble Francesco Gambara, who was his patron. He might have been watching this group for the Inquisitors, although his surviving reports contain no reference to Gambara. Calegari also knew and supplied information to the *novellista* Zuan Paolo Ferrari, who ungratefully denounced him in return. In response to the unanimous chorus of disapproval against Calegari, the Inquisitors arrested him in 1620 and did not release him for two years.

Antonio Olivieri: He unwittingly implicated Antonio Calegari in a plot to leak confidential information from the Senate to the Duke of Parma, and thus sealed his own fate, since he was assassinated in early 1621 by

Pointing Fingers

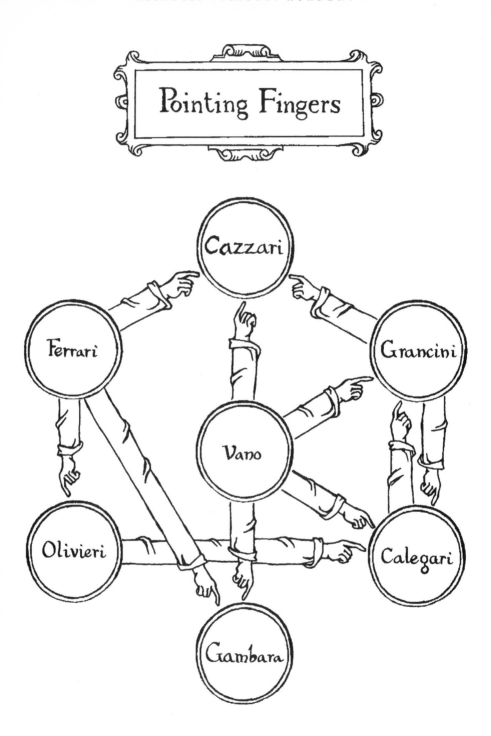

agents sent from Parma. Zuan Paolo Ferrari then investigated the killing for the Inquisitors.

Francesco Gambara: A provincial noble who does not seem to have been actively involved in spying, but he associated with others that were, and hence he appears in surveillance reports submitted by both Vano and Ferrari.

From mid-1621, then, Vano's competitors—Alessandro Grancini, Zuan Paolo Ferrari and Antonio Calegari (in that order of importance)—were all either in prison or inactive. From then on, he was the principal, if not the only, source of information on events inside the Spanish embassy. It was precisely at this point that his reports ceased to be reliable.

14. ALCHEMY

T HE OCCULT SCIENCES—MAGIC, ASTROLOGY, ALCHEMY—
were an important part of early seventeenth-century intellectual
life. Occultists presupposed the existence of a hidden reality, which
corresponded with the visible world but was separate from it, just
as the meaning of an allegory was separate from the painting or
image in which it was figured. This hidden world could be accessed
through various magical rituals, or mathematical manipulations, or by
'decoding' visible phenomena. In effect, alchemists and magicians
wished to spy upon nature and reveal her deepest, darkest secrets.

A possible analogy between alchemists and spies seems to have
occurred to at least one Venetian artist. The allegorical figures carved in
wood by Francesco Pianta in the middle years of the seventeenth century
include one identified as 'The Spy, or Curiosity'. He carries some obvious
iconographic indicators of his status, including a cloak pulled over
the face, but he also wears a winged boot, an emblem associated in

alchemical lore with Hermes, the messenger of the gods. In turn, Hermes wasidentified with the element of Mercury, used in the chemical operations conducted as part of the search for the philosopher's stone. The presence of this emblem on the figure of 'The Spy' is perhaps slightly odd, given that another of Pianta's statues is explicitly identified as Mercury, but the ambiguity is revealing. After all, Mercury was the god of revelation, commerce, communication and thieving. What better patron could Gerolamo Vano wish for, since his activities fell under all four headings? Certainly, a pair of winged boots would have come in handy on the gallows.

One occultist doctrine is worth discussing in more detail: that of correspondences. According to this theory, resemblances between objects or entities indicated an underlying connection and helped to prove a general principle of order and inter-connection in the universe. For example, the organisation of the political system was generally held to duplicate the physical order of the cosmos, which in turn was repeated in the physiology and internal workings of the human body, and this correspondence reinforced the 'rightness' of both arrangements. So the king's place in the polity was equivalent to the sun's place in the cosmos, which equalled the head's dominance of the body, and so on.

What Vano did was reduce politics to a series of correspondences, whereby Spanish policy meant the ambassador Bravo's actions. So, there was no sense of the state as a complex machine with many layers, or of a bureaucracy. Rather, each level replicated the one above it. There was no need to worry about complex manoeuvrings in councils at Madrid, Vano implied. Just listen to Bravo speak, and you would be transported to the heart of the Spanish state. To a degree, this approach reflected more general notions about the personal nature of power and the ways in which an ambassador was thought to 'represent' his master. However, Vano took things further, drastically simplifying the interactions between his characters to isolate Bravo, his secretary and their associates in Venice. Admittedly, the embassy was not entirely sealed off. Vano does mention communications between Spanish officials in Venice and

Milan and he occasionally refers to international events. Nonetheless, his reports are almost as claustrophobic as my choice of quotations suggests. Looking into the Spanish embassy was like looking into a gold-fish bowl. There was no bigger picture—or rather, the implication was that it all came down to this. The big picture would just be the same thing on a larger scale. Bravo related to King Philip III as microcosm to macrocosm.

Correspondences were usually held to be manifestations of divine providence. Underneath a confusing surface reality, whose bewildering variety of forms might otherwise suggest a worrying disorder, there was an essential unity. In turn, this meant that the forms of political life were not arbitrary but a necessary part of God's plan, which it would be sinful to challenge. In Vano's reports, by contrast, the hidden reality underlying appearances was a threat to political order. Indeed, treason was the quin-tessential type of disorder; it overthrew natural hierarchies and denied the bonds that held society together. If Vano's reports disrupted the theory in this sense, they simultaneously suggested another, entirely conventional correspondence: the idea that treason was a sickness of the body politic. What Vano was doing, then, was akin to diagnosing a disease on the basis of its visible symptoms, or at least providing a list of those symptoms for a qualified physician—the Inquisitors—to interpret.

This is not to say that Vano was literally an occultist or indeed a philosopher of any kind. You will search in vain for a theoretical proposition or generalisation in his reports. Nor will you find any use of figurative language or abstractions, even the most banal, such as the 'common good'. Nonetheless, his reports suggest not only the logic underlying occult philosophy but also the criticisms of those who dismissed alchemists as charlatans. Like the alchemists, Vano was preoccupied with the question of how to gain access to a hidden reality on the basis of visible phenomena, which presented themselves as riddles that had to be solved. But conversely, Vano the critical empirick, patient collector of details, was simultaneously trying to 'demystify' and expose the activities of Venetian traitors, who deliberately obscured the truth of their betrayal with disguises and secret signals. The irony of this paradox is that Vano himself was eventually revealed as a charlatan whose secrets were worthless and whose 'revelations' turned out to be another kind of mystification.

15. WINKS AND BLINKS

File 636, 8 January 1621: **This morning ... Oratio Pisani arrived at Rialto via Blacksmith Alley under the portico of the drapers and pretended to blow his nose. He cleared his throat to make a signal to lord Nicolo Rossi, who heard him and made a sign that he should go to the house by staring intently at him and [inclining] his head.**

Report from the informant Gasparo, included as an insert in File 636, 13 July 1621: **The secretary of Spain and Don Giulio [Cazzari] were under the portico of San Giacomo in Rialto when the Clarissimo lord Camillo Trevisan passed and raised his hat to them in salute. They greeted him in return and ... [he] went under the portico to where the nobles were gathered.**

File 636, 2 May 1621: **Don Giulio [Cazzari] left [home], going by way of the main street of San Stae parish, frequently looking over his shoulder, took the ferry [over the Grand Canal] and went down past the church of the Servite friars, via Vinegar Promenade to the parish of San Gerolemo, where he said mass in the church of the Cappuccin friars. Then he left, passed over Vinegar**

Bridge into Boatshed Alley at the Anconetta and knocked on a door where a Venetian noblewoman from the clan of Da Riva stays; Countess Colalto also lives in her house. [Cazzari] stayed for about an hour, then left, and went to see the Mantuan resident.

S PIES, LIKE HISTORIANS AND ANTHROPOLOGISTS, ATTEMPTED to discern meaning by making connections. They looked for patterns, consistencies or irregularities. To paraphrase a famous anthropologist (who was himself paraphrasing a philosopher, an appropriately tortuous attribution), how can you tell a wink from a blink? How do you know if a movement of the eye is an involuntary twitch, a secret signal or even a deliberately misleading parody of such a signal? When is a cough not a cough? When it is a secret signal from Pisani to Rossi. But we can also reverse the question. How can you tell when Pisani is blowing his nose because he has a cold? Under what circumstances can the conspiracy hypothesis be falsified? **I don't believe any more**, as Gomez would say.

There was an important difference between spies and the people studied by anthropologists. For spies, meaning was a private business shared only with a select few. Paradoxically, the actions of the spy were most meaningful when they were made to appear totally meaningless to everyone except the intended recipient of the message. Consider an encrypted despatch. Its surface pattern is apparently random, the written equivalent of white noise or nonsensical gobbledegook, but if you have the key, then there is a hidden order.

For anthropologists, meaning is a broad, inclusive notion. Shared understanding is what defines membership in a community. For spies, by contrast, meaning was exclusive; it was what separated you from the people among whom you moved every day. At the same time, you had to be able to function in the everyday world and understand the everyday meanings that allowed you to perform effectively as a spy by appearing not to be one.

Blink / wink. Click click. How can you be sure of what has been captured on the blurred exposure? You need an interpreter, and not just a photographer. If we accept that at least some of Vano's information is false, then there is also the disturbing possibility that his images were manipulated, or that Vano was deliberately falsifying blinks as winks. For the spy, it was the blink that was the most disturbing possibility. The blink was innocent. The blink was static in the signal. The blink rendered the spy redundant. Only guilt was meaningful and profitable in Vano's world, and the more tortuous the deceit, the more he was needed to unpick its complexity.

Interpreting an action or text requires an understanding of the actor's or writer's intentions, of what they are trying to do or say. This was critical for Vano and the Inquisitors, as it is for us trying to understand their reactions. Pisani coughed while standing near to Rossi, and Vano insisted that it was *with intent*. By contrast, Camillo Trevisan openly and unambiguously greeted Cazzari, but it was not clear if it meant anything at all. At this stage, the commentary does not insist on a particular interpretation. 'Time will tell' is the implicit message. The informant Gasparo was doing routine surveillance at Rialto, because that was where nobles met as well as where ambassadors gathered, so he might as well write it down. It made him look busy. It made him look attentive. The same for duty at San Marco. For example, on 17 August 1621, Gasparo provided a detailed itinerary of the movements of the noble Bortolo Corner in and around San Marco. At no point during his walks did Corner do anything or meet anyone suspicious. There may have been some prior reason to justify this apparently irrelevant accumulation of detail, or there may have been some subsequent event that provided a key to unlock the meaning hidden within Corner's route, but there is nothing in the report itself to suggest either possibility.

Itineraries were a speciality of Vano's. The Imperial resident went here, got in a boat there, got out of the boat somewhere else, walked up and down for twenty minutes, did not speak to anyone, 'seemed' to be waiting for something, went into a church, genuflected at the altar, stayed for mass. Why should anyone care? Because it happened at night perhaps, or simply because the Imperial resident attracted meaning like a magnet. Anyone stepping within Rossi's field of force was likely to be similarly magnetised. Movements were also flagged as interesting because of the attempts made to hide them. Obviously Cazzari's insistence on looking over his shoulder in May 1621 was equivalent to having a sign on his back that said, 'Follow me'. But how could you know Cazzari was not just bored and out for a walk? Or, more disturbingly, how could you tell that he was not drawing you off so Rossi could go out and meet a traitor?

Vano's reports are obsessed with the possibility of hidden meaning, but he usually stopped short of explicit interpretation. The one effect he employed consistently was irony, an effect that asserted both control over and distance from his subject material. His deadpan delivery suggests a refusal to take responsibility for what the Inquisitors did with the information. Vano implied that the Inquisitors were the ones piecing the story together and he was merely the artisan supplying the raw materials.

We should distinguish here between the reports in which Vano watched from 'outside', following targets around the streets of Venice, and those in which we look 'inside' the Spanish embassy, over an informant's shoulder. In the latter, displays of emotion from the targets are often both unambiguous and melodramatic, and they are usually provoked by something Vano has done. In other words, Vano was cautious about identifying unknown visitors to the embassy, but he did not want there to be any ambiguity about what a talented and effective spy he was.

Vano was a connoisseur of the street, but he was one with special tastes; we might even say decadent or perverse tastes. Only guilt and betrayal interested him. He was not, as Baudelaire described the modern poet, the painter of the passing moment and of all the suggestions of eternity that it contains. The first part of the clause certainly applied, but the second seems irrelevant. Vano was not interested in eternal verities, only in immediate, perceptible contingencies that might reveal particular intentions. His reports imply a viewpoint similar to that described by one recent commentator on the Italian Mafia.

> Everything is a message, everything is charged with significance in the world of the Mafia. There is no such thing as a negligible detail. ... We can detect something pathological in this exchange of ceremonies and attention to details. A man who lives in constant danger needs to understand the significance of clues which are, on the surface, totally irrelevant, to interpret them by means of a constant effort of decoding.

Roland Barthes once claimed that art is without noise. In other words, it contains nothing that is not meaningful. If we consider Vano's reports as 'art', we must therefore redefine the latter term, because Vano worked on the boundary between signal and noise, where one disintegrated or coalesced into the other. Here meaning could be postponed or deferred indefinitely.

We can infer how the Inquisitors interpreted Vano's reports on the basis of what they did after reading them, but the connections are not always clear. We can infer that the Inquisitors ultimately interpreted Vano's reports as untrue on the basis that they executed him for writing them.

16. SPECIAL DELIVERY

File 636, 5 June 1621:
My man [Fabritio] went to meet [the informant] Paulo ... in the place where they slaughter the calves and the Spanish secretary arrived ... and said, 'What do you want here, spy? Don't you know that the King of Spain's purse is bigger than that of these [Venetian] lords? I have good spies. You are Gerolamo Vano's man and you're here for Paulo to make some plot'.

Fabritio replied, 'It's not true. I am a man of honour'. And the secretary beat him with a sheathed sword, and there were three others with the secretary ... and he ordered them to thrash his bones with a club and then carry him to the house of Gerolamo Vano.

Anonymous letter sent to Gerolamo Vano, inserted in File 636, 29 November 1621: Your Lordship is the most worthy general of spies for the lords Inquisitors of State, known as such not only in this city but throughout the state. The company of spies begs Your Lordship to provide a replacement for Gregorio de Monti, a recently deceased brother of our company, so that the service does not suffer. Your honour as general of spies demands it.

ABRITIO IS AN HONOURABLE MAN. SO ARE THEY ALL, ALL
honourable men. The word was a mantra, a magic charm to ward
off the word *traitor*, or an ironic reference to the dishonour
inherent in the spy's profession. The more important point here is
that there was more than one way to communicate intentions. The
best way might be to send a message through someone else, a message
flowering with bruises, developing slowly like invisible ink, or a letter
that implied the writer knew more than they were willing to say. What,
then, are the implied messages in the quotations above?

In the first case, the subtext is: If I know about this meeting, then
what else do I know? If I do not intervene in other meetings, with other
informants, it is only because I have my own reasons for not doing so.
If I can hurt your messenger, then I can hurt you. The use of a sheathed
sword and a club for the beating was also part of the message, equivalent
to an insulting slap across the face rather than a confrontation between
equals. However, Vano's subsequent discussion of the secretary's various
plots to assassinate him added an ironic counterpoint, which runs as
follows: The secretary says he is manipulating me, but actually I know
about his plots and I have anticipated or dealt with all of them. I am still
in control. In effect, Vano alters the meaning of the message by a shift of
inflection, or by the tone of voice in which he quotes it.

In the second quotation, the message is: You do not know who we are,
but we know who you are and—since the letter was delivered direct to
Vano's door—we know where you live. We are watching you, but you
cannot see us. The use of 'we' instead of 'I' is obviously meant to imply
a conspiracy or alliance of unknown proportions. The message may also
be satirising Vano's pretensions to be the Inquisitors' **general of spies**.
Hence, it has a second subtext: You think you are important, but actually
your life (including this threat) is a farce that is all the more ridiculous
because of its potentially tragic consequences.

Again, however, Vano could shrug off both the threat and the ridicule
because of the inaccuracy of the reference to Gregorio de Monti, who was
the secretary of Henry Wotton, the English ambassador. He had no

connection to Vano, although he did supply information on the Spanish to the Venetians and once offered to sell English secrets to the pope (possibly with the quite different intention of stealing information on Wotton's behalf). It was the messenger who appeared foolish because, while he claimed to see through Vano's pretensions, this claim was based on incorrect, or at least imprecise, information.

17. FIDDLER'S ELBOW IRISH PUB, 11.00 P.M.

Jon [returning after a considerable interval with three pints of Guinness]: I'm invisible at bars. Sometimes I like to wait—as a game—and see how long it takes to get served. The only rules are that I'm not allowed either to attract attention deliberately or to hide. I place myself in full view; I look straight ahead; I hold a bank note in my hand; then I wait. I think the record is about forty-five minutes.

Phil: It's a conspiracy, damn it!

Jon: Probably [laughs]. But since you're the resident conspiracy-theorist, do you think that fishmongers at Rialto or people doing their shopping noticed the 'secret signals' among spies? And did they care about the Spanish conspiracy?

Jim: I've found nothing to suggest public concern about the Spanish conspiracy, but then obviously the prosecutors in my trials [in civil courts] were not

looking for evidence on that, or asking questions
about it. People's only concern with politics was
focused on the topic of wars, which they used as a
form of dating, as in 'It was just after the war with
Austria'. They had to pay higher taxes during war,
and the guilds were obliged to provide people to
serve on the galleys.

Jon: So they were really only aware of war when it
affected them directly?

Jim: They were actually quite patriotic, but my sense
is that people were more interested in what was going
on in the neighbourhood than in international events.

Phil: Obviously our documents point in the opposite
direction, because the Inquisitors of State *were*
concerned precisely with people talking about politics. But as far as spying was concerned, I'd agree
with Jim. People weren't very conscious of spies,
apart from those who were paid to be, and to monitor
the arrival of foreigners: I mean the police. I've got
reports where spies were posted around the Spanish
embassy, and ordinary people came up and asked them
for directions, you know, things you wouldn't really
ask a spy.

Jon: Anyone asking for directions must have been a
stranger though, which means they wouldn't be able
to tell the difference between a spy and a local.

Phil: During the Spanish conspiracy, government
records reveal a preoccupation among the people
with a possible Spanish invasion. People were looking
out from the belltower of San Marco, waiting for
the arrival of an enemy fleet. They were scared.

Jon: Weren't there demonstrations against [the Spanish
ambassador in 1618] Bedmar?

Phil: I think that, as with the Gunpowder Plot, there's a difference between what was real and what was invented. For example, with Bedmar, what evidence do we really have that there was a riot around the Spanish embassy?

Jon: Well, except that Bedmar requested a bodyguard, because his life was in danger.

Phil: But he was making a point, which is that the people were unruly and the Venetians couldn't control them. In other words, the request was a calculated, implicit insult to the government. It also served to justify Bedmar's rush to leave Venice.

Jon: Do you get any sense that Grancini's and Meschita's neighbours knew what they were up to?

Phil: People were suspicious about Meschita's activities.

Jon: Did they denounce him?

Phil: I don't remember—you up for another round?

Jon: Same again then. I'm only asking because usually people were well aware of what their neighbours were up to. In trials witnesses introduced the local gossip with 'I mind my own business, but ...'. People knew who was beating his wife, or who hadn't consummated the marriage, really intimate things. The business with Grancini's wife, you can bet that the neighbours overheard all the arguments.

Jim: Spies were more like us, the foreign researchers in Venice. We don't have roots. We don't take part in neighbourhood life, but we have certain specialist kinds of knowledge about the city that are not available to the locals.

Phil: Spies also did most of their business in public places, like Rialto, and stayed in inns or monasteries, places where people were constantly coming and going.

They didn't live in the same neighbourhood for years
and years. They were constantly moving around the city.
Jon: Yes, but Vano was different. He owned property in
Venice. He knew other immigrants from his home town of
Salò; he was involved in the local economy. He must
have had a certain profile. I'd love to know what the
neighbours thought of him.
Jim: Yes, that's interesting. Vano was a spy, but he was
also somebody's neighbour, and the community of spies
and ambassadors in Venice was like a special, city-wide
'neighbourhood', whose inhabitants all knew each other.
Phil: I think people who denounced spies were most
likely to be other spies, just as the people most
likely to denounce criminals are other criminals.
Jon: But ordinary people knew that Vano was a spy.
There's something I found right at the last minute—an
interview with a widow who lived near the Spanish
embassy. She saw something suspicious in her local church,
but that's not why I mention her. The important
thing is that she didn't drop a note in one of the
denunciation boxes or go to see the Inquisitors'
secretary. Instead, she walked halfway across the city
to Vano's house and told *him*. She understood that he
would know what to do with the information.
Jim: Whether or not spies were invisible, servants
were sometimes treated as such by their masters, which
was precisely why the servants were able to betray them.
Jon: In Vano's reports, there's a feeling of being
'backstage' inside the embassies. This metaphor was
used by a Spanish diplomat called De Vera to explain
the idea of the ambassador being 'two persons', both the
symbolic substitute of his master and a private individual, just as an actor becomes someone else onstage.

Jim: The accepted wisdom is that, in the seventeenth century, the home was still a public space, or at least semi-public, and that the separation between this private, domestic sphere and the public world 'outside' only happened in the eighteenth century.

Phil: That's why the Venetian state tried to control noble marriages, baptisms and even parties, because these were considered to be 'public' events, with political significance.

Jon: What about secret signals? Did you notice if someone was winking or 'staring meaningfully' at someone else? I mean apart from bartenders whose attention I'm trying to catch.

Jim: Well, in Venice, people were very aware of what particular gestures and costumes meant.

Jon: Yes. Seventeenth-century intellectuals argued that gesture was a kind of universal language, understood by everyone—like insults are.

Jim: Secret signals work differently, because they're addressed to someone in particular, whereas an insult has to have an audience to work. You're making a public declaration.

Jon: And since it has to be understood by everyone, the meaning has to be conventional. With the secret wink or signal, on the other hand, bystanders might recognise our intention to communicate something but they won't know what.

Jim: Another difference is that, with an insult, sometimes the recipient doesn't want to receive the message. I have to force him to notice, or make it impossible for him to ignore it.

Phil: One of the differences between *novellisti* in the generic sense of people who loved gossiping about

news—the *curiosi*—and the more specialised sense of
newswriters who traded information was that the
curiosi wanted to be *seen* knowing and talking about
things. They boasted about all their contacts and the
secrets they knew, and then they ended up in trouble,
because it turned out that they didn't really know
anything.
[Non-applicable conversation follows.]

Fiddler's Elbow Irish Pub

Six pints of Guinness

18. RUNNING ALTERNATIVES

What the map cuts up, the story cuts across.

—Michel de Certeau

HE MOST EXTREME PROBLEMS OF INTERPRETATION IN Vano's reports involve a series of meetings between the Spanish secretary Andrea Irles and Vano's accomplice Domenico in May 1622. As usual, Vano himself does not seem to be overly troubled by the implications of what he reports. He passes the parcel of interpretation to the Inquisitors, who can only hope that there is something left in the middle once all the wrappings are off.

The background is this. By early 1622, Domenico has left the embassy and been promoted to Vano's right-hand man. The Spanish are well aware of this—over the past eighteen months, Vano has proudly passed on news of various plots against his and Domenico's life as proof of his own importance. On 10 April, two days after Foscarini's arrest on treason charges, Domenico meets the informant Francesco, who warns him of a plot against his life.

At this point, Vano and Domenico have five and a half months left to live.

On the morning of 11 April, Domenico goes to Vano's house to pass Francesco's warning on. He does not find Vano. He tries San Marco. He does not find Vano. He doubles back to the house. He reaches the bridge of the Angel.

Rossi is coming towards him accompanied by hired muscle and, on seeing Domenico, shouts, **That's him**, with the force of a pistol crack. *Ecce homo.*

On the page, assassin follows spy at the precise speed that word follows word. The eye runs backwards and forwards in a metronomic rhythm, pursuing the ending. The reader follows a parallel line to that traced by Domenico's feet, through Paradise Alley and over the wood bridge into Santa Maria Formosa. Stop. There is a problem with Domenico's route—or, rather, with Vano's description of it.

The Bridge of the Angel. Paradise Alley. What happens if we try to follow this route on a map? What Vano says is, *at* **the Bridge of the Angel, [Domenico] ran into Rossi coming [towards] San Lio** (my emphasis). This sounds straightforward enough, but it makes little sense visually.

Vano may mean to imply that Domenico entered the Salizzada San Lio via the Bridge of the Angel, walking north, and then kept going until he met Rossi at the junction with Paradise Alley. This hypothetical route is marked on the map by a dotted line. The problem is that Vano cuts the space represented by this line out of his account (he says, *at* the Bridge of the Angel, Domenico runs into Rossi and turns into Paradise Alley, with no gap between these two events). The missing space is approximately two hundred and twenty-five metres, or two and a quarter minutes of Domenico's life. In other words, Vano collapses time and space for dramatic effect.

His technique here is analogous to the manipulation of perspective in a Cubist painting. Artists like Picasso simultaneously display aspects of a three-dimensional object that could not in actuality be viewed from a single viewpoint. In other words, Cubist paintings combine multiple viewpoints by partially 'flattening out' three-dimensional objects onto a two-dimensional plane. Vano similarly misrepresents Venetian geography

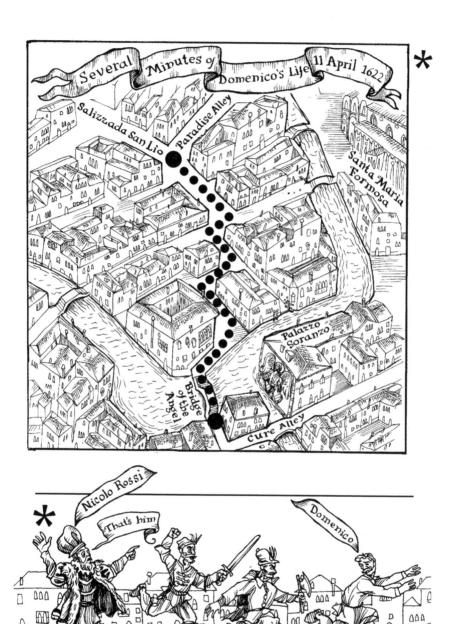

by superimposing two points that were in reality quite separate. Consequently, we simultaneously 'see' two distinct moments in time: that at which Domenico crossed the Bridge of the Angel and that at which he met Rossi. Another artistic comparison might be the apparently hyper-realistic paintings of Venice produced by Gentile Bellini and Canaletto. Their views showed buildings and monuments that would actually be blocked from sight if the artist stuck rigorously to the 'real' point of view apparently adopted. In effect, then, Bellini and Canaletto also combine two or more distinct viewpoints in a single picture.

None of this is particularly shocking.* It is the sort of thing that happens in any story, and it does not necessarily undermine the truth of Vano's account. Why then lavish such attention on a missing two and a quarter minutes, when all historical narratives omit days, months, years, even centuries? The answer is simple. We can only appreciate Vano's artistry if we zoom in until the brush strokes become visible or the integrity of the image begins to break up. And we need to understand his artistry if we are to understand exactly where the truth of his reports lies.

Play. Fast forward to Santa Maria Formosa. Open space stretches sound; time stretches in the echo. Open space offers more options. It prevents assassins appearing around blind corners. It prevents the future closing in. Domenico's feet running; arms stabbing air.

Cut back to early 1620 and the parish of San Giacomo dall'Orio, on the other side of Venice: A robbery in progress; Domenico's feet standing still. His arm stabs down with a stiletto at a prone body lying on the ground: a salutary reminder that Domenico was not averse to handing out the kind of treatment Rossi's men had in store for him.

Forward to April 1622 and across to Santa Maria Formosa: The hunter now hunted. What goes around comes around.

Forward again to September 1622: The day of Domenico's execution: feet kicking on the gallows, running on thin air. No more choices left.

---

* There are three other possible interpretations of Domenico's route (Versions Two, Three and Four below). Version Two is at least as plausible as that discussed in the main text.

Domenico the loyal servant; Domenico the spy; Domenico the victim; Domenico the thug. Where and when will the Wheel of Fortune stop?

April 1622: Domenico's feet running. On to Santa Marina, and then San Cantian. Take the ferry for Murano. Interrupt the journey at the Crosechieri, where there is a monastery, and sanctuary.

Let us assume, just for argument's sake, that Vano's account of what happened on 11 April 1622 is true. Anyway, even if it is not, Vano was still required to make his subsequent reports consistent with what he had already said, as if it was true. So: Domenico escaped from the assassins by the skin of his teeth. He might have been flattered by the attention, but he had no reason to believe that Rossi and Irles the Spanish secretary wished him anything but harm. Why then did Irles ask for a private meeting a month later in early May? What could the two men possibly have to say to each other under the circumstances?

Domenico suspects a trap. The messenger swears on his children's lives that safety is guaranteed. Domenico insists on a neutral location. They agree on the church of San Stae.

Churches occupied an important function in Vano's Venice, and not just because friars and confessors were often denounced as possible spies. Churches were simultaneously public and private space. Vano often met his informants there because he could wait inconspicuously. There were always people coming and going. Moreover, he could see these people relatively easily, which decreased the likelihood of an ambush. Even better, there was always an excuse for visiting a church if someone asked. Even women could visit without suspicion, which made churches similarly convenient for adulterous trysts.

11 May 1622, early morning: Domenico checks the church. He sees the Spanish secretary enter alone. He approaches him near the altar. The secretary asks who he is working for. Domenico says something about

---

Version Two: If we take Vano's words at face value to mean that Rossi was indeed coming towards San Lio, then this might imply that the protagonists were walking in opposite directions to Version One. In this scenario, Domenico would reach the Bridge of the Angel walking south from the

a merchant. He adds that he is planning to take a new job working for a noble. (This might be true, but Domenico does not know where the noble lives and will not give his first name.)

How long since you last saw Vano? says the secretary.

Domenico cannot remember.

The secretary congratulates him. He has passed the first test by not denying the connection. Then comes the pitch.

[Vano] has been paid thousands of ducats, and bonuses on top, and he has a stipend of five hundred ducats, and what about you lot [who work for him]? When's he ever given you a gold coin or two? [No, it's] a *scudo* here, four *lire* there, just enough for a drink, and no more.

Clearly this is not a desirable state of affairs. Perhaps the secretary can do something about it?

Vano is working for the Inquisitors! Really? Domenico is shocked.

Domenico's efficiency is missed around the embassy nowadays. Letters keep getting sent to the wrong address. (Irles does not seem to have considered the possibility that Domenico might be involved in redirecting them). In short: Come back Domenico. All is forgiven.

Domenico needs some time to think about it, and, of course, to discuss the situation with Vano, a silent ironic aside intended only for the reader.

No need to make your mind up now. Just tell the messenger yes or no when you next see him.

11 May, sunset: Irles waits by Domenico's house and repeats the offer, unaware that Domenico has just returned from meeting Vano. Irles suspects that his **servants are stabbing [him] in the back**. Domenico is the man to sort the problem out. (He is indeed uniquely qualified, since he helped recruit the traitorous servants in question.) The only thing he has to do is renounce the works of Gerolamo Vano and all who traffic with him.

Salizzada San Lio and it would be Rossi who was coming up the other way. Upon meeting Rossi, Domenico turns around one hundred and eighty degrees and runs back the way he came, turning off the Salizzada when he reaches Paradise Alley.

15 May: Domenico is still prevaricating, obviously curious to see how long Irles can keep going. He claims that he owes money to his current employer and therefore cannot obtain a permit to change jobs. Irles offers to pay the debt for him.

The secretary said, 'The other day I swore to you on the most holy sacrament and our lord that I would not harm you, and I really wish to do you good if you will serve me'.

Domenico said, 'Sir, what do you order me to do and what can I do?'

The secretary said, 'Promise me loyalty or go away and live your own life. Do the same if you don't believe me'.

Domenico said, 'Your Lordship, tell me what you want'.

The secretary said, 'Be loyal to me and never mention my name'.

Domenico promises (a promise again weighted with an ironic double meaning, since it is recorded by Vano).

Then the secretary ordered him, 'Go and find Gerolamo Vano and tell him that you have managed to persuade Battista ... to reveal the contents of letters from Milan by your efforts at wining and dining him'.

The punchline: Irles wants Domenico to pretend that he is receiving information from Battista.

The worrying thing about this: According to Vano's reports, Domenico really does receive information from Battista.

Alarm bells are already ringing, but this is not all. There is a further complication. According to a letter written by the English ambassador Henry Wotton after Vano's downfall, Battista was an invented source, and any information attributed to him was therefore by definition unreliable. So, in May 1622, the Spanish secretary Irles tells Domenico to pretend that Battista is an informant, while Vano simultaneously pretends the same thing to the Inquisitors.

The problem with this version is that Domenico was supposed to be on the way from San Marco to Vano's house, and Vano's house was somewhere near Santa Marina at this date (off the top of the map). Hence it makes no sense for Domenico to be walking south down the Salizzada, since this takes him straight back to San Marco (just off the bottom of the map). In other words, we have to

What is going on? Bifurcate the possibilities. Either / or. If / then.

Version I: The Spanish offer is genuine and should be taken at face value. If Battista is really supplying information, then Irles is unaware of this fact.

Version I.a: Irles is so stupid or so cynical that he thinks profit is sufficient stimulus for overcoming the bad blood caused by the assassination attempt in April.

Version I.b: Irles thinks that Domenico is unaware of his role in the various assassination plots hatched during the previous year.

Version II: The Spanish offer is not on the level, and Irles knows that Domenico is going to pass everything on to Vano.

Version II.a: Irles is not sure how deeply involved Domenico is with Vano. He uses the offer as a pretext to speak with Domenico, hoping that his reactions will provide valuable clues on Vano's activities. From Irles's point of view, then, Battista is a maguffin. He may or may not be Vano's informant in reality, but in either case Irles is not suspicious of him.

Version II.b: Battista is really Vano's informant. Irles is suspicious of him but is not absolutely sure of his treachery. The proposal of Battista as a 'phantom' agent is a ploy, intended to draw a reaction from Domenico.

Version II.c: Battista is an informant but, unknown to Vano, he is a double agent, feeding Vano false information in precisely the way suggested by Irles here. Irles's proposal to Domenico is therefore a double bluff intended to convince Vano that Battista is a genuine source by deliberately drawing attention to the possibility that he is not.

Version III: The offer to Domenico is provisionally genuine. Irles's next move depends on how Domenico responds.

Version IV: Vano has such overweening confidence in himself or such contempt for the Inquisitors' intelligence that he has invented

---

presuppose an error on Vano's part for this version to be correct, but perhaps an error is more plausible than the 'collapsing of space' effect that Version One requires.

Version Three: Domenico was walking north and Rossi was coming south, as in Version One.

the whole ridiculously implausible story, presumably with Domenico's connivance.

Version IV.a: Vano plants the story because it makes him look clever. In Vano's fantasy, the bumbling actions of the Spanish serve to highlight his genius.

Version IV.b: Battista is a fake informant, invented by Vano, and Vano is creating a fallback position to protect himself against the revelation of this fact. If he is later charged with accusing innocent men, he can claim to have been duped by Battista and Irles, spies even more cunning than himself. In other words, Version IV.b is a triple bluff by Vano, in which he pretends that Version II.c is true, but that he failed to penetrate Irles's double bluff.

Let us list some odds for those who like a flutter on what has already happened, in the belief that it offers greater certainty than what has yet to take place.

Version I.a: 2–1

Version I.b: 2–1

Version II.a: 5–1

Version II.b: 10–1

Version II.c: 10–1

Version III (in combination with any of the above): see author for quotation.

Version IV.a: 1–1

Version IV.b: 10–1

This is all rather arbitrary because the calculations are based on preconceived (rather than scientific) notions of what is probable. For example, we know Vano invented some of his material and we cannot unknow this. This leads us to suspect everything he wrote, when in fact much of his material must have been reliable. The efficacy of Vano's lies

---

However, here they met at the Bridge of the Angel rather than at the turnoff into Paradise Alley. Domenico then ran *at and past* Rossi into the Salizzada San Lio before Rossi and his men had time to react.

depended on him usually telling the truth. The implausibility of Irles's approach to Domenico does not mean it could not have happened, since different definitions of plausibility apply to spies than to normal people. In any case, historians do not have the luxury of dismissing the improbable out of hand. We are obliged to consider all that is theoretically possible, since the improbable occurs frequently enough in human history to confound even the most scientific of calculations.

In short, 1–1 on IV.a. may be unrealistically low.

Cut to the chase.

Every turn that Domenico took in the streets of Venice was a commitment that narrowed his options. Moreover, refusing to choose would be equally fatal. He had to think ahead like a chess player, sketch out possible futures and rewrite them from one moment to the next. The threat not only came from behind; it approached from ahead. It was a hypothetical moment when there were no choices left: the brick wall in the dead-end alley.

Domenico's route maps the line between free will and compulsion, chance and necessity, past and future. It is visible only as a series of dots rather than a line, separate slides that appear as a continuous whole if you run them through the projector fast enough. The Bridge of the Angel. Click. Paradise Alley. Click. Santa Maria Formosa. Click.

There is a contrast between the transience of the event and the (relative) permanence of the streets through which Domenico ran: between the intangibility of Domenico's fear and the persistence of Venetian geography. Can we 'read' Domenico's route by tracing it with our feet as we read Vano's words by tracing them on the page with our fingers? The problem is that the Venice we 'share' with Domenico, or rather its

---

The problem with this version (besides the fact that, again, Rossi is not walking 'towards' San Lio) is that it requires Domenico to have both extremely sharp reflexes and nerves of steel. Moreover, Vano described Domenico as reacting to the situation only after Rossi said, 'That's him!'

Version Four: Domenico was walking north, as in Versions One and Three. Rossi, however, was

architectural frame, has been vulgarised by overexposure, reproduced and trivialised in a million postcards and holiday snaps and overlaid with other, less urgent itineraries. ('Notice, on your left, the beautiful church of the Miracoli', Domenico gasps in this anachronistic world of guide books, waving his umbrella as he runs. The assassins behind pause momentarily to admire the exquisite marble decoration, allowing Domenico the few seconds he needs to pull ahead.)

Move back to 1622, and then forward from 11 April to 11 May. The spreading delta of possibilities raised by the secretary's suggestion that Domenico come back and work for the Spanish appears to take all the forward impetus out of the story, but that is only because it traps us at the moment when we are required to make a choice. Which road? Which interpretation promises a solution? Which leads to a dead end? Can you hear the assassin's footsteps behind?

Choose now.

Domenico's options on the streets of Venice in April were relatively simple. He was a gondolier, so he *knew* Venice. Its geography constrained him but also released him. One street or canal led directly to another. Actions led directly to consequences. Causes led to effects. Our choices are more difficult than Domenico's. They concern interpretation rather than action and there are no grounds in the record itself for preferring one interpretation over another. Vano stares at us with mask-like impassivity, offering no advice. Domenico remains similarly deadpan. In May, unlike in April, he refused to choose. Instead, he put off the moment of decision until the Spanish secretary gave up.

In contrast to Domenico, we know the outcomes in advance. All our choices of necessity lead to Domenico's death on the gallows in September 1622, despite the fact that none of them can be said to cause

---

coming west down Cure Alley [*Calle di Remedio*] and he ran into Domenico at the Bridge of the Angel. Before Rossi reached him, however, Domenico continued north into the Salizzada San Lio and then turned off at Paradise Alley.

The problem with this version is that it is not clear why Rossi should be described as going

it; nor do they really explain it. Every route is literally a dead end in this sense.

From Domenico's point of view (looking forwards) everything is contingent; his choices change what happens. From our point of view (looking backwards) everything is predestined; our choices change nothing. Domenico runs for his life, but we know that his life has precisely five and a half months left to run.

How do we represent what has yet to already take place? That is the contradictory tense in which history is written. Jules Michelet described it as 'when it shall have been': history as future perfect rather than past definite. We must attempt to escape the brick wall represented by facts, their killing banality. Interpretation is our attempt to assert free will when faced with the inevitability of what has already happened.

No one cares any more what happened to Domenico on the morning of 11 April 1622, and perhaps that is the point. It is only when there is nothing at stake that we can enter a pure state of play and fully enjoy the aesthetic and intellectual pleasures that the past has to offer. But there is another point of view, which returns us to the dilemma posed at the beginning of this book. Vano was a storyteller, but his words had real consequences: in his account, a man's life was at stake on the morning of 11 April 1622. Indeed, is not Domenico's run a perfect symbol of all those experiences whose essence is irretrievably lost to the historian, because the sensations are both too immediate and too 'trivial' (or rather personal) to be either represented or remembered? Domenico's route maps fifteen minutes of fear. It is the immediacy of his response that we reach for but never touch. It is the disposability of his body, so easily ruptured by blades and bullets, that moves us.

towards San Lio if he was coming down Cure Alley. It is admittedly not an impossible route for reaching the Salizzada, but it is a rather indirect one.

Whichever version we choose, things become clearer once Domenico turns off into Paradise Alley. Of course, Vano could just have been writing vaguely, effectively 'smudging' the whole area

Not all of Vano's reports generate possibilities in the way that Domenico's meetings with the Spanish secretary do, but there is a basic, insoluble problem with all of them. Every story supplied by an informant is predicated on a lie. If this fundamental, necessary lie was exposed, then the flow of information ceased. Moreover, spies were actively trying to deceive each other, so even if a spy reported honestly to his paymasters there was no guarantee that he had not himself been deceived. Levels of deception that would normally be dismissed as absurdly improbable become troublingly convincing.

Isolate an individual image. Blow it up. Blow it up again. And again. What initially appears crystal-clear and hyper-realistic is revealed by a simple change of scale to be coarse grained and amorphous. The foreground dissolves into the background. Entities that were crisply distinct bleed into each other on the picture plane. The image becomes flat, abstract, artificial. There is also a serious problem with double (quadruple?) vision. Some reports will tolerate more magnification than others, but all of them break down if you zoom in close enough.

In the religious culture of the seventeenth century, entire sermons could be spun out of one or two words from the Bible. Jesus wept, for example. The assumption was that the text could bear an infinite degree of scrutiny, or an infinite weight of interpretation. Vano's words carry no such guarantee. The truth about Vano's lies can be found in the space between the dots that make up the image, the space that the eye fills of its own accord by a cognitive trick. It is the space of doubt, and therefore by definition the space of faith too.

Be precise about the degree of imprecision.

---

represented by the line on the map. All my interpretations may be erroneous in that they overestimate the precision of the effect Vano was aiming for. The sad fact is that I have nothing better to do than pore over Vano's reports trying to work out exactly what he meant. Conversely, Vano had many demands upon his time that may have meant he was unable to obsessively consider every detail.

19. TRACE

T HIS CHAPTER IS A KIND OF FORENSIC ANALYSIS. IT COMPARES the 'fingerprints' left by some of our protagonists in the archive with the marks left by an abstract criminal (time) upon a metaphorical corpse (the city). In Venetian alleyways, some surfaces take prints better than others, but everything has to be dusted with light before it reveals its message. Of course, forensic analysis does not use elements that retain their original and pristine appearance: quite the opposite. Only by studying the process of decomposition can you measure the distance between past and present. There is no material decay in the photographs of documents comparable to that in the shots from the city, although plenty of documents in the archive are eaten through or water damaged. However, there is an analogous decay of meaning, in that words, idioms and references to particular individuals prove difficult or impossible to make sense of.

Walking is an improvised performance, arranging the elements provided by geography as words are arranged in a sentence. Of particular interest is the point at which the pedestrian unexpectedly shifts off the beaten path down a short cut known only to him or her, the equivalent of the 'twist' in the end of a tale that creatively transforms its meaning. Venice is a famously disorienting city, one in which outsiders have to reconcile themselves to being frequently lost. It has remained unconquered by the rational geography of the map, because any serious alteration of its medieval plan would have meant altering the city's unique relationship with the surrounding waters, and this has never been a practical option.

City and archive have things in common. There are demolished and disused spaces in both, sites where you have to pick through rubble. Acid ink eats paper as salt corrodes brick: water-bled documents and damp foundations. The Napoleonic and Austrian administrations who ruled the city after the fall of the republic in 1797 binned thousands of pages, just as they demolished churches and houses. There are dozens of alleys that appear to go nowhere in the city. There are thirty-seven boxes of Miscellaneous Papers that don't belong Anywhere in the archive, which contain hundreds of letters that were originally part of the Inquisitors' records. Doesn't an oar breaking the surface of a canal resemble a pen dipped in ink? The gondolier as calligrapher. Doesn't the curl of a turning sheet of parchment recall a breaking wave? History is on the tip of my tongue as I turn this corner. Geography is at the back of my mind as I turn this page.

What happens if we start from File 636 and move towards the death of Antonio Foscarini in April 1622? It is impossible to get there by taking a straight line through Vano's reports, in which we quickly reach a dead end. So, we work from key junctions and familiar landmarks (confirmed dates and recognisable names). A detour into the Ten's archive. All the junctions and subdivisions ultimately peter out, but they make it possible to produce a sketch of the area around our inaccessible destination. The original authors had access to information that I do not. They had the possibility of switching to a boat when they hit a canal. I am landlocked, forced to negotiate my way around records that were not designed to yield answers to my questions.

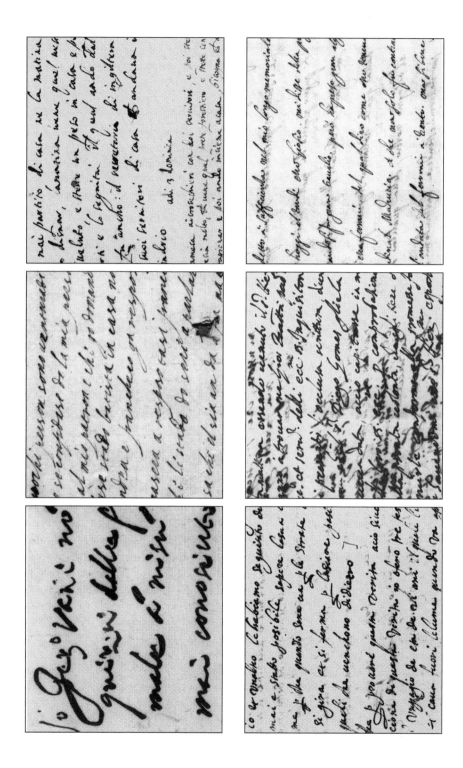

Try all files that cover relevant dates. Paths connect in unexpected ways, revealing different perspectives. I recognised the police captain Francesco Ongarin's handwriting in Vano's file before I knew who the writer was, but once I got a fix on his identity (or at least the way he wrote his 'f's, 'p's and 'd's), then his reports started appearing everywhere, a series of short cuts linking different files. It took a while to connect the 'Menego' interviewed by the Inquisitors in 1619 with the 'Domenico' who appeared as an informant in Vano's reports in 1620, and it was not immediately clear that this was the same man who reappeared as Vano's assistant in 1621. The identification was only possible once the conversation between Domenico and the Spanish secretary in May 1622 reviewed in Chapter 18, 'Running Alternatives', revealed a shared history between them. After this, it was easy to work back and establish that (for example) our Domenico was the man for whom Giulio Cazzari, the secretary to the Imperial resident, wrote a reference in October 1620, which can now be found in File 584. You can reach him from many different directions.

Since there is no map to describe the confused contents of the Inquisitors' damaged archive, we are obliged to tramp out our own paths by moving through and across the pages, trying to reconstruct the routes (and the detours) taken by our characters within, across and sometimes outside the rules established by bureaucratic procedure. There was never a map for the Inquisitors' archive, precisely because there were relatively few rules governing their actions. In a sense, the documents were intended to form an inaccessible labyrinth, through which only the secretaries knew the route, and they frequently forgot it, or failed to pass the relevant knowledge on. The damage the archive suffered after the fall of the republic has only made things worse.

Top left, Santa Maria della Salute, 18 December 2000, 12.30 p.m.; Council of Ten criminal papers, Gerolamo Vano, probably 21 September 1622.
This sample is from the papers Vano wrote in the condemned cell the night before his execution, although it closely resembles his normal hand. The only obvious difference is that the strokes are thicker than

usual here. Vano's italic script is generally highly legible but gives an overall impression of crudeness due to the consistent separation of letters, which consequently appear slightly irregular and crooked.

Top middle, Santa Sofia, 18 April 2001, 1.45 p.m.; insert in File 636, Francesco (Vano's informant in the Mantuan residence), 12 August 1622.
Francesco's language is quite distinctive because many of his phrases are in dialect. Indeed, some of the variations from standard Italian here are quite rare outside contexts closely linked to direct speech, such as transcriptions of testimony in court records or dialogue in plays specially written for 'low' characters. Literate people tended, by definition, to 'clean up' their language when writing. Francesco, by contrast, uses spoken constructions such as **go domandao** for *ho domandato* (I asked) and **vo sinoria** for *vostra signoria* (your lordship). He also spells his own name in four different ways during the course of the same report, firstly as what appears to be **francheco**, followed by **franceco**, **francesco** and **franseco**. In fact, it is different every time it appears! Eclectic spelling is normal in seventeenth-century documents but, even so, this is remark-ably inconsistent. If your sense of a word is dominated by its sound rather than its visual appearance, as was the case for illiterate people, or those who wrote infrequently, then consistent spelling appears less important. Tellingly, Francesco uses almost no abbreviations, although the text here may have been an atypical composition in this respect—we lack any others to compare it with. This absence also suggests that he did not write very much, or at least had little contact with professional copy-ists, who used a whole set of shared notations for common words.

Top right, Ghetto, 15 April 2001, 1 p.m.; insert in File 636, Francesco Ongarin (the Ten's chief of police), 2–3 January 1621.
In some respects Ongarin's hand is similar to Vano's, although the sepa-ration of letters is less marked and their shape departs more from the classic italic form. There is also greater use of looping. There are clear dialect inflections, although they are not as marked as in Francesco's

report—e.g. **vene fora di casa** for *viene fuori di casa* (he left the house), **indrio** for *indietro* (behind) and **doi** for *due* (two). Like Vano, Ongarin consistently renders what would be double consonants in modern Italian as single (or conversely, single as double). Vano and Ongarin both had an interesting relation to literate and intellectual culture, which their hands betray. They occupied a level below that of secretaries, notaries and noble magistrates—men who had either received a classical education or who wrote for a living. Despite this, both men were required to produce written reports on an almost daily basis. This may account for the fact that they give the odd impression of simultaneously being practised and awkward in holding a pen.

Bottom left, San Francesco della Vigna, 16 December 2000, 12.45 p.m.; File 1214, Diego Gomez, 4 February 1620.

Since Gomez's responsibilities in the embassy included translation, it is possible that he also performed secretarial tasks. In any case, the hand here is fluent, albeit workmanlike. Although this sample proves that Gomez had an excellent command of written Italian, there are still a few slips where he was obviously spelling with Spanish pronunciation in mind or just used an irregular form; for example, **enbasiatore** for *ambasciatore* (ambassador), **venchono** for *vengono* (they come), **ofero** for *ovvero* (an elaborate literary variant of or). Reading Gomez is equivalent to listening to someone speak with a Spanish accent, although if you are used to standard Italian this is actually less difficult than following Francesco's dialect.

Bottom middle, Rialto, 27 March 2001, 5.30 p.m.; File 1214, Zuan Battista Padavin, 4 February 1620.

In one respect, Zuan Battista Padavin (secretary of the Inquisitors of State from September 1619 to September 1620) and his successor Roberto Lio (secretary from October 1620 to September 1622) are the most important characters in this book. Their importance lies in the simple fact that they physically produced most of the documents in the Inquisitors' archive during this period and also many of those in the

Ten's archive. The latter documents can be split into two categories: firstly, the official, retrospective section, which was made up of a series of bound, parchment registers, with a parallel set of files containing the draft versions of the register entries, in loose-leaf paper copies; secondly, the material produced on a day-to-day basis, mainly for the purpose of actually making decisions rather than recording them for posterity. The level of care taken in writing out the first section was obviously greater than it was for the second. The Inquisitors' archive, by contrast, consisted only of the second sort of material, which partly explains why Padavin's hand here is rather sloppy. Nonetheless, it is still clearly legible and recognisably the work of a professional writer.

Ironically, then, it is the untidiness of Padavin's hand that testifies to the level of his ease in holding a pen, in contrast to Vano's clearer but more laborious letter formation. The grammar is also more 'correct' than Vano, so, for example, we get Italian rather than dialect forms for names, such as **Gio** (the standard abbreviation for Giovanni) instead of the Venetian Zuanne, or the Latin **Hier.m** (for Hieronimo) instead of Gerolamo. We also get literary terms, such as the pronoun **egli** (he) and **occlusa** (enclosed), which is a Latinism. In a longer extract, the tendency towards Latinate spelling and vocabulary might become more apparent, although it was less obvious in writers of Padavin's generation than in documents written by their sixteenth-century predecessors.

Bottom right, west side of the Arsenal, 18 December 2000, 3.15 p.m.; File 610, Alessandro Grancini, 4 March 1620.
This is one of Grancini's **memoranda** from 1620 and his hand here differs from that used in the more topical and less polished reports from the 1610s. This piece has obviously been written carefully and at leisure, although it is still relatively plain, without elaborate flourishes on loops, or similar decorative features. Grancini was a more sophisticated calligrapher than Vano, as we might expect given that he began his career as a copyist. The style is fluid (with no separation of letters) and the stroke thickness is consistent, with only occasional pooling of ink in loops.

20. PARADISO PERDUTO, 12.05 A.M.

Jim: It's like the bloody *Star Wars* cantina in here.
Jon: This sort of thing is missing from my story: the band playing over there, or the merlot and prosecco you're drinking.
Jim: Or the Croatians arm-wrestling in the corner.
Jon: In whose honour I am drinking this disgusting Jägermeister stuff.
Jim: What you mean is the everyday world that Vano and his targets lived in.
Jon: Yes, what was going on in the streets around them.
Jim: I think Venice would have been like a city in the developing world today—like Fez, in Morocco, where shop interiors and exteriors blend together, and so do industry and retail. As you walk around, you can hear people trading and selling, smiths hammering and carpenters sawing and planing. In Venice there were

shipbuilders all over the city, and silkweavers'
rickety looms clattering away. There were bells in
all the city's parishes, and music. Singing was an
important part of church liturgy, but there were also
operas and smaller, more intimate, private concerts.
There were madrigals and lute playing, and Venice was
famous for its orphan child choirs. Less harmoniously,
there were itinerant salesmen—and women—shouting about
their goods for sale, and lots of gossiping and
'murmuring'. The boatmen and gondoliers were famed for
their rough speech and cursing. You would also be able
to hear the official government heralds at San Marco
and Rialto, announcing the latest proclamations and
sentences.

Jon: But not *every* sentence. One of the really
striking things about the trials of Foscarini and then
Vano is that there were no proclamations. Just dead
silence and dead bodies.

Jim: Well, corpses bring us to smells, and Venice
probably reeked, but on the plus side there was
cooking in all the food stalls: fresh and salted fish,
cheese, milk, meat, blood, frying food coming from the
fritoleri, and the *luganegheri*, with their steamy
soups.

Jon: The *luganegheri* were the sausage-makers, no?

Jim: Yes, but they also sold broths. Then you had the
canals, which were practically open sewers.

Jon: Don't overdo it though. Venice was quite advanced
in comparison to Paris or London—at least the sewage
was removed by the tide!

Jim: The government also kept the most offensive or
odious trades away from the city centre: the tanners,
who used dogshit and scraped animal skins, for

example. Also the glass-workers, although in that case
it was more because of the danger of fire.

Jon: In the centre, the smell of baking bread must
have been common, because there were bakers and ovens
for hire every few streets. Also, the rather less
enticing odour of piss, but at least the perfume and
soaps helped cover that up.

Jim: As did the wafts of the Orient from the spice
shops for which Venice was famous. What's also interesting is all the different styles of clothes everyone
wore. People constantly judged others according to how
they dressed. Clothes revealed which ethnic or social
group you belonged to, much more so than they do today.

Jon: I love the fact that certain kinds of sleeve
were reserved to 'respectable' people to show that
the wearer didn't engage in manual labour (as wearing
a suit does today, now I come to think of it). And
certain colours or dyes were reserved for gowns worn
by senators and other important office holders.

Phil [animatedly]: The first thing people referred to
when asked to describe a respectable person was that
they wore *maniche comode,* sleeves open at the wrist.
But it also meant you could trick people about your
background by changing your dress.

Jim: It was a cliché of the time: appearances were
deceptive.

Phil: They were only deceptive if people didn't know
you or where you came from. Spies were unique in that
their attention was often directed at strangers and
outsiders, people they didn't know already but instead
had to identify.

Jon: The fact that no one knew your history was
the one advantage you had as an outsider. In other

respects, you were at a real disadvantage to Vano and Domenico. On the streets, they could use the background as cover, and move confidently, without paying any attention to it. So all these sights, sounds and smells are missing from Vano's reports because Vano took them for granted and suppressed them as 'noise'.

Phil: Or alternatively the background chatter provided an excuse for failing to overhear conversations that were too dangerous or compromising to pass on. Informants say things like, 'And then I couldn't hear, because he was speaking too quietly, or the street was too noisy'. Or maybe it's the opposite: the conversation was actually innocent, but the spy didn't want to provide proof of that and put himself out of a job.

Jon: Half a conversation is so much more titillating than a whole one.

Jim: What?

Jon: [inaudible]

[Non-applicable conversation follows.]

Paradiso Perduto

One shot of Jägermeister and two glasses of wine

21. STREET THEATRE

File 636, 6 September 1620: **Yesterday evening ... about midnight lord Nicolo Rossi came for the [Spanish] Ambassador and said to him, 'Lord, we are ruined; our affairs go from bad to worse; there is some evil influence that persecutes us'.**

The lord Ambassador, stamping his foot on the floor said, 'Cursed be whoever made me come to [the new location of the embassy]; it was better near San Marco'. He ate half his dinner and got up from the table muttering that he didn't want to eat. ...

[Rossi] threw out a young man who was writing in the study, and ... hissed through his teeth, '[The traitor] is this young Spaniard'.

File 636, 12 December 1621: **At five hours after sunset, a boat came with someone in the back ... [who] wore two swords and a pistol. [The boat] passed backwards and forwards twice and put [the man] down at the Spanish secretary's dock. He climbed up on the prow of the secretary's gondola and attached some paper to the thread, then whistled twice. At this, a gondola arrived and said, 'Who goes there?' He didn't reply, but ripped the paper and**

jumped in his boat, almost falling in the water, then left in the direction of the canal of San Stae. ... Domenico jumped onto [the secretary's] dock and pulled the thread away ... because there was a little bit of paper still attached.

O N THE SURFACE, VANO'S REPORTS CONTAIN NO TRACE OF his inner life. For example, he never discusses how he feels about the constant threats against his life allegedly uttered by the Spanish. Instead of exploring the mental worlds of his characters from the 'inside', Vano constantly invokes images of movements, gestures and actions. Every psychological state is rendered physically. He is not content to narrate information: he dramatises it. He shows as much as tells. In the first report quoted above, a first person narrator (probably Domenico) has silently converted himself into a third person one. Vano the conjuror: a puff of smoke and Domenico is invisible. But isn't the suspiciously melodramatic dialogue designed precisely to draw our attention to his **evil influence** over the Ambassador's affairs; to heighten our awareness of the betrayal taking place and hence of the informant's value to the Inquisitors?

Vano never resorts to melodrama when writing in his own voice. All the lurid phrases in his reports are quotations attributed to others. He is deadpan, but his enemies are gripped by passion. They are melancholic; they cannot eat; they cock pistols in fury and curse their nemesis Gerolamo Vano. They are woefully unprofessional, or so Vano implies. This is his (unarticulated) diagnosis on the basis of the symptoms displayed. Someone who is not in control of his emotions cannot, by definition, be in control of the story.

The characterisation of unidentified traitors differs significantly from that of the foreign ambassadors, as we can see in the second quotation. We might think of the games being played on the streets of Venice for a very select audience as a peculiar version of the *commedia dell'arte*, a semi-improvised Italian dramatic form that involved stock characters, who wore masks. Vano's characters similarly act out variations on the same generic plots—and literally wear masks, or more frequently hold cloaks and handkerchieves over their faces. In particular, the characterisation of the Spanish ambassador, and the clumsy interpolation of Spanish words and phrases into reported speech, may be derived from the *commedia* character of the 'Spanish captain', a boastful soldier who used a deliberately garbled version of the language similar to that of Vano's reports. Vano may also have had the role of the *zanni*—cunning Venetian servants who attempted to outwit their betters—in mind as an implicit reference point for himself and his accomplice Domenico.

The kind of performance involved in the *commedia* differed from the role-playing that occurs in modern social situations, when the persona we adopt (the metaphorical mask we wear) is that of our truer self, the self we would like to be. But it also differed in important respects from the 'performances' offered by Venetian traitors in Vano's reports, whose priority was always to preserve their anonymity rather than to conform to dramatic or other conventions. Hence their 'characterisation' is ultimately more limited than that of the various foreign ambassadors. In effect, traitors were struggling to remove all trace of a truer self from their appearance. Any aspect of their everyday personality or appearance that remained visible could be used by Vano: **The servant saw that he was a man with cheeks as red as apples with black moustaches turned down and of medium height, or [Waiting] in the lagoon with a boat, there was a man with a black jacket and white stockings, without a beard but with moustaches.** The reports are full of such minor details, carefully stored up in the expectation of future revelations.

Insofar as they were aware of him at all, Vano's targets tried to wrest control of their stories back from him and, in doing so, erase themselves from his reports, or at least strip their identifiable characteristics away, leaving only those of 'The Traitor', who was always the same: cunning, suspicious and greedy. We might even argue that the entire cast of Vano's reports (including the narrator) were trying to re-make themselves as people whose truer self was that of a person who wore masks, and was faceless without them. In Vano's world, there was no layer deeper, more authentic, than theatrical self-representation. Vano the family man; Vano the local dignitary; Vano the spymaster: it is not necessary to choose between these different realities. If we only have access to the last, it does not mean the other two did not exist.

Vano's account of events inside the Spanish embassy does, however, rely on an implicit opposition between onstage and backstage activities. Elsewhere, onstage, the Spanish ambassador appeared before the Venetian cabinet in official audiences, and neither party said exactly what they meant. Calculated ambiguity reduced accountability. The effect was the same in official minutes as in official portraiture. Think of Velázquez's many paintings of Philip IV of Spain, a series beginning shortly after Vano's death in 1623. Over a period of thirty years, there is hardly even a change of posture, and certainly none of the dynamism of Rembrandt's self-portraits. In 1665, Philip was reported to be capable of remaining immobile for indefinite periods of time, without a flicker passing over his face.

Backstage, Vano showed the soliloquies, the asides, the private gloating and despair that the public posturing concealed. He switched the register from freezing aristocratic disdain to the sort of vulgar emotion normally confined to genre scenes of peasants. The high and mighty Spanish, renowned throughout Europe for their obsession with honour, were denied their rightful, heroic status and presented as low figures in a comedy. They congratulated themselves for dissembling their intentions in public, unaware that Vano and the Inquisitors were still watching. Most of all, they revealed their fear and resentment of Vano.

This contrast between 'onstage' and 'backstage'—or between Vano's reports and official sources—should not be exaggerated. Official records also (since people are not painted figures) describe outbursts of petulance, anger and grief. Furthermore, rulers and other powerful men might remove their masks in public quite deliberately for strategic effect—or at least pretend to remove their masks. The critical difference is that Vano describes the words and actions of people who believed themselves unobserved. Hence there is a potential contradiction at the heart of Vano's reports, which simultaneously draw on repeated motifs and stereotypes while implicitly claiming to reveal the backstage reality that underlay this role-playing.

Vano's vision of politics is a 'tabloid' one. He tells of plots, not policies. He is concerned with individual intelligence, and not ideals or institutions. He reveals lies and bribes rather than detailing laws and treaties. It is not only a corrupt world, but a grotesquely oversimplified one, rendered in primary colours; in bleeding inks and bodies. Vano is indifferent to official audiences and functions. He ignores ceremonial and precedence disputes. He never mentions banquets or parties in the embassy. Less obviously but perhaps more significantly, he either ignores or ironically mocks questions of principle, especially the Spanish obsession with honour. As a spy, he was arguably outside the honour code, which was precisely why he was useful to the Inquisitors. His world is also resolutely secular. Churches are for secret meetings, and priests (who appear frequently) are potential spies whose religious convictions are entirely irrelevant. It is a world entirely stripped of ritual, unless you count coded coughs. Remarkably, then, Vano seems to distance himself from both poles of seventeenth-century morality: honour and religion.

This is partly a matter of genre. Piety would be out of place in a surveillance report. Thus, if we switch genres, we find that Vano commissions numerous masses for his soul in his will. Nonetheless, his reports have an entirely different flavour to the sectarian rhetoric and motivations of (for example) spies in Elizabethan England. The Imperial resident Rossi tells his Spanish counterpart Bravo, **'Don't order masses to be said so that God [will help]. [Instead,] help yourself [and] I will help you. You need to consider your actions carefully'**.

What men did and said exposed their weakness and their treachery. Vano watched and wrote, but he could not afford to conclude his stories of betrayal too quickly. He needed to put off the denouement until the audience had been properly primed and the trails had been laid. Only then would the Inquisitors appreciate his skills as storyteller; only then would they pay him what he deserved. We might therefore also compare him to the narrator of the *Thousand and One Nights*. By unmasking traitors he rendered himself redundant. Once they had been caught, then why should the Inquisitors keep paying? Vano therefore needed new traitors almost as much as he needed new informants. Despite his best efforts, the attrition rate among all members of his cast was high. The temptation to flesh out the cast list by invention must have been strong, and there is evidence to suggest that Vano succumbed to it. After Vano's execution, the English ambassador to Venice, Henry Wotton, reported that Battista, quoted by Vano as a prominent source throughout 1622, was not in fact his informant and had never even met him.[*]

---

[*] Vano may have learnt other things in the army besides how to recruit and lead men, since officers frequently padded their muster rolls with 'phantom' troops to increase their profits.

22. DESIRE

S

OMETIMES VANO MADE USE OF THE CLASSIC ANALOGY between treason and sexual infidelity, which was common in courtly poetry of the period. In May 1622, for example, besides plotting to thwart Vano's plans, the Spanish secretary was also trying to steal Nicolo Rossi's girlfriend. The iconography of betrayal, an inverted iconography of desire. However, women were apparently more valuable in this symbolic role than as individuals with their own lives and concerns. Elsewhere in the reports, they are confined to walk-on parts, with one or two lines at most.

Since I cannot prove a lover, I am determined to prove a villain.

Thus Vano's reports do not contain a single reference to his wife. We only know that he was married because his will refers to **my dearest companion lady Faustina**. Other men's wives (Domenico's, Grancini's) similarly appear only when they are waiting for word of missing or imprisoned husbands. Because of Vano's silence, it is impossible to imagine his home life. When an anonymous, threatening letter was delivered to him in November 1621, Vano reports that his housekeeper took delivery of it. His wife remained invisible even in her own house. There is a sense of lost opportunity here. Why was it not obvious that courtesans would make excellent sources?

Perhaps there is a connection between the invisibility of women in Vano's world and the subjection of men to a gaze that is traditionally directed at women. According to the critic John Berger, *Men act and women appear. Men look at women. Women watch themselves being looked at.* In Vano's reports, however, with few exceptions, adult males both look and are looked at, and the gaze always expresses aggression, not desire. There is no suggestion—as there had once been in medieval Venetian laws—that homosexual relationships might be linked to other kinds of secret or conspiratorial association. So, for Vano, men both act and appear—indeed, the difference between the two terms constantly threatens to disappear, as men are obliged to watch themselves being watched. But unlike Berger's archetypal woman, who is—it seems—powerless to resist the male gaze, Vano's protagonists are engaged in a constant struggle to reverse the direction of the surveillance.

It was not a matter of staring your opponent down, as it would be in a confrontation based on the principle of honour. On the contrary, the meeting of gazes was to be avoided whenever possible, because it was a kind of mutual unmasking. Such an explicit recognition only happens twice in Vano's reports. The first occasion was when Rossi ran into Domenico in April 1622, shouted **That's him!**, and let loose his assassins. Here, Rossi had the advantage. More ambiguous was a silent, charged meeting in December 1621, when, as Vano put it, **Don Giulio Cazzari ran into me in Eel Alley; [and] fixing me with an evil eye, he went on to the turning at Santa Marina.**

For Vano and his colleagues, it was always better to do things indirectly, to look out of the corner of the eye. The connections between betrayal and desire therefore remain implicit in Vano's reports. The most explicit discussion of the theme is not in an intelligence report at all, but rather in Alessandro Grancini's request for a separation from his wife. The subject could only be addressed openly by switching genres.

23. $2 + 2 = 5$

Council of Ten criminal register, 8 April 1622: **Sir Antonio Foscarini, son of Sir Nicolo, is accused of meeting secretly and frequently with the Ministers of [foreign] Princes by day and night in their houses and elsewhere, in this city and outside, both in disguise and in his own clothes. He has revealed the most intimate secrets of the republic, by mouth and in written notes, and been paid for it. He is to be arrested.**

Despatch of the Florentine resident in Venice, 9 April 1622: **Yesterday evening after the Senate met, the knight Foscarini (ex-ambassador to England and France) was arrested by order of the lords Inquisitors of State and immediately interrogated for five hours continuously. It is still not known if the matter concerns the public interest, or arises from a previous imprisonment of three years ago. [The purpose may be] to purge him of the jealousy and obstinacy he felt towards the republic.**

File 636, 9 April 1622: **Battista, servant of the Spanish secretary, said that last night at four bells a masked man ... knocked and asked urgently for the** secretary ... [and] gave him the news that the Knight F had been imprisoned with his servant. Then he left straightaway. The secretary, greatly enraged and stamping his feet, ran about like a man possessed, and called Nicolo Rossi to give him the news straightaway. Both of them armed themselves and said privately, '*We go to warn our friends*'. Battista took a sword and the secretary said, 'Where do you think you're going, *drunken rogue*? You want to come *with me without being asked*? I'll give you a kick'. And he threw him down four stairs. The secretary and Rossi went out ... When they returned home, the secretary shut Battista up in a room. After a while he returned ... and questioned him at length, saying, 'Battista, tell me *the truth*, I know that some coward has asked you about my affairs ... [O]n the King's *life*, tell me who they are, so that I can punish them and I shall forgive you. You will be like my brother and master of my house. I shall give you as much money as you want. I know that these villainous Venetians have been after you and you'll be thrown in the storeroom [if you don't confess]. Tell me to save your life'. ... The secretary asked him if he knew that [Venetian?] gentleman *from the other night*. ... Battista said, 'Sir, I don't know anyone. I wouldn't know them even if I saw them'. The secretary was enraged, saying, '*I'll make you confess* by force. You won't get away from here', and he shut the room up and left [Battista] there for twenty-four hours without anything to eat or drink. ... [When Battista was released] he went to [see] the servants of Nicolo Rossi and asked them, 'Why the hell did my master lock me up? What am I supposed to have done?' The servants replied, 'We don't know anything about you, but your master is behaving insanely, like ours and Don Giulio [Cazzari]. They've gone cuckoo. They say a gentleman called Foscarini has been imprisoned ... Don Giulio said ... 'We are sure to find that this business was started by Gerolamo Vano and Domenico and no one else. Our friends know Vano and Domenico well ... and we can hang and drown these villains'.

Council of Ten criminal register, 20 April 1622: Tomorrow morning before daybreak, [Antonio Foscarini] is to be strangled by the executioner in the prison where he is now detained, so that he dies. After he is dead, he is to be hung by the foot by the same executioner on a high gallows between the two columns in [Piazza] San Marco and left there all day.

Despatch of the Florentine resident, 23 April 1622: **Sentence was passed ... and executed with greater consternation among this nobility than has ever been seen, since the body of a principal Senator has been exposed all day in this manner ... The investigation was carried out in such a secret manner that the reasons for this rigorous sentence are still not known precisely.**

Report from a novellista in Venice employed by the Duke of Urbino, 23 April 1622: **He was strangled in prison ...** ~~after refusing to confess or submit to the church in any other way. Indeed, some people say that he tried to take his own life by various methods. Others say that he confessed and made a will.~~[*]

Despatch of the papal nuncio in Venice, 30 April 1622: **The reason for Foscarini's death is being kept so secret that not even the most important senators know it. The only thing that's clear is that it was for dealing with foreign Princes and their ministers.**

Despatch from the Venetian ambassador in England to the Council of Ten, 10 June 1622: **His Majesty [James I] added, 'As a favour, give me some idea of what that unhappy man Foscarini did. I knew him here for a long time [in the 1610s, when he was Venetian ambassador in London]. He was certainly eccentric but also courageous and passionately committed to serving your [country]'. ... [The king] became emotional and showed extraordinary compassion. ... [He said that] it seemed impossible to him that [Foscarini] would have betrayed his country.**

Biographical sketch by the noble Gerolamo Priuli, c. 1632: **There was a diabolical sickness, we might even say a devil incarnate [in Venice]. [Those**

---

[*] Crossed out by the writer, who obviously regarded this information as either unsubstantiated or too controversial.

possessed by it] conspired to accuse anyone they could of treason with inventions and lies for profit. Unluckily, [Antonio Foscarini] was struck by such a horrible falsehood. ... [He was] falsely accused ... of secret meetings with the secretaries of the Emperor and Spain ... on the basis of testimony from witnesses who had been corrupted by the wicked man [that is Vano, who is not named here]. Matters of State are so important and sensitive that circumstantial evidence has the force of proof. Three hours after sunset on the night of the 20 April, he was informed of [the sentence]. He was at peace in bed, sleeping without the slightest fear of the sentence, comforted by a clear conscience. He endured his encounter with death with singular strength of mind. During the three hours left to him after sentence was pronounced, his only thought was to insist continually upon his innocence. With these words on his lips, he surrendered his spirit into the hands of the executioner who strangled him in prison.

AS WITH EVERYTHING INVOLVING VANO, THE SOURCES RELATING to Foscarini's second trial in April 1622 are incomplete, fragmentary and sometimes contradictory. Unpick the thread of names; peel back the skin of the story.

Foscarini had been tried once before—on charges of bringing Venice into disrepute during his embassy to London in the early 1610s. In 1618, he was finally absolved of these accusations, after a painfully protracted prosecution, during which he was imprisoned for eighteen months. His personal life had been mercilessly subjected to scrutiny. It was a whispered smear campaign, with no information ever released officially. He stayed in Venice after his release. He was quickly elected to political office by fellow nobles anxious to reaffirm their faith in him.

8 April 1622: Foscarini was arrested outside the Senate, and executed a few days later. The Ten's resolutions on the case are dry as bone. The executioner was paid, as were the men who carried the body away. The sums are meticulously recorded, unlike the accusations. Critically, as the quotations above make clear, the charges were not proclaimed. Of course, arresting Foscarini in the Ducal Palace was in itself a public declaration, and a very dramatic one at that, at precisely the moment when it would make the greatest impact on the maximum number of people. But what was it a declaration of? No one was quite sure.

The despatches written by foreign ambassadors resident in Venice at the time reveal the extraordinary impact of these events, because Foscarini was far more important than Vano's earlier targets. He was not an impoverished nonentity like Zuan Battista Bragadin, or an inexperienced novice like Zuanne Minotto. He had been ambassador to France and England, and he *mattered*, despite his subsequent difficulties. So all the ambassadors in Venice wrote immediately to their masters on the subject of his arrest, but the only thing they could testify to accurately was the size of the disturbance. They could only speculate on its causes and possible consequences. Their initial reports thus describe a decisive action whose air of purpose was unmistakable but whose precise meaning was unclear. Most had heard some version of the accusations contained in the unpublished arrest warrant, but their words reveal a deep uncertainty: **It is still not known, it seems**; **suspicion** is sown; it **stir[s]** in the **shadow** of a crime.

Meanwhile, Vano wrote a report on 9 April 1622, in which he claimed to describe the Spanish reaction to the arrest. Only the Inquisitors and the Ten were privy to its contents, but its timing was surely not a coincidence; that is, Vano waited until the Inquisitors were committed before he named Foscarini on paper. Even so, his report never exactly specifies the nature of Spanish interest in the case. We are clearly meant to infer that Foscarini was in Spanish employ, but any such inference is made at our own risk. We can also observe Vano's regular strategy of attributing identifications to other people, and thus disclaiming responsibility for their accuracy. *They* **say a gentleman called Foscarini has been imprisoned**, Vano writes, but he cannot say if 'they' are correct.

Did anything described in the report of 9 April 1622 actually happen? Presumably Rossi and Irles went out as described, although they may have just been looking for news. Foscarini's arrest was, after all, an extremely dramatic event, whether or not they had any special interest in it. Apart from this basic observation, there is not much to say. We cannot see past the words, or under their surface, into the black box of the Spanish embassy.

No one except the Ten knew what was going on. There was no warning of the arrest, and so the foreign ambassadors tried to make sense of events by looking for portents. They were trying to rewrite the record; trying to remake themselves as men who knew all the secrets and who could find their way around in the dark without stumbling over the furniture. They short-circuited the gaps and fused an unstable, new tale that leaked doubt continually. They used the earlier accusations from 1618 to add verisimilitude and detail to the unconfirmed rumours in 1622. Foscarini was a notorious sceptic, so he must have died impiously. Foscarini was a notorious libertine, so his death must have something to do with a woman. Bruise his reputation and drag it over the stones. Where did this rumour come from? Who were the **probablest voices** referred to by the English ambassador Henry Wotton? They were never identified. No one ever originated rumours; no one confirmed or denied them. They were generated spontaneously, like flies in rotten meat. **It is [publicly said]. This is what is said, but until now without any certainty.**

The tongues o'th'common mouth. I do despise them.

Tidbits of sexual gossip complemented political intrigue. Or rather, sexual intrigue and personal eccentricity were advanced as clues to a deeper political misconduct. What was known was advanced as evidence of what was unknown. People were seeking a shape for the story. It had to make sense somehow but it was not yet clear which bits of information had to be kept and which discarded. The ambassadors were reshuffling clues—not only to determine what had already happened but to divine possible future repercussions.

The tired old metaphors all apply. We are in a hall of mirrors, or perhaps at a masked ball (Vano is somewhere in the crowd, unrecognisable under his disguise.) In the absence of reliable or precise information, we deal in reflections that break apart at the touch.

Ambassadors and ex-ambassadors turn up in each other's pockets and each other's reports, their purposes and cross-purposes interwoven. Foscarini had a place in this group. He was someone they took notice of, someone whose actions and fate signified, in both senses of the word. He was an initiate of their occult world, and they were concerned with his fate because it might in some sense foretell their own.

None of the various readings of Foscarini's character that we are presented with in the comments of the foreign ambassadors was inevitable. None of them, that is, was necessary. They were pieced together from visible fragments. The gaps were filled by speculation and an emphasis on the symbolic possibilities of events. We are obliged to read the Ten's laconic and impersonal deliberations in a way that re-enacts the attempts of seventeenth-century ambassadors and spies to decipher the information available to them. The problem is that the Ten never made connections explicit. They never cross-referenced and they provided little or no context for resolutions and judgements.

The Ten's records note only that Foscarini was instructed to prepare a verbal defence on 13 April 1622. On 20 April, he was condemned, with three proposals for sentencing, of which the most severe was passed. The speed and ruthlessness of this prosecution contrasted strongly with the slow, poisonous accumulation of evidence in his earlier trial. Foscarini was strangled in prison, quickly and discreetly, but his body was **hanged by one leg on a gallows in the public *Piazza* [San Marco], from break of day till sunset, with all imaginable circumstances of infamy, his very face having been bruised with dragging on the ground.**

Most nobles were beheaded, since this was considered a more honourable death. The inversion here, as with the earlier execution of Zuan Battista Bragadin, symbolised Foscarini's alleged reversal or inversion of proper values. The corpse was marked with signs that made his dishonour clear, even if the precise cause of that dishonour remained obscure. The Ten were telling the public how to 'read' his body. From this point onwards, Foscarini is reduced to a ghostly presence whose swinging, inverted corpse cast a shadow over all those associated with him. The execution was supposed to be the end of the matter but, as it turned out, the Ten were unable to fix the meaning of Foscarini's death quite so easily as they had hoped. His ghost could not be exorcised. In the immediate aftermath of Foscarini's death, however, Vano continued to submit reports as if nothing had changed.

File 636, 8 May 1622: **This morning the [Spanish] secretary was washing his hands and said to Rossi, 'Lord Nicolo, yesterday evening *our friends sent** a message in spite of of these [Venetian] lords'. And Rossi said, 'It's a good time to do it because now these Venetians must think that we have nothing and we will actually get whatever we want. Let the devil do what he will!'**

Vano's subtext here is clear. He is telling the Inquisitors: Do not think that you can do without me now that Foscarini is gone. There are new threats that only I can meet. Treason is a hydra. Cut off one head and another springs up to take its place. Vano reiterates his other major theme—his own genius—with equal enthusiasm.

File 636, 6 June 1622: **The Spanish secretary said to Nicolo Rossi and Don Giulio [Cazzari] that he is *totally desperate because of this Vano. He takes away all the nobles from us*.** ... All he needs to do now is come and take our shoes and we won't be able to leave the house.**

How was Vano's deception exposed? The source of the trouble is quite unexpected, because it had nothing to do with Foscarini. In August 1622, one of Vano's old informants—Zuanetto, whose evidence had helped to convict both Zuanne Minotto and Zuan Battista Bragadin back in 1620—returned to Venice and appeared before the Ten on a serious matter. Eight months before, at the end of 1621, Zuanetto had also testified in the trial of Alvise Querini, another of Vano's noble victims, who had been condemned to ten years in prison for visiting the Spanish embassy.

---

* These words are in Spanish in the original.

** The words in italics are in Spanish in the original. After **nobles**, the language is a mixture of Spanish and Italian, but it is hard to recreate this effect in translation.

Now, in August 1622, Zuanetto claimed that he had been suborned to perjure himself in Querini's trial. As a result, Vano and Domenico were arrested. The latter action was officially registered on 22 August but probably took place a few days earlier, since Vano's reports cease on 16 August. In prison, Vano and Zuanetto were brought together on 5 September to test their reactions (an unusual procedure for the Ten). No reason was recorded for Vano's arrest, but it seems likely that Zuanetto identified him as the man responsible for doctoring the evidence against Querini.

Vano turned out to be innocent of this charge, or at least not guilty enough to get Querini off the hook. In fact, the Ten discovered that Querini's brother had bribed Zuanetto to undermine his own testimony in the hope that the case against Alvise would collapse. In other words, Zuanetto had been suborned to *pretend* that he had been suborned. Hence, Alvise Querini remained in prison, although he was freed by the more prosaic means of a purchased blank pardon in 1623. Zuanetto got ten years' service in the galleys for perjury (that is, for pretending to have previously committed perjury). Querini's brother, who initiated the whole thing, apparently got off without punishment.

Despite the failure of Zuanetto's misguided attempt to free Alvise Querini, Vano was now in deep trouble. On 20 September 1622, and again with no explanation, the Ten sentenced Vano and Domenico to death by hanging, a proposal that barely won out over another to drown Vano secretly. An extraordinary meeting of the Ten on the morning of 22 September deferred the executions until the entire council met later in the day, when a suspension of the sentence was suggested to allow the investigation of **things asserted** by Domenico, along with a review of the **necessary** past prosecutions. Again, no details were provided to explain these tantalising phrases. The proposals failed to obtain the necessary majorities and the executions were therefore carried out as decreed.

The most probable scenario here is that Zuanetto's accusations raised wider questions about Vano's credibility, questions that then led the

Inquisitors back to Foscarini's case. Vano would surely have appreciated the irony of the situation: he was caught because of the crime he did not commit.

I begin To doubt th'equivocation of the fiend That lies like truth.

In January 1623, the English ambassador Henry Wotton put together a story that is roughly (but not exactly) consistent with the facts of Foscarini's death as we know them. Here Vano's downfall was linked explicitly to Foscarini's posthumous exoneration, which had just been announced as Wotton wrote. He began with the observation that **the case of the late Cavalier Antonio Foscarini hath been diversely misreported, and perhaps not the least even by those that were his judges, to cover their own disgrace**. Wotton claimed that Vano had accused Foscarini on the basis of information provided by Battista, his main informant in the Spanish embassy in 1622. When Vano tried the same trick again with another noble, the Inquisitors insisted on interviewing Battista directly before taking action. When asked to provide corroboration of Vano's charges, Battista denied knowing him, resulting in a sentence of death against Vano for perjury. If we assume that it was actually Zuanetto's accusations that prompted the Ten to investigate further, and perhaps to interrogate Battista in the course of those investigations, then Wotton's version makes sense.

There is nothing in Vano's final reports that suggests he was about to be arrested, but the last two are all about Battista, and in light of Wotton's suggestion that he was a 'phantom' agent, this emphasis seems significant. As we saw, Battista was the alleged source for Vano's only substantial report on Foscarini, dated 9 April 1622. Significantly, shortly after that report Battista disappeared; that is, Vano does not mention him again for some time. Only in Vano's penultimate reports in August does Battista make a dramatic comeback.

File 636, 15 August 1622: **The Spanish secretary came to see the Mantuan resident two hours before sunset, so angry that he was foaming at the mouth. He couldn't speak because he'd seen Battista his servant with someone who he thinks is a senator's servant. He is scared that [Battista] will reveal all his** affairs. He was tempted to kill him there and then by beating the shit out of him. The resident said, 'Sir, don't do anything … [N]ow I shall tell you. Battista has stayed the night twice here with me and confessed to being friends with Domenico. My servant Francesco has also eaten and dined with them. … I want to get the truth out of him … and then we'll go and make a stink in the cabinet about our servants being suborned by scoundrels'.

File 636, 16 August 1662 (Vano's final report): **[The Spanish secretary said to Battista], 'Is it really true that you've eaten and drunk with Domenico and other Venetians?' Battista replied, 'Sir, I suppose I could have, because I like to drink, but I'm not sure who he is. If someone showed me this Domenico I would tell you if I've spoken to him but in any case I wouldn't have said anything about Your Lordship's affairs … [If] the doge with his hat* came and gave me everything he has, I wouldn't say anything [about you]. I'd rather be drawn and quartered first'.**

What is going on here? Perhaps Vano was trying to prepare a defence against his imminent exposure as a fraud. If he had been lying to the Inquisitors about Battista, then he was going to have a lot of explaining to do when Battista denied knowing him. Using the above reports, he could defend himself with the claim that Battista *used to be* his informant but was now working for Spain and Mantua. Obviously he would deny knowing Vano when questioned, under instructions from Vano's enemies, because anything that undermined Vano's credibility was good for the Spanish.** If this is what Vano intended, then his fictional scenario is a curious inversion of the real situation with Zuanetto that actually precipitated his arrest.

We should also note that the reaction to Foscarini's arrest and the description of Battista's 'defection' quoted above are the two longest

---

* 'Hat' is a rather flat translation. The *corno* was the doge's official, ceremonial headgear. The only obvious alternative is 'crown', which is misleading because the whole point about the doge was that he was head of a republic, and not a monarchy.

** This scenario resembles Version IV.b of the conversation reported in Chapter 18, 'Running Alternatives'.

reports in File 636. Vano becomes more verbose as he gets more nervous. The more he has to hide, the greater the number of words he puts in the reader's way. After his last report in mid-August, we fall off the edge of our flat, paper world. There is nothing more in File 636, and the trial records for both Foscarini and Vano are gone, but there is further circumstantial evidence of the effects of Vano's downfall in the abrupt changes of fortune that many of his victims experienced after his death. Besides Foscarini, consider the following.

December 1622: Alessandro Grancini is released from prison.

6 March 1623: Alvise Querini is released quietly using a purchased blank pardon.

10 March 1623: Lodovico Rhò, a Spanish associate denounced by Vano and arrested in 1620, is released and ordered to leave Venetian territory.

24 July 1623: The Senate secretary Andrea Alberti, previously condemned for treason, is retrospectively absolved of all charges. In a petition asking that his case be reviewed, Alberti explicitly identifies Vano as his (false) accuser.

The pattern is obvious. Vano's evidence had been contaminated, and Foscarini was not the only one of his victims to benefit. The final question is why was there a four-month delay between Vano's execution and Foscarini's public exoneration? According to the English ambassador Henry Wotton, Foscarini's nephews asked that Vano be questioned about their uncle's case in September, just before he was executed.

Letter of Henry Wotton to King James I, January 1623: **[Their request was refused], either because the false witnesses, being now condemned men, were disabled by course of law to give any further testimony, or for that the Council of Ten thought it wisdom to smother an irrevocable error. The petition being denied, no possible way remained for the nephews to clear the defamation of their uncle (which in the rigour of this State had been likewise a perpetual stop to their own fortunes) but by means of the confessor, to whom the delinquents should disburden their souls before their death; and by him, at importunate and strong persuasion of the said nephews, the matter was revealed. ... [T]he nephews have removed the body**

of their uncle from the church of [Saints] Giovanni [and] Paolo, where condemned persons are of custom interred, to the monument of their ancestors in another temple, and would have given it solemn and public burial; but having been kept from increasing thereby the scandal, at the persuasion rather of the Prince than by authority, they now determine to repair his fame by an epitaph.

The nephews and the priest do not appear in official records, but the Ten were obviously keen to prevent Vano from talking to outsiders about something, since they authorised payment for a special guard to be mounted on his cell to prevent anyone speaking to him before his execution. The revelation (allegedly) provided by Vano's confessor was the only link Wotton was able to establish between Vano and Foscarini. There was only a little seed of fact at the centre of the fleshy gossip—if, indeed, it was a fact. It is ironic that our only identifiable source of information was a man who broke his oath as a priest not to pass on information he had heard under the seal of the confessional.

Council of Ten public proclamation, 16 January 1623: **The Providence of the lord God, by means truly marvellous and inscrutable to human minds, has disposed that the authors and ministers of the falsehood and impostures plotted against our late beloved noble Antonio Foscarini ... have now[,] without the intervention or provocation of anyone, manifested themselves.**

Deus ex machina. No one was willing to take responsibility for the course of events. Some nobles even complained that it would have been better to leave Foscarini's honour besmirched than publicly admit to an error. Right to the very end, we are dogged by circumstances that Henry Wotton left **at large**. For example, Foscarini left six thousand ducats **to him that should discover his innocency**. Or did he? There is no such instruction in the copy of his will registered in the records of the Ten on 29 April 1622, although this version was certainly censored.

Other commentators constructed different stories to Wotton's, although all used the same basic elements. The cryptic and fragmentary nature of the surviving records does not allow us to determine which version is true, only to trace variations and possibilities: a genealogy of motifs. The only solid fact is that Foscarini was innocent. He must have been, because otherwise there was no plausible reason for the Ten to compromise their own reputation by clearing his.

In each report, Vano staked himself and dared the Inquisitors to disprove him. In 1622, he bet his life against Foscarini's. Both men lost.

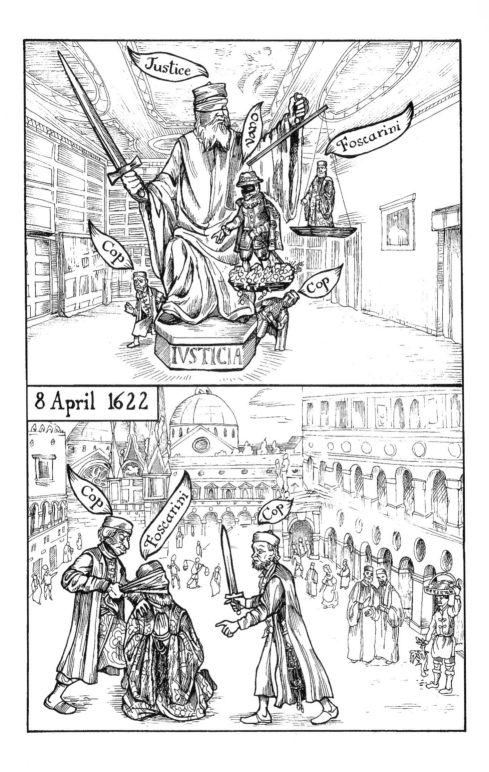

24. DA ALDO, 1.10 A.M.

Jim: House red?

Phil: Here? You must be joking.

Jim: Well then, *tre Campari per favore*, Aldo. *Grandissimi*.

Jon: No, I'll have the house red. I'm not fussy. Was there a Venetian official in charge of wine?

Jim: Of course. They had officials for everything. They were obsessed with collecting information and measuring things, as the vast number of surviving archives proves.

Jon: But what did they do with this information? That's the question.

Jim: Well, one problem was that there was a huge 'black' economy, which the government just couldn't control. Despite the Venetian efforts to measure (and thereby tax) everything, they only managed to get a grip on a small part.

Phil: But that has to do with the nature of a black economy, rather than the efficiency or otherwise of the information gatherers.

Jon: Do you think the same problem existed with political information? Weren't spies members of a 'black' political economy?

Phil: Yes, information was available to those who were willing to pay 'under the counter', but it was probably easier for the Council of Ten to find out about—say, the King of France's mistress—than the black market economy in Venice.

Jim: The danger is to be seduced by the information that's there, as historians have been in the past, into assuming that it's the full picture. Certainly in economic history, it's now recognised that there was a vast amount of smuggling going on in the seventeenth century.

Jon: I think they were more flexible in their methods for gathering political information. That's partly because they were more willing to spend money there.

Jim: Do you think they reflected at all on how measuring things could change the nature of the things being measured? You know, like the 'uncertainty principle' in modern physics.

Jon: Well, they were definitely aware that offering money to spies was going to encourage them to find *something* to tell you. I'm sure that the way the Inquisitors thought about this was in terms of human nature. People were sinful and corrupt and couldn't be trusted. The Council of Ten were also worried that they weren't using their information efficiently: that the archive was in a mess or the indexing system

wasn't up to date. It's difficult to know how grounded
those fears were, but it's also difficult to believe
that they were able to use, or even make sense of,
all the information coming in.

Phil: There are shades of 9/11. You know, the day
after the disaster occurs you find the critical
intelligence report, but it got lost in the pile
until then.

Jon: The same problems arise with the information they
produced and the decisions they took. I don't believe
that everyone read the entire text of bureaucratic
resolutions. The secretaries had a template, and it
was: name here, date there, terms of banishment there,
vote now. I know I skim read when I get to the formu-
laic bits in the registers, so why shouldn't they?
They had to get through a hell of a lot of business.
For example, on the day they officially registered the
arrest of Vano and Domenico, which was 22 August 1622,
the Ten also dealt with many, many other cases. I
made a list of them. So: they debated an assault
by firearms in Padua. They absolved one of Vano's
victims—the noble Zuanne Minotto—of making false
accusations against fellow prisoners. They wrote a
letter to Padua on a prosecution for rape. They wrote
another to Brescia about a denunciation for murder
and intimidation, and yet another to another noble
official regarding a friar who destroyed a pawn-
broker's receipt book.

Jim: What was going on there? A protest against usury
perhaps.

Jon: That's not all. They sentenced eleven people
involved in a bloody feud to death *in absentia*. They
also sentenced a noble widow to death *in absentia* for

poisoning her husband, and dealt with three of her
accomplices.

Phil: That's pretty melodramatic stuff! Noble wives
didn't often poison their husbands.

Jon: Less melodramatically, they gave permission for
a German tourist to see their collection of jewels.
And then they sent even more letters to Brescia
and Verona dealing with procedural questions. Now,
admittedly, 22 August was a busy day for criminal
affairs, but then again, they didn't answer any
letters to Venetian ambassadors abroad or debate any
political issues or legislation.

Phil: How did spy reports become evidence then? I mean,
how were they used in trials?

Jon: I think that excerpts from Vano's reports were
'pasted' or copied into the transcript, sometimes with
names and details suppressed. These excerpts probably
needed to be backed up by direct testimony, but the
relevant interviews might have been gathered months
before the trial officially began.

Jim: Did Vano appear in court to support his written
statements?

Jon: Well, he was definitely present at interviews to
'introduce' testimony from protégés like Gomez and
Domenico, but he wasn't 'cross-examined' on the
contents of his reports because that wasn't how the
legal system worked.

Phil: To get back to the big picture, I think you
have to put Venice in the context of seventeenth-
century Europe, and how naïve the people gathering
information for other states were. In comparison,
Venice, which strikes us as being unable to act
on all the information it gathered, was amazingly

well organised. Because it was a comparatively weak
state—
Jim: They were very conscious of that.
Phil: —they needed to know all the time which troops
were moving, what storms were active in the
Mediterranean. Information was vital for the economy
and for political survival.
Jim: I wouldn't deny any of this. I think they were
amazingly sophisticated in what they tried to do. Their
ambition is striking. What they lacked was a commitment
to providing sufficient bureaucratic and policing
resources to make the system work. But for intelligence
they had sufficient resources to throw at the problem.
Jon: But there, ironically, they were deliberately
exploiting the existence of a black market in political information. They were encouraging servants to
betray their masters and so to break this patriarchal
bond, which was one of the things holding society
together and guaranteeing social order. This is one of
the remarkable things about spying, morally; that, in
a sense, they were gambling with social order, as they
would see it. They were playing a short-term, immediate advantage against the more general principle.
Jim: Were spies always formally in a master- ...,
in a patron-client relation? Or were they on the
margins: hangers-on and parasites rather than trusted
confidantes?
Jon: Many weren't in permanent positions. And that's
precisely why ... They were selling information
because they were vulnerable, because they didn't have
that security. On the bottom rung of this economy, it
was a hand-to-mouth existence, as it is on the bottom
rung of any black economy.

Jim: I think it was a society that really relied on trust, though. The economy worked on credit, where your word was essential. There were formal contracts, but people didn't use them for everyday business. People ran up enormous tabs at their local wine merchants, and it wasn't just the nobles. Maintaining your reputation was essential for your economic existence.

Jon: Even in the world of spies, you had to have some kind of credit, in the sense that the Inquisitors had to believe your information was worth paying for. And often that meant you had to make a downpayment, or at least specify precisely what you had to offer and how you got the information. But the margin of trust was much, much narrower.

Jim: I would still say that spies were exceptional, being prepared to break their word in an era where it had religious significance too. I have court cases [in civil law] which were settled on oath because of the lack of alternative forms of evidence. They made a judgement based on whoever was prepared to swear on the truth.[*] And since we're thinking about the law, there were also two groups of people whose profession was based on keeping their word, and keeping the confidences of their clients, and these were lawyers and notaries. I was wondering if you have any evidence of spies coming from these professions.

---

[*] Witnesses were not automatically sworn to tell the truth in either criminal or civil cases. Rather, the threat to make them swear was sometimes used as a mild form of coercion, on the same principle as threatening them with torture since, once formally sworn, their soul was placed at stake. Witnesses took this threat with widely varying degrees of seriousness. However, a criminal case would never have been decided purely on oath. In depositions to the Inquisitors of State, witnesses were usually sworn to silence but not necessarily to tell the truth.

Jon: No, I would say. In fact, definitely no.

Phil: Not as spies. But again, there was this kind of underworld of information distribution, which was neither spying nor honest. Notaries merged into professional copyists, and *they* merged into *novellisti*, and *they* merged into spies. The boys or apprentices working for notaries—they were the people with the professional skills necessary to forge documents.

Jon: And apprentices were not full members of the profession, and so were not fully committed to its codes of conduct. It makes sense that if you wanted information from a notary's records, you would approach his apprentice, and not the notary himself. Just as Vano didn't try to corrupt the Spanish ambassador directly. Anyway, the cliché about 'The more you learn, the more you realise how little you know' is relevant for the Venetian bureaucracy. It's their anxiety about 'lost' information that proves how sophisticated they were.

[Non-applicable conversation follows.]

25. SPYING AND MODERNITY

ACOB BURCKHARDT IS NOT THE ONLY PERSON WITH A theory about the origins of modernity. More recently, the French philosopher Michel Foucault argued that modernity really began in the transformations of the nature of power in France at the end of the eighteenth century. Using a brilliantly counter-intuitive argument, Foucault suggested that modern notions of individuality were a side-effect of these transformations, which culminated in the application of so-called disciplinary techniques in new institutions such as prisons, police archives and asylums.

> For a long time ordinary individuality—the everyday individuality of everybody—remained below the threshold of description. To be looked at, observed, described in detail, followed from day to day by an uninterrupted writing was a privilege. The chronicle of a man, the account

of his life, his historiography, written as he lived out his life, formed part of the rituals of his power. The disciplinary methods reversed this relation, lowered the threshold of describable individuality and made of this description a means of control and a method of domination. It is no longer a monument for future memory, but a document for possible use.

According to this argument, individuality became the means whereby power gained a hold on its subjects, rather than a sign of their independence. So, what about spies? The dichotomy between surveillance and display is a false one. Rather, display in seventeenth-century society was closely bound up with mutual surveillance and mistrust, in which the sovereign's paranoia about conspiracy and the concealment of true motives met its match in the subject's anxiety about vulnerability to arbitrary power, or the malice of competitors. For all concerned, display could be a form of mystification, designed to conceal darker truths. All courtiers were forced to become spies to some degree, to doubt the motives of others and conceal their own. In Vano's republican Venice, the situation was slightly different because of the absence of both a sovereign and a court. Here private meetings—particularly those involving foreign ambassadors—were considered conspiratorial by default.

In Venice, as elsewhere in Europe, being watched was both a privilege and a curse. Vano's characters were both self-confident heroes and helpless victims. They were not locked into work routines or prison cells (not at first) but were instead constantly slipping out of their watchers' view. In describing the minutiae of individual lives, or at least the physical movements of persons about the city, Vano attributed power to them but also attempted to steal it from them. In the case of ambassadors, power was clearly associated with sovereignty, since they were accredited representatives of their kings, but different kinds of men also appear in Vano's reports: bandits, assassins, servants. It is not quite true to say that all these subjects possessed the same importance, since the most significant thing about the bandits was their proximity to the ambassadors. Even so, Vano's world was a remarkably promiscuous one in which men at the bottom of the social order (servants) sometimes proved to be the most valuable informants.

In Vano's reports, as in the nineteenth-century prison, surveillance sought to individualise its targets. In other words, for the target, individuality was a kind of vulnerability. The targets would have preferred to be known only by the generic characteristics of 'The Traitor': a persona or a mask rather than an identity. For Vano, on the other hand, the reverse was true. Individuality was a strength, or at least a saleable asset, because to be unique was to be indispensable.

For Foucault and those historians who follow him, the structure of the new disciplinary institutions (prisons, hospitals, etc.) was analogous to the structure of their archives. John Tagg describes how

> A vast and repetitive [photographic] archive … is accumulated in which the smallest deviations may be noted, classified and filed. The format hardly varies at all. There are bodies and spaces. The bodies … are … isolated in a shallow, contained space; turned full face and subjected to an unreturnable gaze; illuminated, focused, measured, numbered and named … The spaces, too … are … measured against an ideal space: a clear space, a healthy space, a space of unobstructed lines of sight, open to vision and supervision …

Vano's reports are quite different. For both him and his targets, there was no classification scheme, and no 'norm' against which deviations were to be defined. There was no dissection of individual identity into measurable criteria. Instead, there were repeated, generic motifs, strung together in shifting combinations. Instead of a clear space, a healthy space, a space of unobstructed lines of sight, Vano worked in twisting back alleys and canals, where his line of sight was constantly broken: by closing doors, masks, cloaks, darkness. Instead of the blank stare of the photographic mug shot, the gaze characteristic of Vano's reports was oblique, out of the corner of the eye. Hence we would expect Vano's reports to find a place within a different archival structure, one that corresponded to the structure of the back alleys and dark corners where his power was improvised. The archive of the Inquisitors of State conforms to these expectations.

Classification began to enter into the world of spies in the eighteenth century, if the Parisian police files described by historian Robert Darnton are anything to go by. In these, the format was standardised to a degree, but the crucial innovation was that the archive was organised by target. Each individual under surveillance had their own discrete file, with comments on their habits and morals, and so on. In the archive of the Inquisitors of State, by contrast, surveillance reports are grouped by informant. Among other things, this implied that informants were not anonymous and theoretically interchangeable functionaries, as prison guards (and police photographers) were later supposed to be. They were instead intermediaries, negotiators or translators. Certainly, Vano was interested in producing a document for possible use rather than a monument for future memory, but he did not apply a standardised technique in a controlled setting. On the contrary, he had to constantly improvise and to take care that the direction of the surveillance was not reversed.

What are we to conclude from this? Did the activities of Vano and the Inquisitors 'anticipate' later developments, or represent some kind of transitional point between Renaissance sovereignty and Foucault's idea of disciplinary power? Alternatively, does Vano represent the transition from a naïve and free Renaissance form of individuality to a self-conscious and oppressed Baroque one? Perhaps we might use him to reconcile Burckhardt and Foucault, since his career sits almost exactly halfway between the chronological focus of their respective studies.

By itself, Vano's experience proves nothing, but it is enough to confound both sets of schematic generalisations. Vano cancels all the oppositions that Foucault sets up, and makes a mockery of Burckhardt in much the same way that he made a mockery of the Spanish ambassador. Perhaps Vano does not belong with the artist and the princely despot in the pantheon of heroic creativity, but nor is he a helpless, cowed victim of disciplinary power. His reports were surely written to create a profitable space rather than defend an abstract notion of individuality. However, in achieving this goal, Vano was obliged to remake himself, despite his apparent lack of interest in his own emotions and inward self. As in Foucault's *Discipline and Punish*, individuality was a side-effect of power relations, or of the struggle between opponents, but not in the way that Foucault suggests.

To illustrate this point, we can consider the ways in which Vano became a character in his own reports. During surveillance operations he occasionally played a direct role in the events he described, but there is another way in which he became more and more prominent in his own stories. As time went on, the conversations he quoted tended more and more to be about what a dangerous spy Gerolamo Vano was, while his central theme was more and more the difficulties he had to surmount in supplying information. As Irles, the Spanish secretary, put it, **Cursed be *the servants of these Inquisitors, mad dogs,*** * **but I don't think they have anyone but that coward Gerolamo Vano ... I swear to God, there will come a time [when] I will make him repent**. Similarly, on more than one occasion, Vano quotes someone else describing his physical appearance. These descriptions are always rather vague, probably ironically so. On 8 July 1620, for example, the ambassador Bravo instructed his men to find and kill Vano, a man **of average height and build, whose hair is white at the ends**. Vano knows and understands others, but they cannot truly know or understand him.

---

* These words are in Spanish in the original.

Immediately after this description, Vano made one of his rare reflexive comments, which is all the more unusual in that it is simultaneously an explicit interpretation of events. The ambassador, Vano wrote, **wants me dead even if he has to spend everything he's got**. Was this an admission of fear, or a smug boast as to his effectiveness? No doubt it was both. In this ambiguity lies the secret of Vano's individuality. The only fully realised character in his reports is the narrator, who is at the same time an absent shadow.

26. I SPY, WITH MY LITTLE EYE

File 636, 14 December 1621: **Don Giulio Cazzari ran into me in Eel Alley; fixing me with an evil eye, he went on to the turning at Santa Marina to meet [Si]gismondo the spy.**

I SPY, WITH MY EVIL EYE, SOMEONE BEGINNING WITH 'V'.
Hypotheses: Vano and his enemies summoned suspicion, tracing magical figures with their feet on the streets of Venice, bringing curses down on each other and on men like Foscarini. Their **evil eye** secretly negated the rituals that governments and individuals used to create public consensus. The Ten attempted to limit the damage they could cause to public morality by dealing with them at a distance.

The human search for meaning became pathological in Vano's world. Worse, this pathology was normalised. Paranoia became a rational response. Vano's informants inside the Spanish embassy were continually forced to doubt what others took for granted. Their notion of loyalty was defined by betrayal. Vano watched others, but his primary responsibility was to watch himself with a degree of self-consciousness equal to that of the most sophisticated courtier. Control your lies. Create truth as an act of self-discipline.

Vano was one of the first people in the history of Western Europe to develop spying as a career or profession rather than an occasional activity. He was a man self-fashioned out of nothing, an alchemist able to transform base material (that is, himself) into Venetian gold. In September 1622, the Inquisitors assayed Vano's airy words and found them wanting. His fleshly dross swung lead-like on the gallows, a plumb line to measure the crookedness of his writing.

In the two years before his death, Vano mapped a secret and sometimes fantastic geography. Here be monsters. He traced lines that connected the bottom of Venetian society to the top, lines drawn outside the boundaries of official rhetoric. He and his informants made use of the vocabulary of honour and patriotism because it was the only one available to them and the only shield they had, but honour and loyalty were watchwords that curdled in their mouths.

Vano was a foreigner in his own country, maybe even his own mirror; but then, who knows what Vano saw in the mirror? I have no business trying to look over his shoulder. In the end, I do not know who Vano was. I only know how he wrote (in fact, only how he wrote in his reports to the Inquisitors). But that is more than nothing. It will have to do.

27. INTERRUPTED SENTENCES

N THE WORLD OF THE DETECTIVE NOVEL, JUSTICE MAY NOT be done but the truth is revealed and this truth is authoritative. It retrospectively classifies and labels. There may not be a moral order but there is a narrative order, that of a well-plotted story. **Narrative was my moral language**, says novelist James Ellroy. There is no equivalent truth to be found in Vano's reports because there is no final revelation and no unmasking. There is only gagging, choking and scoring out.

He hath bitten forth his tongue Rather than reveal what we required.

On the day of his death, Vano wrote a will in prison, as Foscarini had done a few months earlier. Notes appended to this will in the hours preceding the execution suggest a man with a bad conscience. Their style contrasts with that of Vano's reports, where he specialised in artful imprecision and outrageous melodrama. With death approaching, Vano instead resorted to bald statements like **I Gerolamo Vano do not know the Clarissimo sir Alvise Querini ... and I didn't speak ill of him to anyone because I've never seen or known him.**

This is a rather surprising comment, since Vano's evidence had undoubtedly helped convict Querini in December 1621. It probably had something to do with Zuanetto's accusations, which brought about Vano's downfall. Vano's will seems to promise contrition and confession, but its contents deliver nothing of any substance. Is this all he had to say for himself hours before his death? It is possible that the comment above was intended as a black joke; that is, Vano refused to admit to accusing Foscarini, an innocent man, and denied responsibility for the conviction of Querini, a guilty man. If I am correct in this interpretation, then I am the first person to 'get' this joke in nearly four hundred years.

Is there a murderer here? No. Yes, I am.

I am a villain. Yet I lie, I am not.

Domenico, in contrast to Vano, had important things to say on the morning of their joint execution. He requested that the sentence be postponed because he wanted to reveal something, even though he knew he had no hope of escaping death by doing so. Domenico did not want to die until the loose ends of the plot were tied up, but by this point the Ten were no longer listening. The execution went ahead but Domenico still tried to find someone else to tell. The English ambassador Henry Wotton said that he revealed Foscarini's innocence to his confessor. Andrea Alberti, another of Vano's victims who was released in early 1623, insisted that Domenico **said to the [police] captains ... [that] Vano had made him testify and swear falsely against me**. Just as Vano could not stop doubt leaking out of his stories, so the Ten could not stop the truth about Foscarini's death undermining their exemplary theatre of justice. Vano's last step into space with a rope around his neck was supposed to be the final full stop at the end of the story, but it turned out to be more like an interruption mid-sentence, a sentence (in both senses of the word) that remained unconcluded until the proclamation of Foscarini's innocence in January 1623. And even that proclamation left many questions unanswered.

We follow a path through the archives marked out by Vano's name. Wherever we go, he was there ahead of us, or someone else was, laying false trails. We are still vulnerable to the false coherence of his reports. It would be easy to adopt a position of total scepticism, but this would be false comfort. The truly unsettling thing about Vano's simulacrum is not that he was a liar but that some of his information was true and that we cannot tell the difference between truth and lies. It may be that the Inquisitors of State had much clearer notions of how to interpret Vano's words than we do. Indeed, *killing* him implies a fairly clear interpretation, but inferring certainty on the basis of decisive actions and identifying the precise cause of that certainty are not the same thing—as the foreign ambassadors who wrote about Foscarini's case discovered.

Take the conventional rules for writing history: and then; and then; an unending superfluity of events, a nauseating surfeit of time. Apply these rules with obsessive attention to detail and with the greatest possible exactitude. Then watch them warp and distort in the fairground mirror of Vano's reports. However, moreover, conversely, paradoxically, possibly, probably: death by a thousand qualifications, the occupational hazard of the historian. When dealing with Vano, add to this list: confusingly, implausibly, surprisingly, incredibly. In short, if you want a neat plot resolution, go and read a novel.

Ask the questions anyway. If I am responsible for what I say about Vano, then Vano must also be responsible for what he said about Bragadin, and Querini—and Foscarini. It matters that Vano brought about the death of an innocent man, but that fact does not define the meaning of his life.

28. PISTOLS! TREASON! MURDER!

> He shall die.
> Shall, was too slowly said. He's dying. That
> Is yet too slow. He's dead.
> —Ben Johnson, *Catiline His Conspiracy*

ET US RETURN TO THE BRIEF HIATUS BETWEEN FOSCARINI'S death and Vano's own, at the high point of Vano's career, before his achievement was exposed as a fraud. Let us celebrate his life and legacy by ending here, with Vano's final triumph, although 'celebrate' is probably the wrong word, since the triumph in question was the murder of Vano's principal adversary on the Spanish and Imperial side: Giulio Cazzari, Nicolo Rossi's so-called secretary.

If Vano was Foscarini's shadow, then Cazzari was Vano's. He instigated, encouraged or assisted virtually every

> Right: Firing mechanism of a wheellock
> pistol filmed at 9,000 frames per second.

anti-Venetian project mentioned in File 636. He had a finger in every poisoned pie. But Vano also had a personal stake in his elimination, for was not Cazzari always the first to propose killing Vano? In May 1622, the Ten and the Inquisitors finally decided to act on Vano's advice and order Cazzari's death.* He was assassinated two months later, on 13 July 1622.

On the day they were going to kill him, Giulio Cazzari left the house about three hours after sunrise. After saying mass in a nearby church, he continued on his way to dine with the Mantuan resident. He did not get far before the assassins struck.

Still life with a stiletto, pistol, powder flask, ramrod and winding key.

Turn the hourglass.

Wind the gunwheel that spins against the metal that produces the sparks that ignite the powder in the flash-pan, which sets off the charge in the barrel that propels the bullet that hits Cazzari.

Who dies.

The powder was a mixture of saltpetre, sulphur and charcoal. When it combusted inside the gun, the gases produced were trapped inside the barrel by the bullet. As a result, internal pressure increased until the bullet started moving, which allowed the gases to expand into the space it left behind.

Tick. Tick.

It took a quarter of a second for the wheel to gain momentum and generate sparks.

---

* The Ten frequently resorted to both assassination and secret execution: 204 people in custody were secretly drowned on their orders between 1551 and 1604. Such actions were justified by ideas on 'reason of state', which were shared by all the major European powers in this period. The Ten's preferred method for assassination was poisoning, when this was practical, and the favoured substances were arsenic derivatives or powdered diamond, which lacerated the intestines in a manner analogous to ground glass.

It took a quarter of a second for the combustion in the flash-pan to spread to the main charge.

It took minutes that no one ever had to reload.

Hold the gun out at arm's length balanced like a sword. Focus the will along the line of the barrel.

Shoot, shoot, Of all deaths the violent death is best.

Cracks whose source passers-by could not fix (although they, unlike us, could never mistake them for a car backfiring). A succession of meditative silences. Burnt wadding floating like fireflies.

No one had the luxury of distance in Venice. The range was poor and the line of fire was always blocked by twisting alleys.

One shot. Hit / miss / misfire.

Get the sword out from under the cloak.

Thnevrythngspedsup.

At the body's periphery, a bullet could easily flick off a finger or an earlobe, shatter teeth or a kneecap. Inside the body, it lacerated and crushed tissue, while its passage created a wave effect similar to that of a stone dropped in water. Flesh 'rippled' away as it passed, creating a temporary cavity—although, at the low (subsonic) muzzle velocities characteristic of

seventeenth-century firearms, the permanent consequences of this were negligible compared with the direct destruction along the primary wound track. If the bullet flattened significantly on impact, it might pick up tissue in a sort of 'snowballing' effect, which increased its surface area and significantly widened the wound track. It could also disintegrate, or ricochet internally if it hit bone.

In the case of a contact wound, where the gun was directly placed against the victim's skin, the entry hole was much larger because the gases issuing from the barrel had nowhere to go except into the wound itself, where (because they expanded faster than the bullet was travelling) they 'blew back' out of the flesh on either side of the entry hole, spraying tissue and bone.

Over thy wounds now do I prophesy—which like dumb mouths do ope their ruby lips to beg the voice and utterance of my tongue.

File 636, 25 May 1621—414 days: **Don Giulio said, 'I have worked a lot for the lord Ambassador of Spain; I've written letters to find out what has been done and planned in this city; and because of this my life is in danger'.**

What's this flesh? a little crudded milk, fantastical puff-paste.

File 636, 29 May 1621—410 days: **Don Giulio said, 'I am all confused ... I want to know how to stay alive because I don't want to lose my life'.**

Ask for me tomorrow and you shall find me a grave man.

File 636, 22 July 1621—356 days: **The lord Don Giulio was in the Mantuan resident's house and said to him, 'I don't want to stay in Venice any more because I'm afraid for my life. I've worked for the Emperor, for the King of Spain and for many other Princes ... For my own safety I want to go to Rome and the court of the Most Illustrious lord cardinal Borgia**[*] **... Lord Nicolo Rossi came to my**

---

[*] Borgia was Spanish ambassador to the papal court at the time.

room and told me that I'm too big for my boots, and that not even the emperor has a room furnished like mine. I replied that I want to spend the money I've earned as I see fit. So I'm going to Rome and I won't be [pushed around] by Nicolo Rossi. I shall escape the threat to my life, because I'm well aware that I've done wrong to these Venetian lords in this city. It's a miracle ... I haven't already been imprisoned'.

He knew it was coming. He knew he was worth killing. His self-importance demanded it. Like Vano, Cazzari offered threats to his life as references to his employers. Fear as inverted egoism: See how much I matter! You would think, then, he would have known better than to leave his house alone that morning. Perhaps the problem was that spies were so sensitive to hints and allusions that they did not recognise cruder and more direct threats. Cazzari was too used to movement in his peripheral vision; he was too habituated to hearing his footsteps doubled by Venetian shadows (the seventeenth-century equivalent of echoes and clicks on a tapped telephone). There were too many people in the street on that July morning, all of them strangers, but don't be paranoid. Keep walking.

Note by Vano, 24 August 1621—323 days: **The [Mantuan] Resident said to [Cazzari], 'Lord Don Giulio, watch what you're doing because you know what these Venetian lords are like. They have your letters'. Don Giulio replied and said, 'These Lords don't know what to do with the letters. They're dickheads. If they'd intended to do anything to me, they would have done it by now. I'm not afraid. When they want to do something against me, I know someone who will tell me everything straightaway'.**

I will not consent to die this Day, that's certain.
Oh Sir, you must.

File 636, 26 April 1622—seventy-eight days: **Don Giulio said to the [Mantuan] resident that he is very afraid that these Venetian lords will grab him and do him an injury because of certain letters that they've intercepted. The resident said, 'Don't worry about it'. Don Giulio said that nothing has been fixed and [he has] only Nicolo Rossi's word [that Rossi will protect him].**

There had been premonitions in the past two years, or rather Cazzari had deliberately invoked the end that eventually overtook him.

Cowards die many times before their deaths, The valiant never taste of death but once.

He decided to leave Venice. He had alternative positions waiting. He would be chaplain to the Empress, or perhaps Cardinal Borgia would get a diocese for him. The moment always passed. He conjured the fear and named it only to exorcise it.

I do dare my fate to do its worst.

Yes, they will kill me, but not today, not today. And that was always true, except on the morning of 13 July 1622, when Cazzari's constantly wavering faith in the meaning of his own life was finally justified by the manner of his death. In the instant before it happened, he knew they had the right man. There was no mistake and no injustice. His career as spy was redeemed in blood. Cut off on a bridge, exposed and unable to either retreat or advance, did time fold in on itself in the instant before the powder flared and the blade pin-pricked skin? Did he experience his death with a profound sense of *déjà vu*? Were all the premonitions relived in that dying moment, remembered images of a hypothetical future now dissolved in an apocalyptic present?

Run and meet death then, And cut off time and pain.

Of course, no one knows what Cazzari was thinking and feeling in the moments before his death. His comments on his own impending end were (if we trust Vano's account) undoubtedly part of an internal drama, or a struggle with himself. But that struggle in turn was bound up with the drama of his relationships with Nicolo Rossi and the Spanish secretary. He was playing to the gallery, and not staring transfixed into a mirror.

Vano was also playing to the gallery by writing Cazzari's words down, but it was a different gallery. Theoretically, the quotations above were only important for their information content, but Vano was certainly exploiting their dramatic nature to grab the Inquisitors' attention. Vano represented Cazzari as his greatest enemy, and therefore (inevitably) Venice's greatest enemy. It was Cazzari's hatred of Vano that symbolised the latter's importance as a source of anti-Spanish information. Even though Cazzari only spoke 'through' Vano, with Vano's inflections and vocabulary, his reactions were used to prove both the existence of plots and (more importantly) Vano's effectiveness in foiling them. Cazzari's anxieties also nicely counterpointed Vano's *sang froid*. Vano never complained when his life was threatened; he never admitted he was at a disadvantage or had been outwitted. He could not be fazed in his own stories. They are going to kill me. Cazzari trembled and sweated. Vano shrugged his shoulders.

Cazzari's obsession was not in fact unusual for the seventeenth century, as shown by the existence of an 'Art of Dying Well' intended to prepare sinners to meet their ultimate fate. What is interesting is that his pronouncements do not fit this model of Christian repentance. The principal reason for such incongruence is that Vano was not writing a work of religious instruction but reports intended to serve as political intelligence, but the full implications of Vano's silence will become clearer if we compare Cazzari's fate to that of the criminals who were publicly executed in seventeenth-century Venice. Moralists of the time pointed out that the condemned prisoner was uniquely privileged in knowing the time of his demise in advance and was therefore able to prepare for it. As a result, he

stood a better chance of meeting it in a state of grace. Moreover, in a metaphorical sense, the prisoner could serve as an 'Everyman' in the morality play of human history. We are all shut up in the prison of this veil of tears ... and we can only leave with death, to which we are all condemned by the justice of God for the sin of Adam. ... every death ... is a [particular] execution of the general condemnation.

The subject of a public execution took part in a communal ritual as well as a personal drama. He became at once a sacrifice to expiate his own sin and a sacrifice made by the community to God. If he accepted his death as just, and if he prepared for it appropriately, he achieved a triple reconciliation: between himself and God, between the community he belonged to and God, and between himself and the community (who prayed for his soul).

By contrast, the victim of an assassination was a sacrifice made to reason of state or political expediency rather than to God. His repentance and his eternal fate were irrelevant since, by definition, he was given no chance to prepare himself. Besides implying a distinction between politics and religion, assassination also underlined the distinction between ruler and ruled, since it defined politics in terms of secret knowledge. It further implied a possible separation of politics from law.

Vano presented Cazzari as if he had already internalised this vision of what his death might mean, as if he had already accepted that the ultimate meaning of his life lay in his role as a pawn in a political game and not a game played between God and the devil. Hence Cazzari appears entirely unconcerned with the judgement of God in Vano's reports. His sole preoccupation is with the judgement of the Venetians, whom his fear flatters and anoints as the arbiter of his fate. By inviting his own death, Cazzari therefore legitimised the vision of politics that made it possible.

13 July 1622—zero hour: There are no surviving representations of Cazzari's death. What do you see when you imagine it? Caravaggio's *Martyrdom of Saint Matthew* perhaps, with the executioner's sword ready to sweep down? Or Artemesia Gentileschi's *Judith and Holofernes*, the female protagonist sawing veins and sinew with a look of grim satisfaction? Paintings like these were attempts to compress all the elements of a narrative sequence within a single, frozen image, a 'pregnant' moment as the theorists of the time put it. If we think of death as such a pregnant moment, then the manner of a person's death would become an allegory of his or her life, a summation and a revelation as well as a termination of its meaning. In the early seventeenth century, this was precisely what death meant in the Christian tradition. It was the moment that decided a person's eternal fate, when each man would discover the secret of his individuality as angels and demons hovered around the deathbed fighting for possession of his soul. Savonarola put it thus: Man, the devil plays chess with you, and he does his utmost to capture and checkmate you at [the point of death]. ... [If] you win here, you will win all the rest, but if you lose, all that you have done before will be worthless.

This notion of death persisted for a long time. In the nineteenth century, the historian Jules Michelet developed a secular version of it.

Caesar under Brutus' knife, Becket under that of Reginald Fitzurse, the Duke of Orléans under those of the Burgundians, the Duke of Guise under that of Henry III—each of these has been himself, achieved his true stature, only once he was dead, lying at his assassin's feet like a new man, mysterious, unaccustomed, different from the old one by all the distance of a revelation, that revelation produced by the ultimate coherence of a destiny.

Here, the focus is still on redemption—not from sin; rather, from meaninglessness. Michelet describes a metamorphosis: death as epiphany, but (since his interest is in history rather than eternity) it is an epiphany that is bequeathed to posterity rather than experienced by the dying

man. The focus is on sudden, unexpected assassination precisely because the consciousness of the victim is not where the meaning of the experience lies for Michelet.

I prefer the Christian tradition, which sees the moment before death rather than the moment after as the one that is significant: the moment in which the knowledge of death is complete but before the fact of death extinguishes that knowledge, the last moment in which a person remains a person (rather than the first moment in which they become a historical character). If, as Pascal believed, humans are thinking reeds whose humanity derives from awareness of our vulnerability, then we are most human at the precise moment when we cease to be so.

There is another, related question. How long did a 'moment' last in 1622? Galileo conducted experiments on the motion of falling bodies using a water clock that measured down to a tenth of a pulse beat, but these measurements could only take place under strictly controlled conditions. Conversely, seventeenth-century watches were so inaccurate that the makers did not bother to include a minute hand, never mind a second hand. But even if 'half a second' could not be measured, it could be perceived; or rather, movements and events that lasted half a second were perceptible. A blink, for example, took one fortieth of a second. The duration did not exist in the abstract, but only in the flash burnt onto the retina; the jerk of the head away from the impact; the spasm of the heart going into shock.

Tick. Tick.

A hundredth of a second was, by contrast, neither measurable nor perceptible in 1622. It can only exist as a hypothetical abstraction imposed upon the past, and it is in this virtual interval that Giulio Cazzari becomes immortal. When the bullet leaves the gun, the space between it and Cazzari's shrinking flesh can always be divided by half; from five metres to 2.5, 2.5 to 1.25, 1.25 to 0.625, *ad infinitum*. The bullet never hits the target; Cazzari never dies.

Different ways of thinking about time correspond to different ways of thinking about death. For some authors, a man's entire life was a preparation for his final moment. Moreover, for many Christians, the souls of the dead did not immediately pass beyond the influence of the living. Ghosts might return; masses could be said for those in purgatory. It is only in the modern photograph, where the prisoner jerks with the electric shock of the bullet's impact or the suicide hovers eerily over the pavement like a table levitating at a seance, that death is reduced to a melting sliver of time, which cannot survive outside the frozen image. And in fact isolating minute cross-sections of time and space is only one of the photograph's functions. It can extend as well as compress the extent of any given 'moment'. On long exposures, it slows perception down rather than speeding it up, cohering time into a unity rather than blowing it into fragments.

We can thicken the moment of Cazzari's death by moving away from it, or rather extending it into a time-lapse exposure, which had its seventeenth-century equivalent in the still life. In the still life, time accumulated with the layers of paint on the canvas. It was not frozen; it congealed. The time depicted, the time in which the brush moved and the time in which the viewer stood in front of the work: they were all superimposed, all extensions of the same meditation upon death.

Let this hour be but A year, a month, a week, a natural day.

The clock did not stop on 13 July 1622. The moment was not yet complete.

Tick. Tick.

Council of Ten public register, 4 August 1622, twenty-two days afterwards: **The continuing investigation has not yet discovered the guilty parties who, last 13 July, wounded and killed Don Giulio Cazzari ... with guns and daggers in Rose Alley in the parish of San Cassian.**
It is essential to ensure that such a serious crime does not go unpunished, so [the following] is to be publicly proclaimed.

[The name of] the person who reveals ... within the next eight days the identity of those wicked men who ... with impious and barbarous cruelty viciously attacked Don Giulio Cazzari ... will be kept secret. If at least one of the guilty men is taken, convicted and punished, providing they were a principal or an employer [and not merely an accomplice], [the accuser] will win ... a blank pardon with permission to free two bandits ...

And if the denouncer is himself an accomplice, provided that he was not a principal or employer, he will win impunity for himself and secrecy.

Secretly, the Ten resolved to assassinate Cazzari. Publicly, they condemned the killers who acted on their orders. Secretly, they paid the assassins in cash, but appearances demanded that the Ten go through the motions of a criminal investigation into the murder. This would have begun with an inspection of the body to determine cause of death, either by a barber surgeon or a court notary supported by a qualified assistant. The scalpel and spatula entered the body along lines scored by the sword and the bullet, re-enacting their passage. The surgeon attempted to project the path of the weapon back to the artificial vanishing point of the assassin's hand. Cazzari's wounds were a map, or a photograph, which the surgeon used to reconstruct the missing dimension of time by a perspectival trick. Still life with butchered meat, scalpel, paper and notary's pen. Wounds do ope their ruby lips. The killer produced pain and death in the body; the surgeon abstracted knowledge from it.

The court officials worked in good faith but the Ten did not care what Cazzari's corpse had to say. They already knew who killed him and their interest was in preventing anyone else from finding out, or at least in making sure no one could prove anything.

File 636, 15 July 1622, two days afterwards: **This morning the Spanish secretary has been to visit the Mantuan resident and they discussed Don Giulio's death. The resident said that the republic might be responsible because [he worked against] [the Venetians] and they have his letters in their possession. The secretary replied, ['I don't know what's going on]; it could be that Don Giulio offended somebody [but] who knows who it was'. The resident** said, 'It's a pity. Many times I told him to leave that house, but he didn't want to move. It's a pity'. The secretary became red in the face and ears and the resident said, 'Mister secretary, you are all red, which is unusual for you'. The secretary replied, 'It upsets me to talk about this matter'.

Despatch by the Mantuan resident, 16 July 1622, three days afterwards: **Don Giulio Cazzari, who worked as secretary for the Imperial resident ... was attacked by three men, whose names are not yet known. The three fled immediately in a gondola, which had been left nearby for this purpose. It is said that they were backed up by another eight people ... On Thursday [Rossi] appeared before the cabinet, ... [who] declared their horror at this turn of events. [They assured him that] they would [not] neglect any possible means by which justice might discover the guilty. However, so far little has been discovered.**

[In code:] It is known for certain that Marquis Rangon was the man who committed the murder under instructions from the Inquisitors of state. ... They believed that Don Giulio masterminded the meetings between the Spanish and the nobles executed here.

Warm. Very warm. Keep going.

Despatch by the Mantuan resident, 23 July 1622, ten days afterwards: **It is said here that the Imperial resident [Rossi] was the one who arranged the murder of his secretary Cazzari, because [Cazzari] criticised him in letters to the [Imperial] court, and because he suspected that [Cazzari] was sleeping with his prostitute.**

No. Cold, colder, freezing.

The Mantuan resident could not tell which of these two versions of the story was correct on the basis of plausibility or coherence. No angel appeared with a trumpet to proclaim the transcendent truth of Cazzari's death.

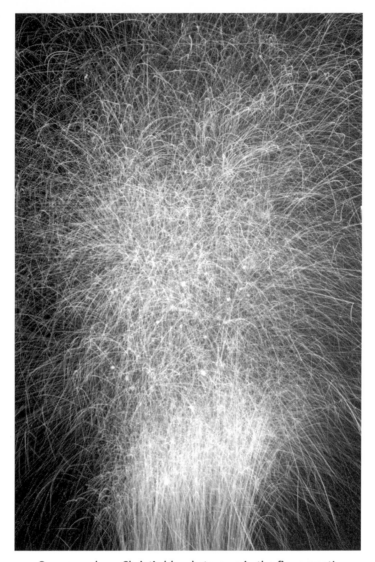

*

See, see where Christ's blood streams in the firmament!

---

* The photograph above was taken on the third Sunday in July 2001 during the traditional fireworks display on the Feast of the Redeemer, which commemorates the lifting of plague from Venice in 1577. The exposure was about thirty seconds.

194

In Christopher Marlowe's play, the dying Doctor Faustus sees Christ's blood in the heavens, and the vision contains both the promise of salvation and the certainty of damnation. Everything depends on how Faustus responds. Unlike the pregnant moment, then, Faustus's vision does not predict or contain its own resolution and, since it is a revelation of divine grace, in a sense it has no cause either. Its contradiction can only be resolved by a choice, which does not concern how to act but rather what to believe. The only unforgivable sin, which Faustus commits, is despair. Unlike Christ, history can only redeem vicariously. It is the historian who must make the leap of faith, in a firework trail through the darkness of time.

Bang.
Bang.

The stars move still; time runs; the clock will strike.

You're dead.

On the day they were going to kill him, Giulio Cazzari left the house about three hours after Sunrise.

He was on his way to dine with the Mantuan resident.

He didn't get very far before the assassins Struck.

Turn the hourglass.

Still life with a stiletto, pistol, powderflask, ramrod and winding key, evoking the evanescence of life.

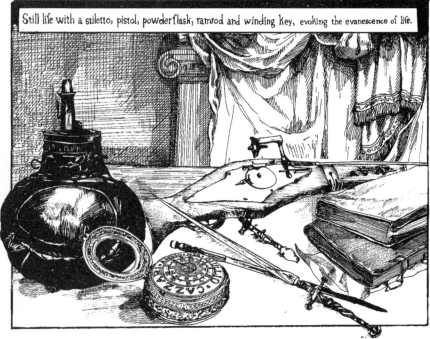

Still life with butchered meat, scalpel, spatula, paper and notary's pen.

A wound in the back, which penetrated the intestines and exited out in front through the stomach, exposing the membrane.

25 May 1621: I have worked a lot for the Lord Ambassador of Spain, and I've written letters to find out what has been done and planned in this City, and because of this my Life is in danger.

Another wound on the Left flank made with an edged weapon penetrating a palm's length or four fingers.

24 August 1621: If they'd intended to do anything to me, they would have done it by now. I'm not afraid.

Two wounds on the head, one on the right side cutting into skin, flesh and bone, the other in front on the point where the skull knits together at the crown cutting into skin, flesh and bone.

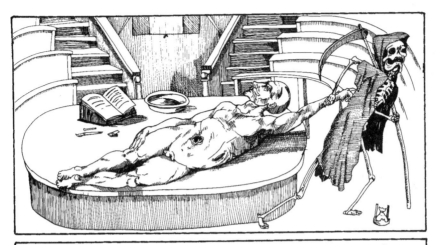

You must keep a picture of Death in your room in a place where it is often before your eyes, but not so that you become so used to it that it no longer moves you. And you say to yourself, "Today, perhaps I shall die". And you must look very well at this figure and see that Death is always opposite you, to pluck you from this life. (Savonarola).

29. LEGACY

F OSCARINI'S EXECUTION LED ULTIMATELY TO AN ACRIMONIOUS debate on the role and powers of the Council of Ten, which became a full-blown constitutional crisis in 1628. There was wild talk of civil war among the nobility, but the crisis was resolved peacefully by a reform that reined in the Ten's powers. Foscarini was not the immediate cause of the 1628 protest but his name was one of its rallying cries. If it could happen to him, the dissenters muttered, it could happen to any of us.

Vano's name, by contrast, had already been forgotten by 1628. It was on nobody's lips then, nor has it been since. Very quickly, as the story was passed on and retold, Foscarini became the victim of an anonymous **wicked man**, whose name was not worth recording. Foscarini was commemorated with an elaborate funeral bust, a number of works of fiction written in his honour and eventually a smattering of scholarly attention (including two twentieth-century biographies). There is even a street named after him in modern Venice—the Rio Terrà Antonio

Foscarini. It is a wide, tree-lined promenade just behind the Accademia gallery, renamed when sentimental interest in the case was at its height. Vano does not even have a dark, malodorous alley named after him. He left only a few hundred surveillance reports, which were immediately buried in a locked chest in 1622 and eventually incorporated into File 636 by a nineteenth-century archivist. There they remained—until I disturbed them.

It is said that every author has an ideal reader in mind. If so, then Vano's was surely a credulous Inquisitor with unlimited funds, and not a sceptical historian with an overactive imagination. Indeed, the earliest reports are undated, or rather the dates have been added by the secretary, as if Vano could not at first conceive that anyone might want to read his words more than a few hours or days into an unimagined future. He was wrong—tragically, gloriously—but his mistake is unsurprising, since his reports are not a 'body of work' in the same way that Dickens's novels are. They were not intended for publication and, even more crucially, they were not Vano's property. He handed them over to the Inquisitors' secretary almost as soon as the ink was dry, and he never saw them again—unless they were placed before him during his own trial for perjury. Vano surely did not intend that his reports become evidence against him, but this unwelcome development underlines the fact that he had no moral or legal rights over how they were used.

Something happened in Venice in the period immediately before 1620: a momentous shift whereby individuals became the target of systematic and ongoing surveillance by other individuals for the first time. Before the early 1600s, the Inquisitors had no 'confidantes'. After Vano's death, the trickle of information coming in turned into a flood.[*]

---

[*] In Cesare Ripa's celebrated book *Iconologia*, which uses allegorical images to personify abstract ideas like Justice or Treason, the figure of the Spy is absent from the first three editions (from 1593, 1603 and 1611 respectively) but was added to the expanded 1618 edition; that is, literary authors like Ripa began to imagine the 'Spy' as a concept at the same time that Vano was working out what it meant to be a spy in practice.

The reasons for the change are obscure, but one thing is sure. Vano was the first person to understand its practical implications and the potential for profit that it brought in its wake. He did not intend to provide a model for others to follow. He wanted only to become indispensable to the Inquisitors. For a brief interval he succeeded, but in the process he made fools of everyone in Venice, and nobody wanted to commemorate that.

30. GENERAL OF SPIES

THE STORY IS FINISHED, EXCEPT TO ASK AGAIN: How 'modern' was Vano really? Superficially, he seems quite different from many of his contemporaries. His reports are utterly indifferent to both religion and honour, and their premises appear similar to those of modern game theory, in that Vano reduces people to isolated individuals, who are rendered vulnerable by their failure to understand the real, hidden motivations of others. He is also cheerfully cynical—you will find no moral judgements anywhere in his reports. Vano despises everyone but disapproves of nothing. Nonetheless, we do him a disservice if we describe him as a man 'ahead of his time'. He was not. He *belongs* in the seventeenth century.

In Vano's time, the desire for complete freedom was seen as either mad or evil. In Jacobean plays such desires are expressed only by Machiavellian villains. Vano had no such aspirations but, rather, wrote to demonstrate his competence in a trade—that of spymaster. Therein lies the paradox—and the real demonstration of Vano's genius—because in the seventeenth century, no one chose to describe themselves as a spy. When dealing with friendly informants, the Inquisitors spared their sensibilities by using polite euphemisms such as 'loyal subject', and so on. The title of spy, like that of atheist or traitor, was always applied to other people and usually intended as an insult. Even Vano was not so bold as to style himself **general of spies**. He left that task to an anonymous letter writer. But if he avoided the *word* when referring to himself, his actions tell a different story. Vano ruthlessly pursued the role of Venetian **general of spies**; indeed, he created it. The post did not exist before he occupied it, and he had no successor, which is to say that no one ever again possessed the authority to have a noble condemned to death on his word alone.

The description is not a literal one. As we have seen, Vano preferred to style himself more modestly as a **captain**, and as far as the Venetians were concerned he held no official position at all. Nonetheless, the phrase **general of spies** does sum up Vano's achievement in co-ordinating the activities of his 'army' of informants. To have a trade in seventeenth-century Venice was to be a member of a community—a guild—but the 'community' of spies had a fluctuating and uncertain membership and was bound only by mutual antagonism and mistrust. The more exclusively a man was identified with that community, the more he was isolated.

There are two hypothetical solutions to this paradox. Firstly, what if spies were actually organised into a trade guild, with their own official hierarchy, apprenticeship system and examinations for professional competence? This never happened, and the very notion is ludicrous. Secondly, the spy could be seen as a prototype of the modern cut-throat entrepreneur, generating profits by speculation in a free market of information. According to the first, unrealised model, information is a product whose quality is guaranteed by shared standards. It is generated, owned and sold by the spy. According to the second, more pragmatic, model, information is a commodity of uncertain and fluctuating value, acquired from others and intended primarily for exchange. Vano's career is the place where these two solutions meet: where the receding medieval past and the distant future pass each other without anyone even noticing. Vano was neither a defender of republican tradition nor a prophet of capitalism. In the end, he stands only for himself, but that is precisely why his decision to pursue spying as a profession was so original and, yes, individual.[*]

---

[*] According to seventeenth-century Italian usage, the word *professione* did not necessarily mean a formal trade like carpenter or butcher but also included any regular activity that took a characteristic form or stamped a man's character. Hence gambling and duelling were professions in this broader sense, as was spying. The issue in question was whether Vano was also a professional in the more limited, modern sense of the word.

31. DOCTOR FRANKENSTEIN

VERSION ONE: I STUDY THE PAST NOT BECAUSE IT IS RELEVANT but because it is dead. It is only because it has ceased to move, and ceased to breathe, that it can be gutted and dissected. It is only when the historian touches no living nerve that bone can be separated from bone and flesh from flesh, that words and biographies and ideas can be chopped and prepared for consumption.

Version Two: *L'histoire est une résurrection*. The past is not dead; it merely sleepeth.

This book aims to demonstrate two contradictory theses. Firstly, the perjurer Gerolamo Vano is justly forgotten. Although he is certainly connected in some way to the 'birth of the individual', whenever that mythical event occurred, and he may have been the first professional spy in Europe, by itself his career proves nothing. It is not **scientifically eloquent**. Secondly, this ultimate failure to connect Vano with larger historical trends is irrelevant. On the contrary, the analysis of larger trends is only important insofar as it illuminates Vano's experience. Without Vano, seventeenth-century Venice does not matter.

The first thesis is undeniable. The second is unprovable. It is a declaration of faith.

Have I resurrected Vano? Or have I merely subjected his body to a series of galvanic shocks, giving him a semblance of life: a severed leg twitching in a laboratory? Like Dr Frankenstein, I am stitching together a corpse made of disparate fragments, a simulacrum equivalent to the one Vano offered to the Inquisitors. The dead speak through blood, like the trees in Dante's Wood of the Suicides. To give them voice, we must re-open the wound that killed them. History is a gorier spectacle than the crudest revenge tragedy. Here, everybody dies—no exceptions, and no reprieves. If I remain to speak the epilogue and offer this moral, it is only because I have a brief stay of execution.

CAST OF CHARACTERS
(IN ALPHABETICAL ORDER)

Andrea Alberti: a secretary to the Venetian Senate. He was convicted of treason in 1621 on the basis of Vano's evidence but later absolved and released.

Battista: an alleged informant of Vano's in the Spanish embassy.

Zuan Battista Bragadin: a Venetian noble and traitor who sold information to the Spanish and was arrested and executed in 1620.

Don Luis Bravo: the Spanish ambassador to Venice in 1619 and 1620.

Antonio Calegari: an opportunistic spy from Bergamo (a town in Venetian territory, near the border with the Spanish-controlled Duchy of Milan).

Don Giulio Cazzari: a secretary to the Imperial resident in Venice (Nicolo Rossi) and also a crony of the Mantuan resident and the Spanish secretary (Andrea Irles). He was assassinated by the Venetians in July 1622.

Bartolomio Comino: a secretary to the Council of Ten during the period covered by this book, except for an interlude from October 1620 to September 1621, when he was temporarily demoted as a result of a procedural reform. He was also secretary to the Inquisitors of State until September 1619 and again from October 1622, in which capacity he presided over the posthumous absolution of Antonio Foscarini.

Nicolo Contarini: an important Venetian politician, who shared political goals with Antonio Foscarini. Between 1612 and 1623, he served as Inquisitor of State three times, including the period in which Foscarini was posthumously exonerated. Later, he was elected doge (head of the Venetian state).

The Council of Ten: *see* Inquisitors of State.

Domenico [Zanco]: Vano's right-hand man from late 1621 and originally one of his informants in the Spanish embassy, where he worked as a gondolier.

Zuanetto a.k.a. Zuanne Facini: an informant of Vano's in the Spanish embassy during 1620. He reappeared before the Council of Ten in 1622, claiming to have been suborned by Vano to offer false evidence in the trial of the Venetian noble and traitor Alvise Querini. His claims were judged to be false and Querini remained in prison.

The Duke of Feria: the governor of the Duchy of Milan (at this time under Spanish control). He was thus an important point of contact for the Spanish ambassador in Venice.

Zuan Paolo Ferrari: a spy who supplied information to the Inquisitors of State during 1621, notably on the circle of the provincial noble Francesco Gambara and on Giulio Cazzari. He was executed by the Council of Ten in 1625.

Antonio Foscarini: a Venetian noble; elected successively as ambassador to Paris and London in the early 1600s; associated with the anti-Spanish party in Venice; first prosecuted for improprieties in his conduct as ambassador in London and exonerated of these charges in 1618. He was convicted of treason in 1622 in a second, independent trial, and executed as a result. In 1623, he was posthumously exonerated.

Francesco: an informant of Vano's in the Mantuan residency during 1621 and 1622.

Diego Gomez: an informant of Vano's in the Spanish embassy during 1620. He was exposed, and subsequently executed by the Spanish in Milan in December 1620.

Alessandro Grancini: a newswriter and spy who sold information to many customers. He was Vano's most important predecessor and rival until Grancini's arrest in mid-1620.

The Inquisitors of State: the Venetian magistrates responsible for protecting state secrets, whose remit therefore included what we would now call counter-intelligence. They were a sub-committee of the Council of Ten, a magistracy with a wider mandate for ensuring public order and state security. Decisions taken by the Inquisitors had to be ratified by the Ten, so although the Inquisitors and the Ten had separate archives, the membership and activities of the two councils overlapped. The Ten had four secretaries, one of whom was also simultaneously secretary to the Inquisitors of State.

Andrea Irles: originally the principal secretary to Don Luis Bravo but then replaced him as official Spanish representative in Venice upon Bravo's recall at the end of 1620.

Roberto Lio: promoted to the rank of secretary of the Ten in October 1620 and simultaneously appointed secretary to the Inquisitors of State. He remained in the latter post until September 1622.

The Marquis of Bedmar: the Spanish ambassador to Venice until 1618 and head of an effective intelligence network organised by the apostate priest Antonio Meschita. Bedmar left Venice in 1618 in disgrace after the exposure of a conspiracy to topple the Venetian government in which he was implicated. After his departure, he wrote a bitter and incisive commentary on Venetian politics, which was widely distributed in manuscript form in Venice and throughout Europe.

Antonio Meschita: *see* the Marquis of Bedmar.

Zuanne Minotto: a Venetian noble and traitor who was arrested and imprisoned in July 1620.

Antonio Olivieri: a Venetian *novellista* in exile in the small independent Italian state of Parma.

Captain Francesco Ongarin: the head of the Council of Ten's private police force, but he was also involved in surveillance operations on behalf of the Inquisitors of State.

Zuan Battista Padavin: a secretary to the Council of Ten until September 1620 and again from October 1622. He was also secretary to the Inquisitors of State from October 1619 to September 1620.

Alvise Querini: a Venetian noble and traitor. He was active in the latter capacity during 1620 but was not arrested until December 1621.

Piero Querini: the brother of Alvise Querini.

Nicolo Rossi: the Imperial resident in Venice.

The Senate: the Venetian council responsible for most foreign policy decisions. It was much larger than the Council of Ten, consisting of more than two hundred men. Most of the leaks that preoccupied the Inquisitors of State originated here. The Venetian cabinet served as a steering committee for the Senate, setting its agenda. The most important members of the cabinet—the doge and six ducal councillors—were simultaneously members of the Council of Ten.

Gerolamo Vano: a spy in Venetian employ, who specialised in supplying information on the Spanish embassy in Venice.

Henry Wotton: the English ambassador to Venice on three occasions: 1604–10, 1616–19 and 1621–23. During the latter embassy, he reported on Antonio Foscarini's execution and exoneration.

Francesco Zappata: a Spanish associate of Don Luis Bravo and Andrea Irles. He was the designated 'contact' for the Venetian traitor Zuanne Minotto.

A NOTE ON CONVENTIONS

All archival documents and other sources quoted or referred to in the text, notes and bibliography are real. The references to historical facts, sources and events in the dialogue chapters are also accurate to the best of my knowledge but the circumstances of their presentation are fictional. The comic strips dramatise narratives assembled from primary sources but their content too is fictional.

Translations from documents are my own, unless otherwise indicated. They are often rather loose, since fluency seemed more important than pedantic accuracy. I altered and modernised punctuation, including the addition of divisions into paragraphs and the use of quotation marks. I also edited and cut freely. Uncertain readings or additions necessary to clarify sense are indicated by square brackets. Particular problems are indicated in the endnotes. I sometimes omit introductory remarks like 'he said' (which Vano almost always uses in lieu of quotation marks) without noting this.

With regard to courtesy titles, 'Sigr' is usually translated as 'lord' (in lower case to distinguish it from the English meaning of the word that implies a specific degree of nobility). A small 's.' is translated 'mister', although sometimes as 'sir' in direct dialogue or in relation to Venetian nobles, where 'mister' does not really give the right impression in modern English. A particular problem arises with the abbreviation 's^r', which can mean either mister or lord depending on context (that is, it can indicate both *ser* and *signor*). When it is used in relation to the Spanish ambassador and Nicolo Rossi, I have translated it as 'lord'; when used in relation to Andrea Irles I have either omitted it or translated it as 'mister'.

The Venetian year (*more veneto*, or m.v.) started on 1 March, so what would be January or February 1622 in our system was January or February 1621 in theirs. I have modernised dates but noted this alteration in the endnotes to avoid ambiguities in the identification of sources.

In quoting plays, I used various commonly available modern versions, which have been edited according to different criteria. All have modernised spelling, and one or two also have modernised punctuation. For my purposes, such minor inconsistencies did not seem critical. I also abbreviated a few such quotations without using the conventional indications of ellipsis.

ABOUT THE ILLUSTRATIONS

The Polaroids in Chapter 19, 'Trace', and the photograph of the fireworks in the title chapter were taken by the author. All other illustrations (besides the photographs of archival documents) were scripted and storyboarded by the author and drawn by Dan Hallett. Most are based in some way on sixteenth- and seventeenth-century paintings, woodcuts and engravings. The clothes in particular are derived from late sixteenth-century costume books produced in Venice. These would have been slightly out of date in 1622, but since printers of the period had no compunction about continuing to use the designs well into the seventeenth century, I too felt justified in using them. It is not clear if Cazzari dressed in a priest's habit in actuality. He is shown in secular garb. Some of the topography has been fictionalised.

Cazzari's autopsy report does not survive. The quotations relating to his wounds in the comic strip that accompanies the title chapter are taken from a roughly contemporaneous report (from 1604), which can be found in Archivio di Stato di Venezia, Consiglio dei Dieci, Processi delegati ai Rettori, busta 2, Processo ispedito contra Christoforo, Scipion et Alfonso, fr[at]elli Gandini, fos 3r–4v.

ACKNOWLEDGEMENTS

This book has a long history. I began it at the University of Wales, Swansea, in 1998/9, where Nina, Kes and Siân made sure that I was not a complete failure as a teacher. Debating with Ulrik Vintersborg in Venice was a crucial source of inspiration. Later, in Cambridge, Asle Toje made helpful comments on early, unreadable versions of the manuscript, while Robert Rosenstone gave much needed encouragement. He and Alun Munslow overruled hostile peer reviews to publish excerpts as articles in their journal *Rethinking History*. In 2002, Helen Slater introduced me to Dan Hallett (our work appears together for the first time in her edited collection *Works on Paper*).

I was supported during my research by a British Academy postdoctoral fellowship at the University of Cambridge and subsequently by a sesquicentennial post-doctoral fellowship at the University of Sydney. I am grateful to these institutions for their support and to the Australian Academy of the Humanities for a generous publishing subsidy.

In Australia, I would like to thank Mary Cunnane, Cressida Hall, Louise Adler and my editor Elisa Berg, but most of all I am indebted to Iain McCalman, whose decisive intervention turned the project around when all seemed lost.

Martin Peglar of the Royal Armouries at Leeds fired a replica wheellock pistol for me on a range provided by West Yorkshire Police, while Adrian Walker filmed the firing with a special camera provided by the Rutherford equipment pool at Oxford. Everyone involved kindly indulged my requests to fire the gun over and over again. Adrian Newman helped edit the resulting footage into its current format. Alan Williams provided important technical information on guns.

Paolo Preto's *I servizi segreti di Venezia* provided invaluable references to archival material that I would not otherwise have found, while Gigi Corazzol's *Cinegrafo di banditi sul sfondo di monti* brought flip books to my attention and gave me the idea of incorporating a dialogue with other historians. I am also indebted to Claudio Povolo's *Il romanziere e l'archivista* for insights into the history of the Inquisitors' archive during the nineteenth century.

Special thanks are due to James Shaw and Filippo de Vivo, who provided invaluable material for the dialogue chapters but bear no resemblance to the caricatures depicted therein. Even greater credit is due to Dan Hallett, who rose to the occasion in spectacular fashion.

The photographs of documents in the chapters 'Idiolect' and 'Trace' are reproduced by permission of the Archivio di Stato di Venezia (concession number 70/2005), and are based upon images provided by the archive's photographic reproduction section. The first is a report by Gerolamo Vano dated 4 August 1620 from Inquisitori di Stato, busta 636. The second is a montage of fragments from six separate documents: (top left) a detail from a document in Consiglio dei Dieci, Parti Criminali, filza 49, entry dated 5 October 1622; (top middle) a detail from a document dated 12 August 1622 in Inquisitori di Stato, busta 636; (top right) a detail from a document dated 2–3 January 1620 (m.v.) in Inquisitori di Stato, busta 636; (bottom left) a detail from a document dated 4 February 1619 (m.v.) in Inquisitori di Stato, busta 1214, no. 57; (bottom middle) a detail from a document dated 4 February 1619 (m.v.) in Inquisitori di Stato, busta 1214, no. 57; (bottom right) a detail from a document dated 3 March 1620 in Inquisitori di Stato, busta 610.

Portions of this book originally appeared in the following:

Walker, Jonathan, 'I spy with my little eye: interpreting seventeenth-century Venetian spy reports', *Urban History*, vol. 29, Cambridge University Press, 2002, pp. 197–222.

Walker, Jonathan, 'Pistols! Murder! Treason!', *Rethinking History*, vol. 7.2, Routledge, 2003, pp. 139–67.

Walker, Jonathan, 'Antonio Foscarini in the City of Crossed Destinies', *Rethinking History*, vol. 5.2, Routledge, 2001, pp. 305–34.

SELECT BIBLIOGRAPHY

Abraham, Lyndy, *A Dictionary of Alchemical Imagery*, Cambridge University Press, Cambridge, 1998.

Accetto, Torcetto, *Della Dissimulazione onesta*, Giuseppe Laterza and Sons, Bari, 1928 (originally published in 1641).

Andreini, Francesco, *Le Bravure del Capitano Spavento divise in molti ragionamenti in forma di dialogo*, ed. R. Tessari, Giardini, Pisa, 1987 (originally published in 1607).

Archer, John Michael, *Sovereignty and Intelligence: Spying and Court Culture in the English Renaissance*, Stanford University Press, Stanford, Ca., 1993.

Ariès, Philippe, *Western Attitudes toward Death: From the Middle Ages to the Present*, Johns Hopkins University Press, Baltimore and London, 1974.

——, *The Hour of Our Death*, trans. H. Weaver, Allen Lane, London, 1981.

Barbaro, Antonio, *Pratica Criminale*, Venice, 1739.

Barthes, Roland, *Michelet*, trans. R. Howard, Hill and Wang, New York, 1987 (originally published in 1954).

——, *Camera Lucida: Reflections on Photography*, Vintage, London, 2000 (originally published in 1980).

Bellarmine, Robert, *The Art of Dying Well*, ed. D. M. Rogers, English Recusant Literature 1558–1640, vol. 314, The Scolar Press, London, 1976 (originally published in 1622).

Benjamin, Walter, *The Arcades Project*, trans. H. Eiland and K. McLaughlin based on the German edition by R. Tiedeman, Cambridge, Mass., and London, Belknap Press, 1999.

Benzoni, Gino, entry on 'Alessandro Granzino', in *Dizionario biografico degli italiani*, vol. 58, Istituto della Enciclopedia Italiana, Rome, 2002, pp. 556–61.

Berger, John, *Ways of Seeing*, BBC and Penguin, London and
Harmondsworth, 1972.

Bossy, John, *Giordano Bruno and the Embassy Affair*, Jonathan Cape,
London, 1992.

Burckhardt, Jacob, *The Civilization of the Renaissance*, Phaidon, London,
1995 (originally published in 1860).

Canosa, Roberto, *Alle origini delle polizie politiche: Gli inquisitori di stato
a Venezia e a Genova*, Sugarco Edizioni, Milan, 1989.

Cassini, Giocondo (ed.), *Piante e vedute prospettiche di Venezia (1479–1855)*,
La Stamperia di Venezia, Venice, second edition, 1982.

Chiarelli, Luigi, 'Il marchese di Bedmar e i suoi confidenti come risul-
tano dalla corrispondenza segreta del "novellista" Alessandro
Granzini con gli Inquisitori di stato a Venezia', *Archivio
Veneto–Tridentino*, vol. 8, 1925, pp. 144–73.

Corazzol, Gigi, *Cineografo di banditi su sfondo di monti, Feltre 1634–1642*,
Edizioni Unicopli, Milan, 1997.

Cozzi, Gaetano, *Il doge Nicolò Contarini: Ricerche sul patriziato
veneziano agli inizi del Seicento*, in *Venezia barocca: Conflitti di
uomini e idee nella crisi del Seicento veneziano*, il Cardo, Venice,
1995 (originally published in 1958), pp. 3–245.

Darnton, Robert, 'A Police Inspector Sorts His Files: The Anatomy of
the Republic of Letters', in *The Great Cat Massacre and Other
Episodes in French Cultural History*, Penguin, Harmondsworth,
1991 (originally published in 1984), pp. 141–83.

Davidson, Nicholas S., '"In Dialogue with the Past": Venetian Research
from the 1960s to the 1990s', *Bulletin of the Society for Renaissance
Studies*, vol. 15, 1997, pp. 13–24.

Davis, Natalie Zemon, *The Return of Martin Guerre*, Harvard University
Press, Cambridge, Mass., 1983.

——, *Fiction in the Archives: Pardon Tales and Their Tellers in Sixteenth-
Century France*, Polity Press, Cambridge, 1988.

De Certeau, Michel, *The Practice of Everyday Life*, trans. S. Rendall,
University of California Press, Los Angeles and London, 1984.

De Vivo, Filippo, *Wars of Papers: Communication and Polemic in Early Seventeenth-Century Venice*, PhD, University of Cambridge, 2002.

Delumeau, Jean, *Sin and Fear: The Emergence of a Western Guilt Culture 13th–18th Centuries*, trans. E. Nicholson, St Martin's Press, New York, 1990.

Elias, Norbert, *The Civilizing Process*, trans. E. Jephcott, Blackwell, Oxford, 1994 (originally published in 1939).

Ellroy, James, *My Dark Places*, Arrow, London, 1997.

Falcone, Giovanni with Padovani, Marcelle, *Cose di Cosa Nostra*, BUR, Milan, 1993.

Foucault, Michel, *Discipline and Punish: The Birth of the Prison*, trans. A. Sheridan, Penguin, Harmondsworth, 1991 (originally published in 1975).

French, Peter J., *John Dee: The World of an Elizabethan Magus*, Routledge & Kegan Paul, London, 1972.

Frigo, Daniella, 'Introduction', in *Politics and Diplomacy in Early Modern Italy: The Structure of Diplomatic Practice, 1450–1800*, ed. Daniella Frigo, trans. A. Belton, Cambridge University Press, Cambridge, 2000, pp. 1–24.

Fulin, Rinaldo, *Studi nell'archivio degli Inquisitori di stato*, Marco Visentini, Venice, 1868.

Garzoni, Tomaso, *La piazza universale di tutte le professioni del mondo*, Olivier Alberti, Venice, 1616.

Geertz, Clifford, 'Thick Description: Toward an Interpretive Theory of Culture', in *The Interpretation of Cultures*, Basic Books, New York, 1973, pp. 3–30.

Ginzburg, Carlo, *The Cheese and the Worms: The Cosmos of a Sixteenth-Century Miller*, trans. J. and A. Tedeschi, Routledge & Kegan Paul, London, 1980.

Goffman, Erving, *The Presentation of Self in Everyday Life*, Woodstock, The Overlook Press, New York, 1973 (originally published in 1959).

Greenblatt, Stephen, *Renaissance Self-Fashioning, From More to Shakespeare*, University of Chicago Press, Chicago and London, 1980.

——, 'Psychoanalysis and Renaissance Culture', in *Learning to Curse*, Routledge, London and New York, 1990, pp. 131–45.

——, 'Towards a Poetics of Culture', in *Learning to Curse*, Routledge, London and New York, 1990, pp. 146–60.

Grubb, James, 'When Myths Lose Power: Four Decades of Venetian Historiography', *Journal of Modern History*, vol. 58, 1986, pp. 43–94.

Hacke, Daniella, *Marital Litigation and Gender Relations in Early Modern Venice (ca. 1570-1700)*, PhD, University of Cambridge, 1998.

Hale, John R., *War and Society in Renaissance Europe 1450–1620*, Fontana, London, 1985.

Heard, Brian J., *Handbook of Firearms and Ballistics: Examining and Interpreting Forensic Evidence*, John Wiley & Sons, Chicester, 1997.

Hinds, Alan B. (ed.), *Calendar of State Papers and Manuscripts relating to English Affairs, existing in the Archives and Collections of Venice*, vol. 17, H. M. Stationery Office, London, 1911.

Hotman, François, *The Ambassador*, V[alentine] S[immes], London, 1603.

Infelise, Mario, 'Professione reportista. Copisti e gazzettieri nella Venezia del Seicento', in *Venezia. Itinerari per la storia della città*, eds S. Gasparri, G. Levi and P. Moro, il Mulino, Bologna, 1997, pp. 183–209.

Koestler, Arthur, *The Ghost in the Machine*, second edition, Hutchinson, London, 1976.

Levi, Giovanni, 'On Microhistory', in *New Perspectives on Historical Writing*, ed. P. Burke, Polity Press, Cambridge, 1991, pp. 93–113.

Loredana, *L'ambasciatore Antonio Foscarini*, Edizioni Cosmopoli, Rome, 1941.

Luzio, Alessandro, 'La Congiura Spagnola contro Venezia nel 1618 secondo i documenti dell'Archivio Gonzaga', in *Miscellanea di Storia Veneta*, ed. R. Deputazione Veneta di Storia Patria, third series, vol. 13, R. Deputazione Veneta di Storia Patria, Venice, 1918, pp. 1–204.

Mackenney, Richard, "'A Plot Discover'd?" Myth, Legend, and the
    Spanish Conspiracy against Venice in 1618', in *Venice
    Reconsidered: The History and Civilization of an Italian City-State,
    1297–1797*, eds J. Martin and D. Romano, Johns Hopkins
    University Press, Baltimore and London, 2000, pp. 185–216.

Mallett, Michael, and Hale, John R., *The Military Organization of a
    Renaissance State: Venice, c. 1400 to 1617*, Cambridge University
    Press, Cambridge, 1984.

Martin, John, 'Inventing Sincerity, Refashioning Prudence: The
    Discovery of the Individual in Renaissance Europe', *American
    Historical Review*, vol. 102, 1997, pp. 1309–42.

Martin, John, and Romano, Dennis, 'Introduction', in *Venice
    Reconsidered: The History and Civilization of an Italian City-State,
    1297–1797*, eds J. Martin and D. Romano, Johns Hopkins
    University Press, Baltimore and London, 2000, pp. 1–35.

Mattingley, Garrett, *Renaissance Diplomacy*, Jonathan Cape, London, 1955.

Mazlish, Bruce, 'The *Flâneur*: From Spectator to Representation', in
    The Flâneur, ed. K. Tester, Routledge, London and New York,
    1994, pp. 43–60.

Molmenti, Pompeo, 'Le relazioni tra patrizi veneziani e diplomatici
    stranieri', in *Curiosità di storia veneziana*, Nicola Zanichelli,
    Bologna, 1919, pp. 25–63.

Moss, G. M., Leeming, D. W., and Farrar, C. L., *Military Ballistics:
    A Basic Manual*, Brassey's, London and Washington, 1995.

Muldrew, Craig, *The Economy of Obligation: The Culture of Credit and
    Social Relations in Early Modern England*, St Martin's Press,
    New York, 1998.

Nani, Battista, *Historia della Republica Veneta*, Combi & La Nou, Venice,
    1662.

Niccolini, Giovanni Battista, *Antonio Foscarini. Tragedia*, Piatti,
    Florence, 1827.

Nietzsche, Friedrich Wilhelm, 'On the Uses and Disadvantages of
    History for Life', in *Untimely Meditations*, ed. D. Breazeale,

trans. R. J. Hollingdale, Cambridge University Press, Cambridge, 1997 (originally published in 1874), pp. 57–123.

Paglia, Vincenzo, *La Morte confortata: Riti della paura e mentalità religiosa a Roma nell'età moderna*, Edizioni di Storia e Letteratura, Rome, 1982.

Pindemonte, Ippolito (but referred to as Melpomenio, Polidete on title page of the following work), 'Antonio Foscarini e Teresa Contarini', in *Novelle*, ed. P. Napoli-Signorelli, Simoniana, Naples, 1792, pp. 3–25.

Povoledo, Elena, 'I comici professionisti e la Commedia dell'Arte: Caratteri, Tecniche, Fortuna', in *Storia dell cultura Veneta*, eds G. Arnaldi and M. Pastore Stocchi, Vicenza: Neri Pozza, vol. IV/I, 1983, pp. 381–408.

Povolo, Claudio, *Il romanziere e l'archivista: Da un processo veneziano del '600 all'anonimo manoscritto dei Promessi Sposi*, Istituto Veneto di Scienze, Lettere ed Arti, Venice, 1993.

——, 'The Creation of Venetian Historiography', in *Venice Reconsidered: The History and Civilization of an Italian City-State, 1297–1797*, eds J. Martin and D. Romano, Johns Hopkins University Press, Baltimore and London, 2000, pp. 491–519.

Preto, Paolo, *I servizi segreti di Venezia*, Il Saggiatore, Milan, 1994.

Priori, Lorenzo, *Prattica Criminale secondo il ritto delle leggi della Serenissima Republica di Venetia*, Gio. Pietro Pinelli, Venice, 1644.

Pullan, Brian S., 'Service to the Venetian State: Aspects of Myth and Reality in the Early Seventeenth Century', *Studi Seicenteschi*, vol. 5, 1964, pp. 95–147.

——, *Rich and Poor in Renaissance Venice; the Social Institutions of a Catholic State, to 1620*, Blackwell, Oxford, 1971.

Raines, Dorit, 'Office Seeking, Broglio and the Pocket Political Guide-books in Cinquecento and Seicento Venice', *Studi Veneziani*, new series, vol. 22, 1991, pp. 137–94.

Richards, Kenneth and Richards, Laura (eds), *The Commedia dell'Arte: A Documentary History*, Blackwell, Oxford, 1990.

Ricoeur, Paul, *The Rule of Metaphor: Multi-disciplinary Studies of the Creation of Meaning in Language*, trans. R. Czerny with K. McLaughlin and J. Costello, Routledge & Kegan Paul, London, 1978.

Ripa, Cesare, *Iconologia*, Per gli Heredi di Gio, Gigliotti, Rome, 1593.

——, *Iconologia*, Lepido Faeii, Rome, 1603.

——, *Iconologia*, ed. Stephen Orgel, Garland Publishing, New York and London, 1976 (facsimile of the 1611 Padua edition).

——, *Iconologia*, ed. Piero Buscaroli, vol. 2, Fogola, Turin, 1987 (facsimile of the 1618 Padua edition).

Romanin, Samuele, *Storia documentata di Venezia*, vol. 7, Pietro Naratovich, Venice, 1858.

Romano, Dennis, *Housecraft and Statecraft: Domestic Service in Renaissance Venice, 1400–1600*, Johns Hopkins University Press, Baltimore and London, 1996.

Sarpi, Paolo, *Opere*, eds G. and L. Cozzi, Riccardo Ricciardi, Milan and Naples, 1969.

Secchi, Sandra, *Antonio Foscarini: Un patrizio veneziano del'600*, L. S. Olschki, Florence, 1969.

Siri, Vittorio, *Delle memorie recondite*, vol. 5, Anisson and Posuel, Lyons, 1679.

Skinner, Quentin, 'Meaning and Understanding in the History of Ideas', *Meaning and Context: Quentin Skinner and his Critics*, ed. J. Tully, Polity Press, Cambridge, 1988 (originally published in 1969), pp. 29–67.

Slater, Helen and Mansell, Thomas (eds), *Works on Paper*, University Printing Services, Cambridge and London, 2002.

Slights, William W. E., *Ben Jonson and the Art of Secrecy*, University of Toronto Press, Toronto, 1994.

Smith, Logan Pearsall (ed.), *The Life and Letters of Sir Henry Wotton*, 2 vols, Clarendon Press, Oxford, 1907.

Spini, Giorgio, 'La congiura degli Spagnoli contro Venezia del 1618', *Archivio storico italiano*, vol. 107, 1949, pp. 17–53.

——, 'La congiura degli Spagnoli contro Venezia del 1618', *Archivio storico italiano*, vol. 108, 1950, pp. 159–74.

Steedman, Carolyn, *Dust*, Manchester University Press, Manchester, 2001.

Tagg, John, *The Burden of Representation: Essays on Photographies and Histories*, Macmillan, London, 1988.

Tassini, Giuseppe, *Curiosità Veneziane*, Filippi, Venice, 1988 (first edition published in 1863).

Tiepolo, Maria Francesca et al., 'Archivio di Stato di Venezia', in *Guida generale degli Archivi di Stato italiani*, vol. 4, eds E. A. Magliozzi, M. Cacioli and L. F. Moro, Ministero per i beni culturali e ambientali, Ufficio centrale per i beni archivistici, Rome, 1994, pp. 857–1148.

Tillyard, E. M. W., *The Elizabethan World Picture*, Penguin, Harmondsworth, 1972 (originally published in 1943).

Trevor-Roper, Hugh, 'The Outbreak of the Thirty Years War', in *Renaissance Essays*, Fontana, London, 1986 (originally published in 1962), pp. 275–94.

Vera [Zúñiga] Y Figueroa, Juan Antonio de [Conte de La Roca], *Il perfetto ambasciatore*, trans. M. Ziccata (a pseudonym of the author), Giusto Wisseldick, Venice, 1649 (originally published in Spanish in 1620).

Villari, Rosario, *Elogio della dissimulazione: La lotta politica nel Seicento*, Laterza, Bari, 1987.

Walker, Jonathan, 'Gambling and Venetian Noblemen, c.1500–1700', *Past and Present*, no. 162, 1999, pp. 28–69.

——, 'Antonio Foscarini in the City of Crossed Destinies', *Rethinking History*, vol. 5.2, 2001, pp. 305–34.

——, 'Legal and Political Discourse in Seventeenth-Century Venice', *Comparative Studies in Society and History*, vol. 44, 2002, pp. 800–26.

——, 'Let's Get Lost: On the Importance of Itineraries, Detours and Dead Ends', *Rethinking History*, vol. 10.4, 2006, pp. 573–97.

Walker, Jonathan, with de Vivo, Filippo, and Shaw, James, 'A Dialogue on Spying in Seventeenth-Century Venice', *Rethinking History*, vol. 10.3, 2006, pp. 323–44.

Weissman, Ronald F. E., 'The Importance of Being Ambiguous: Social Relations, Individualism and Identity in Renaissance Florence', in S. Zimmerman and Ronald F. E. Weissman (eds.), *Urban Life in the Renaissance*, University of Delaware Press, Newark, 1989, pp. 269–80.

White, Hayden, *Tropics of Discourse: Essays in Cultural Criticism*, The Johns Hopkins University Press, Baltimore and London, 1978.

——, *The Content of the Form: Narrative Discourse and Historical Representation*, The Johns Hopkins University Press, 1987.

Yates, Frances A., *Giordano Bruno and the Hermetic Tradition*, Routledge & Kegan Paul, London, 1964.

Zago, Roberto, entry on 'Antonio Foscarini', in *Dizionario biografico degli italiani*, vol. 49, Istituto della Enciclopedia Italiana, Rome, 1997, pp. 361–5.

Zagorin, Perez, *Ways of Lying: Dissimulation, Persecution, and Conformity in Early Modern Europe*, Harvard University Press, Cambridge, Mass., 1990.

——, 'The Historical Significance of Lying and Dissimulation', *Social Research*, vol. 63, 1996, pp. 863–912.

The following manuscript sources were consulted.

Archivio di Stato di Venezia (hereafter cited as ASV)
  Miscellanea Codici, Serie 1, no. 75, *Condennati a morte sino al 1791*.
Museo Correr, Venice (hereafter cited as MCV)
  Codici Cicogna, 3782, G. Priuli, Pretiosi Frutti del Maggior Consiglio.
  Mss. P. D. 171C, Specifica dei Processi che si trovarano nell'Archivio degl'Inquisitori di Stato dal 1573 fino all'anno 1774 e 75. Compilata da Gius[epp]e Gradenigo.
  Mss. P. D. 679.

Biblioteca Marciana, Venice (hereafter cited as BMV)

Mss. Italiani, class VII, 121-2 (8862–3), Gian Carlo Sives, *Cronica Veneta*.

Mss. Italiani, class VII, 1596 (7712), *Registro de Giustitiati, Condanati à mMorte e suspesi, e di quelli che gli anno tramutata la sentenza. Principia l'anno 810 e segue.*

Mss. Italiani, class VII, 1604 (8554), *Congiura del Duca d'Ossuna* (besides an account of the Spanish conspiracy, this includes three texts written by the Marquis of Bedmar after his departure from Venice).

Mss. Italiani, class VII, 1664 (7542), *Miscellanea*.

The following articles contain extra material on Vano and / or Foscarini that does not appear in this book.

'Antonio Foscarini in the City of Crossed Destinies', in *Rethinking History*, vol. 5.2, 2001, pp. 305–34; and subsequently reprinted (but with incorrect marginal illustrations, which were changed without my knowledge by a copy editor) in *Experiments in Rethinking History*, eds A. Munslow and R. Rosenstone, Routledge, London and New York, 2004, pp. 124–55.

'A Dialogue on Spying in Seventeenth-Century Venice', *Rethinking History*, vol. 10.3, 2006, pp. 323–44, contains three extra excerpts from the dialogue.

'Let's Get Lost: On the Importance of Itineraries, Detours and Dead Ends', *Rethinking History*, vol. 10.4, 2006, pp. 573–97, describes the adventures of Francesco Zappata, a Spanish defector and double agent.

Copies of these articles can be obtained via the *Rethinking History* journal website:

http://www.tandf.co.uk/journals/titles/13642529.asp

NOTES

The following abbreviations used in the notes refer to material from the ASV. X, *Consiglio dei Dieci*, followed by Co., *Comuni*; Cr., *Criminali*; Sec., *Secreti*; Inq., *Inquisitori di Stato*; Sen., *Senato*, followed by Sec.; *Deliberazioni, Secreta*; Coll., *Collegio*, followed by Esp. Prin., *Espositioni Principi*; Comm., *Communicazioni dal Consiglio dei Dieci*; reg., *registro*; b., *busta*; bb., *buste*; r, *recto*; v, *verso*; fo., *folio*; fos, *folios*.

Material from the Public Record Office in London is prefixed with PRO.

1. Between the Columns

What glory ... flies beyond my reach: Christopher Marlowe, *The Massacre at Paris*, ii. 40–42.

2. Why Vano Matters

On Foscarini's story: Most of the literary accounts suggest that he died to protect the name of a married lover who lived next door to the Spanish embassy, a rather implausible story to anyone who has read the accusations from his first trial, which describe his outrageous behaviour as Venetian ambassador in London in the 1610s. Regarding Foscarini's second, fatal trial, the account in this book's Chapter 23, '2 + 2 = 5', adds numerous details not previously mentioned by other historians and refutes some common but inaccurate assumptions ultimately derived from Romanin, *Storia documentata*. A useful selection of translated (but often heavily edited) primary sources relating to Foscarini's death can be found in Hinds, *Calendar* and Smith, *Life and Letters*, while Romanin, *Storia documentata*, pp. 584–606, reproduces excerpts from despatches written by the foreign ambassadors resident in Venice at the time.

There have been two twentieth-century books on Foscarini. Loredana, *L'ambasciatore Antonio Foscarini*, largely repeats the romantic myth, glossed with some archival references and quotations from documents and minus any generalised critique of the republic. She identifies Foscarini's alleged lover as Alethea Talbot, Countess of Arundel, an Englishwoman then resident in Venice. The Countess was implicated by gossip in Foscarini's downfall, as Romanin describes in some detail, but there is no direct evidence of a relationship between them (Walker, 'Antonio Foscarini in the City of Crossed Destinies'). Secchi, *Antonio Foscarini*, is a bone-dry adaptation of an undergraduate research thesis, which downplays the scandalous aspects of Foscarini's career.

On the 'myth of Venice': The literature is endless, and by now tediously repetitive, but useful summaries can be found in Grubb, 'When Myths Lose Power', Davidson, 'In Dialogue with the Past', and Martin and Romano, 'Introduction'. The 'anti-myth' has received less attention recently, but some of its nineteenth-century manifestations are discussed in Povolo, 'The Creation of Venetian Historiography', and Preto, *I servizi segreti*.

On Vano's guilt: In 1622, the English ambassador and the Mantuan resident both named him as Foscarini's accuser, while an index of the trial records extant at the end of the eighteenth century in the archive of the Inquisitors of State officially identified Vano and Domenico as Foscarini's false accusers [*calunniatori*]. See MCV, MSS. P.D. 171C, *Specifica dei processi che si trovarano nell'Archivio degl'Inquisitori di Stato dal 1573 fino all'anno 1774 e 75. Compilata da Gius[epp]e Gradenigo.* Nonetheless, there is nothing in the reports that proves his guilt definitively. I choose to believe that he was guilty because it is the most plausible explanation for his prosecution and death.

On previous references to Vano: Paolo Preto 'discovered' his reports but did not explore them in any great depth or make anything of the connection with Foscarini.

On references to Foscarini by Vano: There is an earlier, ambiguous mention of a **Most Illustrious Foscarini**, who is described as the **patron** of Oratio Pisani in a note dated 17 Feb. 1621 (1620 m.v.), and a few casual, indirect references postdating 9 April 1622. Indeed, there is actually a suspicious gap in Vano's reports in the period immediately preceding 9 April 1622, so it is possible that there were other explicit references to Foscarini predating the arrest and that they were separated from the others in 1622 for incorporation into the trial record, which was then lost.

On the current numeration of files in the Inquisitors' archive: The continuous sequence running from b. 1 to b. 1269 is relatively recent (post-1868), as can be seen from the different form in which citations are given in Fulin, *Studi nell'archivio*. The previous system had separate numeric cycles for individual series (letters, etc.), but the subdivisions were broadly similar, if not quite identical.

privately: *in camara*

'I ... they': the odd shift from singular to plural is in the original, which reads *io so che qualcheduno velliaco ti avera ricercado di fatti di mia casa, et ti no[n] avera pe[n]sado sarai cascado, pero p[er] vida del Reii dimi chi sono esti che li faro castigar.*

storeroom: *magazin*

night: the Spanish is plural, but this is not idiomatic in English.

Why the hell ... What am I supposed to have done?: I have slightly altered the content and order of this phrase to make the translation more idiomatic. The original reads *che diavolo dise il mio patro[n] di fatti mii che mi á serado*.

Don Giulio said: This starts off as indirect quotation by the servants but shifts halfway through into direct quotation. The slightly confusing transition is therefore in the original.

The servants replied ... these villains: Some of the language here is difficult, especially when Vano is drifting between Italian and Spanish, so the translation is uncertain. The second reference to Foscarini is in the abbreviated but nonetheless unambiguous form of *fosc.ni*.

gold coin: *cechino*

just enough for a drink: *da bever*

On 'tone of voice': We are dealing here with what Quentin Skinner would call the report's illocutionary force: what it is designed to *do*, or what effect it is intended to produce.

Montaigne is quoted in Archer, *Sovereignty and Intelligence*, p. 25. I draw upon the latter's argument here.

Quotation on Marlowe from Greenblatt, *Renaissance Self-Fashioning*, p. 220. Besides Marlowe, another important reference is *The Revenger's Tragedy*, a play variously attributed to Cyril Tourneur or Thomas Middleton, first published in 1607, and from which my title is drawn.

3. DISSECTION / RESURRECTION

Can these bones live?: Ezekiel 37: 3.

4. THE HERO

of average height and build, whose hair is white at the ends: description given by the Spanish ambassador to the informant Zuanetto (Inq., b. 636, report dated 8 July 1620).

Vano was a serious writer: In the 1620s, the primary value of Vano's reports—to both the writer and their readers—had nothing to do with their aesthetic qualities. Nobody would have thought it appropriate to analyse them under the heading of literature. By doing so here, I am not asserting a universal truth but posing a hypothetical 'What if?' to be elaborated and qualified later.

On Vano's age: ASV, Miscellanea Codici, Serie 1, no. 75, Condennati a morte sino al 1791, no. 326. This manuscript is not always reliable, but I choose to believe it in the absence of contradictory evidence.

The copy of Vano's will that I initially consulted can be found in X Cr., filza 49, under 5 Oct. 1622, although the relevant resolution is not recorded in the criminal register, but in X Co., reg. 72, fos 151v–152r. Possibly there was some uncertainty about whether to classify it as 'Criminal' or 'Ordinary'. The original (in Vano's hand) can be found in the notary's archive ASV, Notarile, Testamenti, b. 1244, Giulio Ziliol, no. 354.

Was Vano a soldier? I have so far failed to find any evidence of his enrolment in the Venetian army. For example, his name does not appear in ASV, index 469, 'Capi di guerra'; nor in index 456, 'Nomi di condottieri ed altri capi di milizia che si trovano nei Notatori di Collegio'. Nor is it in the (incomplete) nineteenth-century card index of *condottieri* compiled from the secret registers of the Senate for the period 1401–1630. Finally, there is nothing from Vano in ASV, Capi del Consiglio di Dieci, Lettere di rettorie ed altre cariche, b. 308, Condottieri e gente d'armi, P–Z. (no equivalent *busta* exists for correspondence addressed to the Inquisitors).

On Vano's title: In the archive of the Inquisitors, Vano is referred to not as 'captain' but as either **mister** [*ser*] or **lord** [*signor*]. This is an apparent contradiction, since (although the connotations of both words were imprecise) the former usually referred to respectable artisans and tradesmen, while the latter was reserved for men of higher social standing. In the Council of Ten's registers, which are both more sparing and consistent in their use of courtesy titles, Vano is referred to as the **loyal Gerolamo Vano** in the resolutions granting him rewards, whereas in the decisions regarding his condemnation in 1622 he is given no title at all. **Most loyal** [*fedelissimo*] was a standard prefix for secretaries, and **loyal** was often used for bureaucrats of lower standing (notaries, for example).

Its use for Vano might imply a status deriving from services rendered to the state, but on an informal basis. In any case, Vano's social status remains ambiguous.

On the dowry index entry: ASV, Notarile, Atti, Crivelli, b. 2686.

On the contract for dowry restoration: ASV, Notarile, Atti, Crivelli, b. 2673. Thanks to Luca Molà for his help in interpreting this information.

On leaving letters at the warehouse: Inq., b. 636, report dated 3 Oct. 1620.

In the Archivio di Stato di Brescia, I consulted Notarile, Salò, b. 139, Silvio Filippini q.a Bernardino, Not.o di Volziano, IV, 1599–1605 and Notarile, Salò, b. 140, Silvio Filippini q.a Bernard.o, V, 1606–1618, although I did not have time to look beyond 1611 in the latter. Vano appears for certain five times between 1599 and 1611 in Filippini's records, excluding his father's will, the division of the *fraterna* and three other occasions on which there is some ambiguity about the reference. By means of these appearances, we can place him in Salò in 1604, 1605, 1607, 1609, 1611, and possibly in 1599 and 1603, the latter dates ambiguous because of the existence of another Gerolamo Vano, possibly our man's cousin. The peace settlement brokered by Vano is dated 1 Dec. 1605. Besides references to Vano's family, numerous surnames and individuals mentioned in Vano's will in relation to credits, debts and legal disputes also recur in Filippini's records. None of these references contains any indication of what profession Vano or his brothers may have been employed in, except for that of minor land and property owners in the region.

On Latin in Vano's reports: There is one report—an undated retrospective summary of events in 1620—where he uses two Latinate terms: **etiam** and in **carceribus**. He also regularly wrote **et** for 'and', but this was a common usage of the period among Italian writers.

5. Idiolect

On T. S. Eliot: 'I know that some of the poetry to which I am most devoted is poetry which I did not understand at first reading'. [Eliot] said that he was passionately fond of certain French verse long before he could be confident of translating it (Southam, B. C., *A Student's Guide to the Selected Poems of T. S. Eliot*, sixth edition, Faber & Faber, London and Boston, 1994, p. 3). Possibly I am distorting Eliot's point here.

On words as things: Ricoeur, *The Rule of Metaphor*, p. 209: In poetic language, the sign is looked at, not through. In other words, instead of being a medium or route crossed on the way to reality, language itself becomes 'stuff', like the sculptor's marble.

6. Odd One Out

Some of the quotations have been edited.

7. Caffè Rosso, 7.00 p.m.

On the 1610s as similar to the 1930s: Trevor-Roper, 'The Outbreak of the Thirty Years War'.

8. The File

On paper spike holes: The reports written in May 1620 that have been diverted to Inq., b. 638 do not have such holes, although the secretary Zuan Battista Padavin certainly read them, because most of their dates have been added in his hand.

Vano's earliest surviving communication is in Inq., b. 1213, no. 40.

Vano's 1619 petition is in X Sec., filza 33 under 11 Mar. 1619.

matters of the highest importance: *negotii importantissimi*

Vano's petition from 1622 is in X Sec., filza 35, filed under 23 May.

Am I not here? … your creature?: Ben Jonson, *Volpone*, I. v. 78.

The letters to and from Grimani are currently included as inserts under the despatches of 20 Nov. 1619 and 8 Jan. 1620 (1619 m.v.) in Inq., b. 462. They cover dates from March to August 1619, although the Venetian resident in Naples had previously made his own arrangements to intercept Grimani's correspondence in 1618 (some of the letters he intercepted appear in Inq., b. 461).

On the 'separate file': The only current principle of organisation in this section of the Inquisitors' archive is alphabetical, and even this is an anachronism, since in the seventeenth century the Ten and the Inquisitors used first names, not surnames, as the basis for alphabetical indexing. At least some of the original reports are missing (see e.g. Inq., b. 201, fo. 194r, which lists a report dated 24 Apr. 1620, predating the first report in b. 636).

9. THE INQUISITORS OF STATE

On the history of the archive in the nineteenth century: Tiepolo *et al.*, 'Archivio di Stato di Venezia', pp. 902–4; Povolo, *Il romanziere e l'archivista*.

On the Inquisitors as a unique institution: There was in fact a similar tribunal in Genoa, explicitly inspired by the Venetian example (Canosa, *Alle origini delle polizie politiche*).

On intelligence and patronage: The 1630 edition of Cesare Ripa's guide to iconography noted on its picture of a spy that such men were motivated by the desire to acquire the grace of their patrons (quoted in Archer, *Sovereignty and Intelligence*, p. 6—this comment is missing from the earlier editions that I consulted).

Roberto Lio was appointed simultaneously as secretary to the Ten and to the Inquisitors. There was no official registration of the appointment, but Lio's hand replaces Padavin's in all the document series in the Inquisitors' archive after 30 Sept. 1620.

The Ten's police performed a limited amount of intelligence work (Preto, *I servizi segreti*, pp. 193–4). For example, their captain, Francesco Ongarin, besides providing some of the manpower for Vano's surveillance operations, spoke directly to Domenico on at least one occasion. He also met with other informants (see Inq., b. 1214, no. 57, reports dated 20 Mar. and 16 June 1620). Ongarin also monitored foreigners in general and the residences of ambassadors in particular (see Inq., b. 758 and especially b. 606, which contains a bound folder of eighty-eight surveillance reports on the Spanish embassy from the first half of 1611). His reports have a wider focus and offer less detailed information than Vano's. In other words, he was not a specialist in the way that Vano was, since he had many other official responsibilities, including normal police duties and supervision of the Ten's prisons. The piecemeal nature of his involvement in spying is suggested by the fact that his reports are currently dispersed between a number of different files (e.g. Inq. bb. 606, 608, 609, 636, 638, 663, 758, 1214, as well as the Ten's *filze*).

On complaints from informants: A summary of a letter from Alessandro Grancini described in an annotated index in Inq., b. 606 stated that **he shows signs of discontent that the Most Illustrious lords Inquisitors of state gave only forty ducats and he expected at least one hundred ... he speaks of the difficulties and dangers he faces in supplying information.**

reward irregularly ... an uncertain or unreliable income produces better results: The quotation is via Preto, *I servizi segreti*, p. 457. The sense is clear, but the translation is slightly uncertain in the latter part.

For Vano's accounts: Inq., b. 953 and also Inq., b. 636, report dated 14 Apr. 1622. A brief account sheet from Alessandro Grancini dated 23 Apr. 1620 can be found in Inq., b. 610.

Vano's blank pardons included two awarded on 11 Mar. 1619 (see X Co., reg. 69, fo. 5v) for unspecified services, possibly related to Hieronimo Grimani; one on 14 July 1620, almost certainly for information contributing to Zuanne Minotto's arrest (X Sec., reg. 17, fo. 14v); two on 23 May 1622, almost certainly for information leading to Foscarini's arrest (X Sec., reg. 17, fos 87r–v). The *voce* awarded on 8 Sept. 1620 to the **secret denouncers** of Zuan Battista Bragadin also almost certainly went to Vano and Gomez (see X Co., reg. 70, fos 130r–v). The going rate depended on the conditions (that is, on how serious a sentence the pardon could be used to negate). To give an indication, the *voce* awarded for assassinating Giulio Cazzari, which was wide-ranging but excluded sentences with special conditions issued by the Ten, was converted to a cash reward of one thousand *zecchini* (see X Sec., reg. 17, fos 84v, 94v–95r), which converts to approximately two thousand ducats.

On blank pardons used as supplements to or in lieu of salary. The Ten's captain of police, Francesco Ongarin, received a steady flow of them in addition to his salary. In 1621, he received two, along with numerous cash reimbursements (see X Co., reg. 71, fos 16v–17r, 257r–v); in 1622, he received a further two, including one for arresting a member of the group who murdered Antonio Olivieri (see X Co., reg. 72, fos 72r, 227r).

On bandits in the Spanish embassy. Smith, *Life and Letters*, i, p. 67 and note 4; Inq., b. 1214, no. 57, various material dated 11–13 June 1620. For a similar situation in the French embassy, see X Cr., reg. 38, 11 Jan. 1622 (1621 m.v.), fo. 91v and various material in X Cr., filza 48 under this resolution; also X Sec., reg. 17, 7 Mar. 1622, fos 77v–78r and the papers in X Sec., filza 35 under this resolution.

Vano will tell you everything in more detail by mouth: Gomez's comment appears in Inq., b. 1214, no. 57.

On enemy surveillance of Vano's visits to the Ducal Palace: Inq., b. 636, report dated 19 May 1622. The Inquisitors sometimes met informants in private houses in order to minimise the risk of exposure.

10. DIPLOMACY

On ambassadors and residents: Hotman, *The Ambassador*, p. 5. In the case of Venetian representatives, the distinction was quite clear for another reason: the former were always nobles, while the latter were always secretaries from the ducal chancery.

Princes … possessions: Hotman, *The Ambassador*, p. 92.

honourable Spies: Hotman, *The Ambassador*, p. 119. The phrase was used by Philippe de Commines and subsequently borrowed by Henry Wotton (Smith, *Life and Letters*, i, p. 110). On spies and honour, see also Preto, *I servizi segreti*, pp. 455–67.

The nobles complain … a minister can legitimately use spies, but not exploit treachery such as this: Luzio, 'La Congiura Spagnola', p. 142.

Montaigne is quoted in Archer, *Sovereignty and Intelligence*, p. 27.

For contradictory advice on ambassadorial immunity: Hotman, *The Ambassador*, confidently asserts that if an ambassador worketh any plottes or practises, either by attempts on the person of the Prince to whom hee is sent, or any enterprise uppon his Estate, he forfeits his immunity. Fifteen pages later, he claims, with equal confidence, that Ambassadors which under colour of negotiating some affaire, or entertainment of. amitie, doe spie out the secrets of the estate to an ill intent … [are nonetheless] infallibly within the sanctuarie of the Lawe of Nations (pp. 103, 118). Mattingley, *Renaissance Diplomacy*, pp. 272–8 makes the same point.

The summary in the conclusion is based on Frigo, 'Introduction'. I depart here from Mattingley, whose account is structured around the rise of resident embassies and who therefore saw the sixteenth and early seventeenth centuries as a period in which institutional structures were inadequate in the face of new political realities.

11. Honour Among Spies

On Inq., b. 1214, no. 57: Much of the material it contains corresponds to entries in a seventeenth-century index now extant in Inq., b. 201, so it may originally have been stored together. Previously (at least until 1868) the series was lised under the broader, and in this case more accurate, rubric of Criminal Prosecutions and Papers [*Processi e Carte Criminali*]. See Fulin, *Studi nell'archivio*, p. 17 and note, which quotes from documents now stored in Inq., bb. 1213 and 1214 but which are cited under the earlier classification.

It is not clear if the minutes of the Christmas Day meeting with Gomez include a transcript or a paraphrase of Gomez's comments. The text lacks features normally associated with a formal deposition.

On gift exchanges: Preto, *I servizi segreti*, suggests that spies who were particularly sensitive about honour *were* occasionally paid with gifts rather than cash, especially if they were of high social status. However, this does not seem to have been the case for anyone associated with Vano, with the partial exception of Domenico, who occasionally received small items like gloves and shoes in addition to cash payments.

On Vano's control of access to his informants: Domenico did in fact pass information through Ongarin on at least one occasion (see Inq., b. 638, report dated 13 May 1620). He also appeared before the Inquisitors without Vano at least once (see the deposition dated 6 Oct. 1620 in Inq., b. 522).

middleman: The Venetian term is *mezano* or *sanser*.

On indirect communication with informants: Vano may have been the exception rather than the rule on this point. For example, the *novellista* Zuan Paolo Ferrari (see Inq., b. 597) addressed many of his reports directly to the Inquisitor Zuan Battista Foscarini (although they may nonetheless have been delivered by Padavin, to whom one of Ferrari's early reports is also addressed). Like Grancini, but unlike Vano, Ferrari had first-hand contact with his targets.

he is too slippery: Gomez's summary of the as yet unidientified traitor's actvities is in Inq., b. 1214, no. 57, report dated 4 Feb. 1620 (1619 m.v.).

I'll see before I doubt; when I doubt, prove: William Shakespeare, *Othello*, 3. iii. 194.

On Padavin's appendices: There is a linguistic shift halfway through his reporting of events on 4 Febuary. Padavin starts off by quoting Vano indirectly and using the first person to refer to himself but then changes without warning to direct quotation (or paraphrase), so that the 'I' becomes Vano.

On Bragadin's priestly disguise: This may have been designed to exploit a degree of ambiguity regarding whether this prohibition applied to nobles in holy orders, who were excluded from direct participation in Venetian politics (Molmenti, 'Le relazioni tra patrizi veneziani e diplomatici stranieri', p. 50).

The arrangement with the servant girl is described in an undated retrospective report on the events of 1620 included in Inq., b. 636.

gondolier: *servitor di mezo* (the Italian phrase indicates the position Domenico customarily rowed in).

What is your name?: The questions and answers are all verbatim from Domenico's deposition but the introductory remarks in the original do not take the form of Q&A. Gomez claimed to have recruited Domenico on Christmas Eve 1619 (Inq., b. 1214, no. 57, report dated 2 Mar. 1620).

Menego from Venice: Domenico had worked in the Spanish embassy since at least 1615. See Inq., b. 609, folder 3, report of Alessandro Grancini dated 24 May 1615 for an early reference to him.

On the arrest warrant: A copy can be found in Inq., b. 1214, no. 57, but I have been unable to locate any original in X Sec. or X Cr., which suggests that it was never formally registered.

gold coins: *zecchini*

On Bravo's soldierly naïvety: This was Bravo's characterisation of himself, at least according to Vano's undated summary of events in 1620 (in b. 636). It was, however, an opinion shared by many (see Luzio, 'La Congiura Spagnola', p. 143).

'You are a brave man' ... 'I've never met this captain': Similar conversations can be found in the reports dated 3 Oct. 1620, 25 Jan. 1622 (1621 m.v.), 9 Apr. 1622 and 10 Apr. 1622.

On Zuanne Minotto's arrest warrant: X Cr, reg. 37, fos 34r–35r. See also fos 37r–v.

[there is enough evidence to convict him]: *restando egli convinto*. A literal translation would be misleading in English, because Minotto had not yet been formally condemned.

close familiarity and secret dealings: *stretta prattica, et intelligenza*.

On the hypothesis that Zuanne Minotto was Zuan Battista Bragadin's accomplice: There is only one source that explicitly links the two men, but I choose to believe it because the connection simplifies things. See BMV, MSS. Italiani, class VII, 1664 (7542), *Miscellanea*, fos 98–107, 'Conspiratione de molti Nobili Venetiani contro la Republica, con il tradimento del Bragadino, il tutto successo l'anno 1620'. A date of composition of 1624 is given in the text, but I have been unable to find any other indications as to its provenance. Romanin, *Storia documentata*, relies heavily upon this chronicle, which does not mention Vano's role in Bragadin's downfall. There is a similar account in BMV, MSS. Italiani, class VII, 121–2 (8862–3), Gian Carlo Sives, *Cronica Veneta*, book 4, fo. 185r, except that Sives does not connect Bragadin with Minotto.

that big dickhead fuck Minotto. My master wants to have him killed: *quel be cazo fotuo di zuane minoto mio patro[n] si vol far amazar*.

On Spanish plans to smuggle Gomez to Milan: Inq., b. 636, reports dated 19, 27 and 28 July 1620.

On Zuanne Minotto's sentence: X Cr., reg. 37, fos 39v–40r.

On Gomez's interrogation: Inq., b. 636, report dated 28 July 1620.

On Zuan Battista Bragadin's sentence: X Cr., reg. 37 (1620), fos 50r–v, 51v–52r.

country: *patria*

On Bragadin's last words: Luzio, 'La Congiura Spagnola', pp. 143–4. The Mantuan resident maintained that the confession was critical, since otherwise there was only circumstantial evidence against Bragadin. If so, then this meant Vano was unable to gain either documentary evidence or first-hand testimony to confirm what Bragadin and Bravo talked about in their meetings.

The quotation on Gomez's death is from the undated summary at the end of 1620 in Inq., b. 636, where Vano implies that Gomez went willingly to Milan, trusting in his legal status as a cleric to protect him. Presumably he was in lesser orders, since there is otherwise no indication that he was a priest. The information on Gomez's execution is in Inq., b. 450, despatch dated 30 Dec. 1620 and Senato, Secreta, Dispacci degli Ambasciatori, Milano, filza 58 (1620) under the same day.

12. DA BAFFO, 8.45 P.M.

Ongarin's expense claims can be found in Inq., b. 953. In 1620, he almost invariably paid forty *soldi* or two *lire* a day to casual employees.

The ringleader of Cazzari's assassins, Giulio Rangon, signed a receipt for one thousand *zecchini* (each *zecchino* being worth approximately two ducats) on 10 Aug. 1622 (Inq., b. 953).

On Domenico's wages: He claimed in Inq., b. 1214, no. 57, interview dated 5 Feb. 1620 (1619 m.v.) that the ambassador paid him **30 soldi a day for expenses, and twelve L[ire] a month in salary.**

On noble salaries and dowries: Raines, 'Office Seeking, Broglio and the Pocket Political Guide-books' and Pullan, 'Service to the Venetian State' respectively.

On gambling debts: Walker, 'Gambling and Venetian Noblemen'.

On Badoer's stipend: Spini, 'La congiura degli Spagnoli', 1949, p. 23.

13. RIVALS

On Grancini: Benzoni, 'Alessandro Granzino'; Chiarelli, "Il marchese di Bedmar e i suoi confidenti'; Preto, *I servizi segreti*, pp. 125, 127; Luzio, 'La Congiura Spagnola', pp. 155–61. Vano mentions Grancini on a few occasions, but Grancini never mentions Vano. Information relating to or supplied by Grancini can be found in Inq., bb. 606–10. The etiquettes on these *buste* are misleading, since a lot of other material is mixed in with Grancini's reports, notably extensive surveillance reports from Ongarin and watchers under his supervision. Below I have numbered the internal folders according to their current order. The dates on the *buste* etiquettes encompass everything kept within, and not just the reports produced by Grancini. However, some of the additional material is obviously related to investigations initiated on the basis of Grancini's information. See e.g. Inq., 606, folder 6 and Inq., b. 608, folder 10, surveillance on Andrea Calbo and Anzolo Ceruti by Ongarin; folder 9, surveillance on Meschita by Ongarin et al.; Inq., b. 608, folder 4, surveillance on Fausto Verdelli by Ongarin et al.

The sketch of Grancini's life is based on an autobiographical *memoriale* that can be found in Inq., b. 610.

On Grancini's father: The index of Grancini's reports in Inq., b. 606, folder 11, notes in an annotation to an early report dated 12 May 1612 that he **hints at having received favours from [Nicolo Contarini] on behalf of his father, who is locked up in prison, and he says that he serves the Spanish Ambassador to obtain his [father's] freedom.**

most important agent ... but he gives no public indication of this: Inq., b. 157, despatch to Milan dated 16 June 1618.

The arrests in 1612 were related to the exposure of the Venetian traitor Anzolo Badoer. In 1616, Grancini claimed that Nicolo Contarini had protected him during this period (Luzio, 'La Congiura Spagnola', pp. 155–6). In fact, Grancini had already made an unsuccessful approach to the Inquisitors as early as 1608 and he had begun to report on one Anzolo Ceruti in late 1611.

On the supposed bad blood between Grancini and Meschita: Although Grancini almost immediately denounced Meschita in May 1612, a paraphrase of an interview dated 24 May 1615 in Inq., b. 609, folder 3, noted suspiciously that **no mention of any sort is made by Grancini of Don Antonio Meschita.**

On Contarini's fastidiousness: Inq., b. 607, folder 1. On other occasions, he insisted on passing material from Grancini on to the Inquisitors (see b. 609, folder 1, note dated 24 May 1614) and discouraged him from sending more. Although Grancini repeated the claim of an association with Contarini on numerous occasions, his accounts of the relationship differ (Luzio, 'La Congiura Spagnola', pp. 155–6).

On Grancini's anxiety: See the initial letter to Vido Diedo dated 11 May 1612 in Inq., b. 607, folder 1 and the reference in the annotated index of Inq., b. 606 to a communication dated 18 May 1612.

On the death of Grancini's father: The annotated index in Inq., b. 606 notes that Grancini was still demanding his father's release in July 1613, but in an interview in Inq., b. 609, folder 3, dated 21 May 1615, Grancini described himself as **born in Milan but moved as a little boy to Venice, where his father died in prison**. Nicolo Grancini therefore died sometime between July 1613 and May 1615.

On the alternative account of Grancini's introduction to Bedmar: Luzio, 'La Congiura Spagnola', pp. 155–6, 159–60.

On Gomez's denuniation of Grancini: Inq., b. 1214, no. 57, deposition dated 25 Dec. 1619.

On Grancini's correspondents: Inq., b. 561, letter dated 27 July 1620. Inq., b. 608, folder 2, contains a paraphrase of an interview with Grancini dated 9 Feb. 1614 (1613 m.v.), in which he admitted passing information to the Duke of Mantua and the English ambassador.

On *novellisti*: Infelise, 'Professione reportista'; Preto, *I servizi segreti*, p. 89. Some sample *avisi* can be found in Inq., b. 704, but Filippo de Vivo suggests that these had been presented for official approval (even though the trade was officially illegal) and are therefore bowdlerised.

The definition of news is quoted in Preto, *I servizi segreti*, p. 456.

On the Duke of Savoy's high opinion of Grancini: Inq., b. 488, despatch from Turin dated 25 Sept. 1618.

For Bedmar's remarks on Grancini: Luzio, 'La Congiura Spagnola', p. 101. For the Mantuan resident's warning, *ibid.*, p. 139. For the nuncio, I am relying on Benzoni, 'Alessandro Granzino'.

his news is not the ordinary stuff: Inq., b. 561, letter from Antonio Calegari dated 27 July 1620.

with hints, promises and suggestions: *con apparenze, e con promesse e speranze* (Inq., b. 609, folder 3). There are persistent complaints by the Inquisitors to this effect throughout Inq., bb. 607–9.

some tolerance ... greater public good: Inq., b. 171, despatch to Turin dated 3 Nov. 1618.

On the reason for Grancini's move: Luzio, 'La Congiura Spagnola', pp. 156, 160.

For Vido Diedo's recommendations: On 27 May 1615, the Inquisitors' secretary noted **that the Noble man mister Vido Diedo has continually [insisted], at every opportunity presented to him or that he could create himself—now with one and now with another of the Most Illustrious lords Inquisitors and even with me the secretary—... that some recognition be given ... to Grancini, so that he has a reason to stay in Venice, other wise he will leave. [Diedo] exaggerates that a great subject will be lost**. Examples of Diedo's persistent and vocal support run through Inq., b. 609, folder 3. He often served as Grancini's cut-out. For example, a report in Inq., b. 609, folder 5, is inscribed: **1616. 6. December presented by Noble man mister Vido Diedo and [written] by Alessandro Grancini.**

On Inquisitorial scepticism regarding Grancini's good faith: Inq., b. 609, folder 3. On 10 July 1615 they warned him **that we have not obtained [*non si cavava*] the advantage he claims from his writings and words, and that we nonetheless believe, that he knows the things we are interested in [*ch[e] sempre si sono aspettate*], particularly regarding the people who frequent the Ambassador's house.**

He claims to write ... according to his own interpretations: Inq., b. 488, despatch from Turin dated 25 Sept. 1618.

On the plan to expose Grancini by taking out a fake subscription: Inq., b. 488, despatch from Turin dated 26 Nov. 1618. Despite their initial negative response to this proposal, the Inquisitors asked the ambassador in Rome to explore the possibility further in Inq., b. 165, despatch of 15 Dec. 1618.

The only thing that holds us back ... cunning fictions: Inq., b. 171, despatch to Turin dated 1 Dec. 1618.

On Inquisitorial caution regarding the interception of Grancini's *avisi*: Inq., b. 165, despatch dated 21 Apr. 1618.

Grancini on Minotto: Inq., b. 610, report dated 20 July 1620.

For the Mantuan resident's account of Grancini's downfall: Luzio, 'La Congiura Spagnola', p. 143.

On Vano's immediacy: The exceptions to this were the limited material relating to Spanish foreign policy (that is, intelligence rather than counter-intelligence), which was necessarily more abstract, the retrospective report at the end of 1620, and a report (Inq., b. 636, dated 20 June 1621) paraphrasing information supplied by the informant Paulo dal Dolo.

On the secretarial reform: X Sec., reg. 16, fos 114v–116r, 117r–v. Until August 1619, secretaries to the Ten had been appointed for life. Henceforth, the period of office was to be restricted to two years, followed by a period of exclusion before reappointment was possible. The immediate consequence of this reform was the temporary demotion of one of the secretaries, while two Senate secretaries were elected to take over the empty posts. (The Ten were short of a secretary at this point, so they only needed to demote one man.) For subsequent resolutions and appointments relating to this reform, see also X Co., reg. 71, fos 5r–v, 16rv, 168r–v; X Co., reg. 72, fos 115r–116r. The changes may have been a pretext intended to get rid of the demoted man, Pietro Darduin, whom the doge apparently loathed. The reform was abandoned two years later, in August 1621, when Bartolomio Comino was re-elected after only one year's suspension. However, similar measures were re-introduced in 1628 after a broader constitutional reform.

Comino's handling of Grancini's reports explains the chronological overlap between Inq., bb. 606–9, and the frequent interpolation of large series of reports from other writers. The interpolations in b. 636 seem much more random.

On Grancini's recycling: The reports in Inq., b. 610 dated 5 Feb. and 18 Feb. 1620 (1619 m.v.) appear to be successive drafts or updated revisions of the same piece. This was a habit of Grancini's. On 27 May 1615, for example, he offered copies of letters written by Bedmar that he had already supplied in 1612 (see Inq., b. 609, folder 3).

On Grancini's warnings about Bedmar's informants: Inq., b. 610, reports dated 4 Mar., 27 Mar., 15 June and 20 July 1620.

On Vano as a spymaster: There are some slight hints that Vano gathered information from sources in other cities, in a manner similar to a *novellista*, but the only such source mentioned in any of the surviving reports is his brother.

On Grancini's comments about the Jewish Ghetto: Inq., b. 610, reports dated 15 June and 20 July 1620 and Inq., b. 1214.

On names that Grancini mentions: Fausto Verdelli (Inq., b. 1213, no. 32; Inq., b. 522 and X Sec., reg. 17, 8 Feb. 1621 (1620 m.v.), 41v–42r; see also Inq., b. 636, report of Vano dated 12 May 1621); Anzolo Giosio (Inq., bb. 201 and 522). Verdelli was also investigated at length in 1613 and 1614 (see Inq., b. 608, folder 4).

The man warned against associating with Spaniards was Vicenzo Tuccio (see Inq., b. 522).

On Grancini's trial in 1622: X Cr., reg. 39, 24 Nov. 1622, fo. 97v; Luzio, 'La Congiura Spagnola', p. 161.

On Grancini after his release: Luzio, 'La Congiura Spagnola', p. 148. He did, however, revive his career as an informant in the Spanish embassy in the early 1630s (Preto, *I servizi segreti*, p. 133).

On denunciations of Grancini by Vano: Inq., b. 636, reports dated 28 July 1620 and 9 June 1621.

On letters to Ferrari: ASV, Miscellanea Gregolin, bb. 6–7. These were transferred to their current location from the Inquisitors' archive in the late nineteenth century.

The bulk of Ferrari's reports are in Inq. 597. Other archival references to him include a blank pardon for the arrest of a priest in 1618 (see X Co., reg. 68, fos 27r–v, 65r) and a proposal for infiltrating monasteries (Inq., b. 1214, no. 57, 16 May 1620). Two more blank pardons were awarded to him in January 1621 (1620 m.v.—see X Co., reg. 70, fos 2v, 31r, 50r, 72r). A solitary report dated 3 June 1620 can also be found in Inq., b. 714, folder headed 1599–1620. It concerns the provincial noble Giulio Rangon, who was later employed by the Inquisitors to assassinate Giulio Cazzari. Another report dated 21 Apr. 1621 is interpolated in Inq., b. 636. Someone with the same name as Ferrari was the victim of an assault in 1622. See X Co., reg. 71, 19 Jan. 1622 (1621 m.v.), fos 280r, 281r.

On Ferrari's execution: X Cr., reg. 41, fos 72v, 81r, 89r–v. The Ten's registers confirm that the Inquisitors of State were the prosecuting magistrates in this case and that there were unusually severe arrangements to prevent access to the trial record. BMV, MSS. Italian, class VII, 1596 (7712), *Registro de Giustitiati, Condanati à Morte e Suspesi, e di quelli che gli anno tramutata la sentenza. Principia l'anno 810 è segue*, suggests that Ferrari was executed as a **double agent [*spia doppia*]**.

For some references to Calegari: Inq., b. 636, reports dated 2 May, 30 June, 23 July, 17 Aug. and 7 Sept. 1620; Inq., b. 638, reports dated 22 May and 26 May 1620.

Ferrari's report on Olivieri's assassins is currently misfiled among Vano's reports in Inq., b. 636, while some correspondence between Olivieri and the noble Vido Diedo is among Grancini's reports. As usual, it is not clear if these locations are significant.

14. ALCHEMY

The temptation to cite Yates, *Giordano Bruno*, in the context of a discussion on spies and the occult is impossible to resist—not because Bruno was an alchemist, but because he was a spy, at least according to Bossy, *Giordano Bruno*. The occult philosopher, mathematician and alchemist

John Dee also dabbled in cryptography and was the subject, if not the author, of spy reports by agents in Francis Walsingham's service.

Francesco Pianta seems to be under-researched. He does not rate a mention in most of the general art histories of the period, and when his work in the *Scuola Grande di San Rocco* does get a line or two, it is dismissed with a derogatory epithet such as 'bizarre' or 'eccentric'. I was not able to find any scholarly work on the carvings; hence the vague dating. However, Pianta's spy is very obviously derived from the similar figure in Ripa, *Iconologia*, ii, pp. 181–2. On the Venetian *scuole*, which were charitable institutions resembling confraternities, see Pullan, *Rich and Poor in Renaissance Venice*.

[The] god of revelation, commerce, communication and thieving: Abraham, *A Dictionary of Alchemical Imagery*, p. 127. The winged boots are also present in Ripa, *Iconologia*, but they are not explained in the commentary to the 1618 edition.

A classic account of the theory of correspondences can be found in Tillyard, *The Elizabethan World Picture*, pp. 91–108.

15. WINKS AND BLINKS

by staring intently at him: *con schizarli l'ochio*

where the nobles were gathered: *broglio*

Don Giulio [Cazzari] left [home]: It is not clear if the house in question was Cazzari's or that of Andrea Irles, the Spanish secretary.

the main street of San Stae parish: *Salizzada San Staii*

the ferry [over the Grand Canal]: *traghetto*

went down past the church of the Servite friars, via Vinegar Promenade to the parish of San Gerolemo: The punctuation in the original renders the sense here a little unclear.

On Cazzari's route: As in Domenico's run (see Chapter 18, 'Running Alternatives'), there are some problems with this itinerary, which has Cazzari walking towards the church of the Cappuccini along the Fondamenta dil Aseo. No such *fondamenta* is marked on the most detailed maps available (those of 1729 and the Napoleonic census). However, there is a Calle dell'Aseo, so I assume that the relevant fondamenta is that onto which this *calle* opens. After the Cappuccini, Cazzari doubled back down Calle dell'Aseo. Vano says that he went **per il ponte dal aseo, in calle dil squero al [anconetta]**, but again, I can find no Calle del Squero. However, since Calle dell'Aseo leads directly into the Campiello dell'Anconetta, I assume that this was the route intended and that the house Cazzari visited was in the *campiello*.

On winks and blinks: Geertz, 'Thick Description', pp. 6–7. The philosopher paraphrased by Geertz is Gilbert Ryle.

Despite Vano's persistent references to suspicious behaviour on the part of Oratio Pisani, I can find no reference to any arrest. The Ten obviously did not consider the evidence to be as unambiguous as Vano did. Vano himself was suspected of using a cough to signal the Spanish by Francesco Ongarin (see Inq., b. 1214, no. 57, report dated 20 Mar. 1620).

On interpretation: Geertz, 'Thick Description'; Tully, *Meaning and Context*.

Gasparo's surveillance report on Bortolo Corner is inserted in Inq., b. 636.

Baudelaire is quoted in Mazlish, 'The *Flâneur*: From Spectator to Representation', p. 49.

The comment on the Mafia is from Falcone, *Cose di Cosa Nostra*, pp. 49–52.

16. Special Delivery

man of honour: *galantomo*

On references to plots against Vano's life: Inq., b. 636, reports dated 8 July and 31 Oct. 1620, 9 Jan., 2 Feb., 20 Apr. and 31 July 1622.

On Gregorio de Monti: Inq., b. 1213, no. 44 and b. 638; Smith, *Life and Letters*, ii, pp. 473–4. He died on 22 Nov. 1621.

17. FIDDLER'S ELBOW IRISH PUB, 11.00 P.M.

On neighbourhood awareness of intimate family matters: Hacke, *Marital Litigation and Gender Relations*.

On the widow's visit to Vano: Inq., b. 1213, no. 54.

On the 'two persons' of the ambassador: De Vera, *Il perfetto ambasciatore*, p. 203.

18. RUNNING ALTERNATIVES

The epigraph is from De Certeau, *The Practice of Everyday Life*, p. 129.

The reports discussed regarding Domenico's conversations with the Spanish secretary are principally those from the period 11 May 1622 to 29 May 1622 in Inq., b. 636, while the route of Domenico's run is recorded in a report dated 10 Apr. 1622 (referring to the date on which the events narrated began; it is clear from the contents that Vano actually wrote it two days later).

coming [towards] San Lio: *che veniva alla volta di santo lio*.

On Vano collapsing time and space: Another problem with this interpretation is that Rossi was not really coming towards San Lio if he met Domenico at the turn into Paradise Alley; rather, the opposite: he was coming from the direction of San Lio. We could solve this problem if we translated *alla volta di* as **at the turn of** (*volta* is used analogously to designate the sharp turn in the Grand Canal). The *volta* of San Lio would then be the bend in the Salizzada at the turn-off with Paradise Alley. However,

Vano uses **alla volta di** to mean 'towards' consistently elsewhere in his reports. The presence nearby of Calle del Volto, superficially encouraging, is misleading because this actually means 'Vault Alley' (Tassini, *Curiosità Veneziane*, pp. 695–6).

On Domenico's route after Paradise Alley: He is described as heading for Santa Marina **through** or **via** Santa Maria Formosa. In actuality he almost certainly took a short cut, since entering the Campo would have extended his route significantly to no end, offering his pursuers an opportunity to cut him off. Vano was presumably describing the route using a sort of shorthand, allowing him to simplify and speed up the narration by reducing the geography of Venice to a few 'key' points (De Certeau, *The Practice of Everyday Life*, p. 101).

On a robbery in progress: In 1620, Domenico was prosecuted for an assault by the Criminal Court of the Forty and was also arrested for carrying a stiletto. The second charge was dropped at the request of the Spanish ambassador (see X Sec., reg. 17, 4–5 June 1620, fos 6r–v), although it did lead to Domenico being mentioned in an ambassadorial despatch (see Sen., Sec., reg. 116, fo. 92v). I do not know the outcome of the trial for the assault, but excerpts can be found in Inq., b. 1214, no. 57, folder headed '1620 6 Giugno proc[ess]o di xl.ta contra Domenego de Zannon serv[ito]r dell'Amb[assado]r di spagna che fù ritento, et rilassato p[er] arme'.

On denunciations against clerics: Inq., b. 1214, no. 57, report of Francesco Ongarin dated 16 June 1620; b. 609, folder 9, headed '1618 e 1619—circa Il Convento di Frari Osservat[io]ni'. Moreover, Giulio Cazzari was a priest and Antonio Meschita (the mastermind behind the intelligence network of Bravo's predecessor) an apostate priest. Rossi's brother and predecessor was also a religious, while Gomez was probably in minor orders. On professional religious as spies, see also Preto, *I servizi segreti*, pp. 472–6.

stabbing [him] in the back: *mi sasinano*. I have changed the quotation from the first to the third person.

On the events of 15 May 1622: All the phrases in bold are verbatim from Inq., b. 636, report dated 15 May 1622, but I have modernised the punctuation and omitted part of the text.

On Battista as an invented source: Smith, *Life and Letters*, ii, pp. 261–2.

On Version II: The conversations Vano quotes between Irles, Rossi, Cazzari and the Mantuan resident subsequent to 11 May imply that the offer was genuine. However, this would only become apparent in retrospect. Moreover, even though Irles speaks *as if* he was on the level (according to Vano), it is still implausible that he should actually have been so.

Jules Michelet is quoted in Steedman, *Dust*, p. 167.

On Domenico's fifteen minutes of fear: If Vano's report was a lie, then what it described was something even more ghostly—that is, Vano's idea of what Domenico's experience would have been like if it had been real, his sketching of the possible posing as actual.

Jesus wept (John 11: 35) is notoriously the shortest verse in the Bible. In the seventeenth century, there was great concern about 'stabilising' biblical interpretation to deny authority to radical preachers. James I cautioned that The Scripture is ever the best interpreter of it self; but press not curiously to seek out farther then is contained therein; for that were over unmannerly a presumption, to strive to be further upon Gods secrets, then he hath will ye be (quoted in Slights, *Ben Jonson*, p. 8).

19. TRACE

On narrative detours and **coups**: De Certeau, *The Practice of Everyday Life*, p. 79.

City and archive have things in common: The decayed and crumbling state of Venice is often exaggerated. My point is actually a positive one, and not a repetition of romantic clichés. Weathering in Venice is meaningful: it speaks not of shoddy workmanship or decadence but of a history earned and retained in surfaces and materials.

vene: It is not clear to me if Ongarin here intended a present tense construction (*viene* in modern Italian) or a past perfect one (*venne*).

21. STREET THEATRE

at the Spanish secretary's dock: *alla riva dil secretario di spagna*

On the aftermath of events described in the report of 12 Dec. 1621: When informed of this fiasco, the Spanish secretary was anxious to recover the message, to the extent of dredging the canal for it. The piece recovered by Domenico had nothing of any use on it. See Inq., b. 636, reports dated 13 and 14 Dec. 1621.

He showed as much as he told: I am indebted to Davis, *Fiction in the Archives*, here and below.

On the Mantuan resident's melancholy: Inq., b. 636, report dated 14 May 1621.

On the *commedia*: Richards and Richards, *The Commedia dell'Arte*; Povoledo, 'I comici professionisti e la Commedia dell'Arte'.

On masks: The verbs 'disguise' [*travestire*] and 'mask' [*maschere*] do not necessarily imply the use of actual masks, but *imbautare* does, since it refers to a particular mask design (the same one Vano wears in the illustrations). All three terms are used in the sources.

On the Spanish captain: Andreini, *Le Bravure del Capitano Spavento*.

our truer self, the self we would like to be: Robert Park, as cited in Goffman, *The Presentation of Self in Everyday Life*, p. 19.

On the anonymity of traitors: Significantly, the *bauta*, apparently the preferred mask among traitors, was not associated with a specific character from the *commedia*, and thus did not oblige the wearer to adopt a persona.

The descriptions of unidentified targets are from Inq., b. 636, reports dated 9 Dec. 1621 and 3 June 1621 respectively.

no layer deeper, more authentic, than theatrical self-representation: Greenblatt, 'Psychoanalysis and Renaissance Culture', p. 143.

official audiences: These were recorded in a file series now entitled Espositioni Principi in the archive of the Venetian cabinet [*collegio*]. The contents of these records are compared with Vano's reports more directly in Walker, 'Let's Get Lost'.

It was not only a corrupt world but a grotesquely oversimplified one: Vano did supply a limited amount of strictly political information, as opposed to counter-intelligence. It generally concerned Spanish policy in northern Italy and also large-scale political/military plots against Venice.

Priests were potential spies whose religious convictions were entirely irrelevant: A number of those under surveillance did attend mass (or, in Cazzari's case, say mass), but this is only mentioned in passing.

This is partly a matter of genre: The obvious contrast to Vano's reports would be the trials conducted by the church Inquisition, but early modern criminal records also contain many references to popular superstitions, while witnesses used secondary accusations of impiety and blasphemy to impugn the credibility of their enemies.

Vano commissioned numerous masses for his soul in his will: X Cr., filza 49, entry under 5 Oct. 1622.

He needed to put off the denouement until the audience had been properly primed: Vano did sometimes push for action on the part of the

Inquisitors, as in Zuan Battista Bragadin's case, presumably because he was worried about the traitor getting away (or someone else exposing him, which might result in Vano losing the reward).

22. DESIRE

The Spanish secretary was also trying to steal Nicolo Rossi's girlfriend: Compare Inq., b. 636, 13 Dec. 1621, where Irles and one of his informants botch a message drop involving a letter tied to a piece of string, and the Mantuan resident rebukes Irles for behaving **like lovers do**.

Since I cannot prove a lover, I am determined to prove a villain: William Shakespeare, *Richard III*, i. i. 28, 30.

my dearest companion lady Faustina: X Cr., filza 49, insert within resolution dated 5 Oct. 1622.

Other men's wives: Inq., b. 636, reports dated 29 May and 17 Aug. 1620, 9 June 1621 and 10 Apr. 1622; Inq., b. 714, petition of Lodovico Rho dated 4 Sept. 1621.

On courtesans as informants: The Spanish 'defector' Francesco Zappata did mention **whores [*puttane*]** among Bravo's sources of information in one of his interviews with the Inquisitors, but without elaborating (see Inq., b. 522, transcript of interview dated 29 Sept. 1620). On this theme, see also Preto, *I servizi segreti*, pp. 479–81.

Men act and women appear ... Women watch themselves being looked at: Berger, *Ways of Seeing*, p. 47.

Thanks to Guido Ruggiero for reminding me that homosexual 'conspiracy' was a concern for the Council of Ten in the fifteenth century.

fixing me with an evil eye: Inq., b. 636, report dated 12 Dec. 1621.

23. 2 + 2 = 5

Council of Ten criminal register, 8 April 1622: X Cr., reg. 39, 12r.

Despatch of the Florentine resident in Venice, 9 April 1622: Romanin, *Storia documentata*, p. 584.

For discussion of the various problematic points regarding the translation of the passage from Vano's report of 9 Apr. 1622, see the notes to Chapter 2.

Council of Ten criminal register, 20 April 1622: X Cr., reg. 39, fos 14r–v.

Despatch of the Florentine resident, 23 April 1622: Romanin, *Storia documentata*, p. 586.

Report from a novellista in Venice employed by the Duke of Urbino, 23 April 1622: Biblioteca Apostolica Vaticana, Urbinati Latini 1091, Avvisi al Duca d'Urbino Francesco Maria della Rovere Anno 1622, fo. 298. Thanks to Filippo de Vivo for this quotation.

Despatch of the papal nuncio in Venice, 30 April 1622: Quoted in Loredana, *L'ambasciatore Antonio Foscarini*, p. 169.

[country]: *Patria*

Despatch from the Venetian ambassador in England to the Council of Ten, 10 June 1622: ASV, Capi del Consiglio dei Dieci, Lettere di ambasciatori, b. 14, 10 June 1622.

Biographical sketch by the noble Gerolamo Priuli, c.1632: MCV, Codici Cicogna, 3782, G. Priuli, *Pretiosi Frutti del Maggior Consiglio*, fos 29v–30r.

On the sums paid to the executioner and others: X Co., reg. 72, 12 May 1622, fo. 52v.

In the discussion of the aftermath of Foscarini's execution, the distinction between what the Council of Ten knew and what the foreign ambassadors who commented on the case knew is critical. The Ten were working on the basis of a specific accusation from a trusted informant that was legally acceptable because **matters of state** allowed judicial discretion in the interpretation of evidence. Foscarini was convicted and executed unjustly but legally. His condemnation by public opinion, based on the gossip relayed by ambassadors, was an entirely distinct process but one that the Ten were willing to take advantage of.

It is still not known: *Despatch of the Florentine resident Nicolo Sacchetti, 9 Apr. 1622* in Romanin, *Storia documentata*, p. 584.

it seems: Sacchetti, 16 Apr. 1622, in *ibid.*, p. 585.

suspicion: Sacchetti, 12 Apr. 1622, in *ibid.*, p. 584.

stir: Letter of Henry Wotton, 15 Apr. 1622, in Smith, *Life and Letters*, ii, p. 232.

shadow: Sacchetti, 16 Apr. 1622, in Romanin, *Storia documentata*, p. 585.

His death must have something to do with a woman: **He is said likewise to have led a courtesan to Monsignor de Leon's [the French ambassador's] house vizarded, and then calling himself Bernardo Tiepolo; which change of name doth stir suspicion** (letter of Wotton in Smith, *Life and Letters*, ii, p. 232).

It is [publicly said] ... without any certainty: Sacchetti, 23 Apr. 1622, in Romanin, *Storia documentata*, p. 586.

The tongues o'th'common mouth. I do despise them: William Shakespeare, *Coriolanus*, 3. i. 22.

On the defence: X Cr., reg. 39, 13 Apr. 1622, fo. 12v.

On Foscarini's sentence: X Cr., reg. 39, fos 14r–v.

hanged by one leg on a gallows: Smith, *Life and Letters*, ii, p. 262.

Zuanetto: His name appears in the Ten's registers in 1622 as Zuanne Facini but I am sure that it is the same man referred to by Vano as

'Zuanetto'. Indeed, on 7 Sept. 1622, the Ten used the diminutive form 'Zaneto' too (see X Cr., reg. 39, fo. 72v). For his early appearances in Vano's reports, see for example 18 and 19 July 1620.

On Querini's trial: X Cr., reg. 38, fo. 82v. See also fos 85r–v for resolutions regarding the torture of Querini, and fos 92v–93r for his conviction. Henry Wotton believed that he was arrested **for a secret journey to Ferrara, and conference there with the Cardinal Governor** (Smith, *Life and Letters*, ii, pp. 221–2), but in fact Alvise came from a branch of the Querini clan with property in Ferrara, and he therefore needed to meet with the Cardinal-Legate to discuss matters relating to this. He did so with permission from the Ten (see X Co., reg. 70 (1620), fo. 89v).

On Querini's and Zuanetto's juxtaposition in Vano's reports: Inq.,b. 636, 28 July 1620, **Zuanetto saw and recognised Querini on the stairs with the lord Ambassador. He was quite sure who it was.** On some occasions, the identification refers even more specifically to Alvise Querini. The Spanish 'defector' Francesco Zappata also confirmed that Querini was a regular visitor to the embassy (Inq., b. 522, interview dated 29 Sept. 1620).

On Vano's and Domenico's arrest: X Cr., reg. 39, fo. 61v. Records from the trials of Alvise Querini and Zuanne Minotto (but *not* Antonio Foscarini) were examined in response to Zuanetto's claims, although both men ultimately remained in prison (see below).

On Querini and Zuanne Facini a.k.a. Zuanetto: X Cr., reg. 39, fos 69r–70r, 72v, 73v–74v, 79r–v, 115r–v. On the former's pardon in 1623, X Co., reg. 73, fos 5v–6r, 8v. Two other men may have been peripherally involved in Zuanetto's scheme, since they were arraigned and judged exactly contemporaneously with him. However, both were absolved by large majorities. See X Cr., reg. 39, 79r–v, fo. 115v.

On Vano's and Domenico's condemnation: The corpses were not to be hung upside down by the foot, as Foscarini's had been. This suggests that they were not accused of treason, or at least that the Inquisitors did not wish to label them as traitors.

On the reconfirmation of the sentence: X Cr., reg. 39, fos 76r–77r.

On the course of events in late August and early September: Vano was arrested on 22 August, and Facini / Zuanetto did not physically turn himself in to the Ten until 3 September. However, he had written to the Ten earlier.

I begin To doubt th'equivocation of the fiend That lies like truth: William Shakespeare, *Macbeth*, 5. v. 41–3.

On Wotton's version of events: Smith, *Life and Letters*, ii, pp. 261–2. Compare the Mantuan resident's account in Luzio, 'La Congiura Spagnola', pp. 146–8.

Wotton calls Zuanetto a.k.a. Zuanne Facini 'Zuan Battista', but I am again assuming that it was the same man. Wotton also names the noble Marco Miani as Vano's prospective victim, but that name does not appear in any other source. By contrast, the Mantuan resident refers to false accusations against Sebastian Venier, Agostin Nani and an unspecified senator from the Emo family (Luzio, 'La Congiura Spagnola', p. 148). The late eighteenth-century index of the Inquisitors' archive confirms that Francesco Emo was the victim of a false accusation in 1622, but it distinguishes the consequent prosecution of his accusers from that of Vano and Domenico, which means that they were distinct cases. See MCV, MSS. P.D. 171C, *Specifica dei processi che si trovarano nell'Archivio degl'Inquisitori di Stato dal 1573 fino all'anno 1774 e 75. Compilata da Gius[epp]e Gradenigo.*

foaming at the mouth: *buttava bava alla bocca.*

by beating the shit out of him: *darli tante zapate che li salti le budelle dil corpo.*

make a stink: *ha strepitar.*

On Grancini's release: Luzio, 'La Congiura Spagnola', p. 148, and X Cr., reg. 39, 24 Nov. 1622, fo. 97v. As we have already noted, it is not clear if

Vano played any role in Grancini's imprisonment, but the timing of both his arrest and release are suggestive.

On Querini's pardon: X Co., reg. 73, fos 5v–6r.

On Rhò's release and expulsion: X Sec., reg. 17, fo. 111v; X Co., reg. 73, fo. 15r.

On Alberti's absolution: X Co, reg. 73, fos 59r–v; X Cr., reg. 40, fos 52v–53r.

Alberti's petition is in X Co, filza 343, within the entry dated 24 Apr. 1623. With this in mind, it might be significant that rumours at the time of Foscarini's arrest linked him to Alberti (Romanin, *Storia documentata*, p. 585). In other words, there was a perceived connection between the only two cases in which Vano was subsequently explicitly identified as the (false) accuser.

For the text of Wotton's letter: Smith, *Life and Letters*, ii, pp. 262–3. On 18 Jan. 1623 the Savoyard ambassador reported that **Yesterday the great Council was held and the doge and all of the said Council declared Foscarini to be innocent ... now his relatives can enjoy those honours that the gentlemen of this republic enjoy, which they could not before this declaration was made** (quoted in Romanin, *Storia documentata*, pp. 590–1). This was not literally true, since men could not be deprived of their rights as nobles for a relative's crime in Venice, but was probably intended to suggest the revival of the family's reputation. The delay is even more mysterious given that the Mantuan resident was confident that Foscarini would be posthumously cleared in September 1622, immediately after Vano's death, although the sources of this rumour are just as mysterious as those regarding Foscarini's guilt. See Luzio, 'La Congiura Spagnola', pp. 147–8.

On the guard in front of Vano's cell: X Co., reg. 72, 52v, fo. 136v.

On Vano's confessor: The priest Christoforo Orseti, attached to the confraternity responsible for ministering to prisoners, is recorded as a witness for Vano's will, and perhaps took his final confession. See X Cr., filza 49, entry under 5 Oct. 1622.

For the text of the proclamation of Foscarini's absolution: X Co., reg. 72 (1622), fo. 234v.

For the cynical suggestion that the truth be suppressed: MCV, MSS. P. D. 679, no. 13 (or possibly 14—the numeration is actually unclear).

For Wotton's comments on Foscarini's will: Smith, *Life and Letters*, ii, p. 263.

Regarding possible censorship of the will: The Ten noted on 29 April 1622 that it was not **appropriate ... that the will made by the late Sir Antonio Foscarini ... is released in the form in which it is found and has now been read to this council**. Consequently, they released only portions of it, keeping the full text **under seal**. See X Cr., reg. 39, fos 15v–17r.

For alternative versions of Foscarini's absolution: One of the most popular, with obvious affinities to Wotton's, can be found in an early form in Siri, *Delle memorie recondite*, pp. 380–1. Here an unknown member of the Ten going through trial records noticed that an unnamed man condemned for perjury some months after Foscarini's death appeared as a witness in the earlier trial. When challenged on the details of his testimony against Foscarini, the perjurer confessed its falsity. A similar version can be found in MCV, Codici Cicogna, 3782, G. Priuli, *Pretiosi Frutti del Maggior Consiglio*, fos 29r–30v. Here the outline is even more vague: the execution of unnamed false witnesses leads by unexplained means to Foscarini's posthumous absolution.

24. DA ALDO, 1.10 A.M.

For Minotto's plot to secure himself a pardon by **impostures**: Luzio, 'La Congiura Spagnola', p. 147; X Cr., reg. 39, fos 35v, 60r, 61v. X Sec., reg. 17, fo. 90r is probably related. He narrowly escaped conviction and execution. As in Querini's case, his non-noble accomplice was not so lucky.

On the relationship between economic and social credit: Muldrew, *The Economy of Obligation.*

25. SPYING AND MODERNITY

For a long time ordinary individuality … a document for possible use: Foucault, *Discipline and Punish*, p. 191.

The dichotomy between surveillance and display is a false one: Here and below, I draw upon Archer, *Sovereignty and Intelligence.*

On the illegality of private meetings between foreign ambassadors and Venetian nobles: The relevant laws state that it was forbidden for any of our Nobles of any rank or condition whatsoever (1542), with no exceptions (1612) to visit the house of a foreign ambassador without permission from the Ten (Inq., b. 1, fos. 12, 28–30).

A vast and repetitive [photographic] archive … open to vision and supervision: Tagg, *The Burden of Representation*, pp. 64, 76.

For more discussion of the Inquisitors' archive, see Walker, 'Let's Get Lost'.

On eighteenth-century Parisian police files: Darnton, 'A Police Inspector Sorts His Files'.

On grouping of files by informant: Again, I should point out that the current classification of Vano's reports is not original but they must orig-inally have been stored together. The files discussed by Darnton offer more precise and detailed biographical information on their subjects than Vano's reports do, partly because each concerns a person who had already been identified, whereas Vano's reports were more concerned with the process of identification itself. Moreover, the targets of the

French reports were not spies so much as gossips and *libellistes*, the sort of people who in fact also dominate eighteenth-century reports in the Inquisitors' archive.

the servants of these Inquisitors, mad dogs: Inq., b. 636, report dated 1 Feb. 1622 (1621 m.v.).

[The ambassador] wants me dead even if he has to spend everything he's got: Inq., b. 636, report dated 8 July 1620.

The only fully realised character ... an absent shadow: This situation is reminiscent of accounts of modern consciousness, such as Koestler, *The Ghost in the Machine*, pp. 212, 219: The self which directs the searchlight of my attention can never be caught in its focal beam. ... the experiencing subject can never fully become the object of his experience ... Consciousness has been compared to a mirror in which the body contemplates its own activities. It would perhaps be a closer approximation to compare it to the kind of Hall of Mirrors where one mirror reflects one's reflection in another mirror, and so on.

26. I Spy, with My Little Eye

spy: *spionario*.

27. Interrupted Sentences

Narrative was my moral language: Ellroy, *My Dark Places*, p. 127.

He hath bitten forth his tongue Rather than reveal what we required: Thomas Kyd, *The Spanish Tragedy*, 4. iii. 193–4 (slightly edited).

On Vano's will: X Cr., filza 49, entry under 5 Oct. 1622. For Foscarini's will, see X Cr., reg. 39, fos 15r–17r and below.

On Vano's final joke: This interpretation could be falsfied by the missing trial record. Possibly Vano confessed fully therein, and the note regarding Querini was merely an afterthought, meant to clarify something in his earlier testimony.

Is there a murderer here? ... Yet I lie, I am not. William Shakespeare, *Richard III*, 5. iii. 185, 192.

On Domenico's final request: X Cr., reg. 39, fos 76v–77r. The suspension of the executions required a majority of two-thirds (a lower ratio than was usual in such cases) because Domenico's appeal was **in the interests of justice and not a [personal] entreaty or in expectation of any reduction of the punishment of the aforementioned Domenico, as he explains in his petition**.

For Alberti's petition: X Co., filza 343, within the entry dated 24 Apr. 1623.

[An] unending superfluity of events: Nietzsche, 'On the Uses and Disadvantages of History for Life', p. 66.

28. Pistols! Treason! Murder!

The epigraph is from *Catiline His Conspiracy*, 3. 663–5.

On Cazzari's anti-Venetian activities: The reports of the informant Zuan Paolo Ferrari back Vano up here, although Ferrari was largely restricted to 'external' observations, which describe who Cazzari met and talked to. See Inq., b. 597.

On the resolution to assassinate Cazzari: X Sec., reg. 17, fo. 84r. The material included in X Sec., filza 35, entry under 9 May 1622 regarding this decision is not a comprehensive account of the case against Cazzari, which interestingly involved reading the trial of Antonio Calegari. The material currently extant includes (besides Vano's reports) depositions from the investigation against Andrea Alberti and a quotation from an interview with the Spanish 'defector' Francesco Zappata. On 10 May, the Ten further resolved that the assassins would receive immunity from prosecution and a blank pardon as a reward (*ibid.*, fos 84v–85r). The reward was later converted to two thousand *zecchini*. On assassination in general and for the figures quoted in the note, see Preto, *I servizi segreti*, pp. 329–74. The decision followed earlier abortive resolutions to arrest Cazzari, which could never be carried out because he remained under Rossi's protection (see X Sec., reg. 17, fo. 99r). Ironically, it was easier to kill him than to interrogate him.

On reports of Cazzari's assassination: Inq., b. 636, report dated 15 July 1622; Luzio, 'La Congiura Spagnola', p. 146; PRO, State Papers Venetian, 99/24, fos 107r–v.

Shoot, shoot, Of all deaths the violent death is best: John Webster, *The White Devil*, 5. vi. 113–14.

Over thy wounds ... to beg the voice and utterance of my tongue: William Shakespeare, *Julius Caesar*, 3. i. 259–61.

What's this flesh? a little crudded milk, fantastical puff-paste: John Webster, *The Duchess of Malfi*, 4. ii. 125–6.

Ask for me tomorrow and you shall find me a grave man: William Shakespeare, *Romeo and Juliet*, 3. i. 98–9.

File 636, 22 July 1621: Part of this passage was included in the material in X Sec., filza 35, entry under 9 May 1622.

[pushed around]: A very uncertain translation of *imbutato*, which means 'soaked' or 'impregnated' in modern Italian. Unless Cazzari was using a peculiar idiomatic turn of phrase, I assume that this modern sense is a red herring and that, in this context, *imbutare* is related to *buttare*, 'throw' or 'throw out'.

Note by Vano, 24 August 1621: This report does not survive in Inq., b. 636 but is quoted in X Sec., filza 35, as above.

These Lords don't know what to do with the letters: *si hanno smenticato le l[ette]re*.

dickheads: *coglioni*. The exact translation is 'bollocks', but it is not idiomatic in this context.

I will not consent to die this Day, ... Oh Sir, you must: William Shakespeare, *Measure for Measure*, 4. iii. 59–61.

injury: *affro[n]to*.

Don't worry about it: *non dubite di nie[n]te*.

Cowards die many times ... The valiant never taste of death but once: William Shakespeare, *Julius Caesar*, 2. ii. 32–3.

On Cazzari's career options: Luzio, 'La Congiura Spagnola', 146; Inq., b. 636, report dated 22 July 1621.

I do dare my fate to do its worst: John Webster, *The White Devil*, 5. iv. 141–2.

Run ... And cut off time and pain: Thomas Middleton, *Women Beware Women*, 5. ii. 169–70.

On Cazzari as Vano's sworn enemy: e.g., Inq., b. 636, report dated 20 July 1621.

We are all shut up in the prison ... every death ... is a [particular] execution of the general condemnation: I quote an eighteenth-century moralist cited in Paglia, *La Morte confortata*, p. 86, but the attitude expressed here would have been familiar in the seventeenth century too.

On reason of state and political expediency: Assassinations could have religious motives and the Ten did on occasion authorise the elimination of notorious and troublesome heretics in this manner. But since Venice was opposed to Catholic Spain and potentially allied with England and the German Protestant princes, in international affairs it was in her interests to separate religion from politics. As I have already noted, Venetian spies like Vano entirely eschewed sectarian rhetoric, unlike those in Elizabethan England.

each man would discover the secret of his individuality: Ariès, *Western Attitudes toward Death*, pp. 51–2.

Man, the devil plays chess with you, ... if you lose, all that you have done before will be worthless: Savonarola is quoted in Ariès, *The Hour of Our Death*, pp. 109–10. On the deathbed experience, see also Ariès, *Western Attitudes toward Death*, pp. 33–6, 46, and Delumeau, *Sin and Fear*, p. 60.

Caesar under Brutus' knife, ... the ultimate coherence of a destiny: Barthes, *Michelet*, pp. 82–3.

On different ways of thinking about death: Bellarmine, *The Art of Dying Well*, and Ariès, *The Hour of Our Death*, pp. 300–5.

Let this hour be ... a natural day: Christopher Marlowe, *Doctor Faustus*, 5. ii. 63–4.

daggers: *pistolesi*. The *pistolese* was a dagger with a triangular shape, wide at the base and tapering sharply to a point.

Rose Alley: *Calle della ruosa* (now known as Calle della Rosa).

employer: *mandante*.

For the proclamation against Cazzari's killers: X Co., reg. 72, fo. 103r. I have altered the sentence structure of this quotation considerably to clarify sense and improve the flow in English, as well as removing much technical information.

For the payment to Cazzari's assassins: X Sec., reg. 17, 4 Aug. 1622, fos 94v–95r. The policy of not letting the left hand know what the right hand was doing is clear from an audience held by the Venetian cabinet for Rossi on 14 July 1622. The cabinet included the doge and the six ducal councillors, who were also *ex officio* members of the Ten and were therefore aware of the order to assassinate Cazzari. Nonetheless, they made no comment as their colleagues suggested to Rossi that **since the murder was committed by foreigners armed with arquebuses, who came here**

specifically to carry it out, it must have been ordered by some powerful person (Coll. Esp., b. 30).

Cazzari's autopsy does not survive. The only available description of Cazzari's wounds is from Henry Wotton, who wrote in a letter to the English Secretary of State that Cazzari's assassins had each stabbed him in the kidneys and then **cut his heade in pieces** (PRO, State Papers Venetian, 99/24, fos 107r–v).

[he worked against]: The verb used is *offendere*.

['I don't know what's going on']: *no[n] so come la si sia*.

It's a pity: An uncertain translation in this context of the phrase *suo danno*, which is used without a verb.

Despatch by the Mantuan resident, 16 July 1622: Luzio, 'La Congiura Spagnola', pp. 146–7.

[Rossi] appeared before the cabinet, … However, so far little has been discovered: *tutti quei S[igno]ri mostrarono di sentire acerbamente questo fatto, né si manca d'ogni possibile diligenza acciò la giustitia venga in cognitione dei delinquenti, ma sinhora poca notizia se n'è potuto havere*.

Don Giulio masterminded the meetings: *Don Giulio fosse causa dell'intelligenza*.

Despatch by the Mantuan resident, 23 July 1622: Luzio, 'La Congiura Spagnola', p. 147. I have omitted the concluding phrase *et artificiosamente vien publicato* because I am uncertain how to translate it in this context. It may imply that the rumour was deliberately spread as misinformation.

See, see where Christ's blood streams in the firmament!: Christopher Marlowe, *Doctor Faustus*, 5. ii. 70.

The only unforgivable sin, which Faustus commits, is despair: This interpretation only holds for the 'A' text of *Doctor Faustus*. The variant 'B' text does not appear to admit the possibility of last-minute repentance.

The stars move still; ... the clock will strike: Christopher Marlowe, *Doctor Faustus*, 5. ii. 67.

29. LEGACY

For more on the 1628 crisis and its proximate causes, see Walker, 'Legal and Political Discourse'.

Vano's name ... was on nobody's lips: Apart from (briefly) Samuele Romanin's, and (equally briefly) Paolo Preto's.

wicked man: MCV, Codici Cicogna, 3782, G. Priuli, *Pretiosi Frutti del Maggior Consiglio*, fo. 29v, written *c.* 1632. Priuli seems to have been the first person to suggest that there were *three* false witnesses who testified against Foscarini, a suggestion repeated by later commentators. Probably the confusion arose from the ambiguous and uncertain role played by Battista, Vano's 'phantom' agent. Bizarrely, Romanin, *Storia documentata*, seems to imply that the 'third man' was Giulio Cazzari. Perhaps he was misled by the existence of a file under Cazzari's name in the *Riferte dei Confidenti* series of the Inquisitors' archive (b. 584). Its contents do not suggest that Cazzari ever worked for Venice. On the contrary, they are intercepted letters, probably misfiled in the nineteenth century.

Rio Terrà Antonio Foscarini: Before 1863, it was the Fondamenta Foscarini; that is, it was previously named after the family, but not Antonio specifically (Tassini, *Curiosità Veneziane*, p. 8).

30. GENERAL OF SPIES

The title of spy ... was ... usually intended as an insult: This generalisation is based on the use of the word *spia* in Italian and Venetian sources. I cannot say whether it applies to the use of analogous terms in English or French. Venetian sources do sometimes refer to men in their own employ as spies. For example, the expense claims submitted by the Ten's captain of police in Inq., b. 953, refer thus to individuals employed on an *ad hoc* basis for surveillance operations. However, it is doubtful that the word was used to their faces. The fact that no one referred to Vano as a spy in his reports is actually rather suspicious. On the vocabulary of spy reports, see also Preto, *I servizi segreti*, pp. 41–9.

31. DOCTOR FRANKENSTEIN

the first professional spy in Europe: I am sure there are many other claimants for this dubious honour, notably Francis Walsingham.

scientifically eloquent: The phrase is from Levi, 'On Microhistory', with whom I disagree on the necessity of being 'scientifically' anything.